DECADE *of* CHAMPIONS

Edited by
Gene Myers
and
Tracee Hamilton

Detroit Free Press

1989

ACKNOWLEDGEMENTS

Editors

Gene Myers, Tracee Hamilton

Coordinator

Dave Robinson

Research and copy editing

Brad Betker, Bill Collison, Reid Creager, Toni Cybulski, Bernie Czarniecki, Owen Davis, Joe Distelheim, Rich Hava, Jane Jankowski, Ken Kraemer, Tom Panzenhagen, Janie Reilly, Steve Schrader, Free Press sports copy desk

Special thanks

Kent Bernhard, Diane Bond, Scott Bosley, Mark Brazaitis, Tom Coe, Ed Duffy, Bob Hall, David Lawrence, Bob McGruder, Helen McQuerry, Heath Meriwether, Beth Myers, Guy Powers, Marcia Prouse, Pat Riepma, Tom Watts

Free Press sports staff, September 1989

Mitch Albom, Brad Betker, Bill Collison, Reid Creager, Steve Crowe, Joe Cybulski, Pat Cybulski, Toni Cybulski, Bernie Czarniecki, Owen Davis, Jim Dwight, Bob Ellis, Perry A. Farrell, Matt Fiorito, Keith Gave, Gene Guidi, Tracee Hamilton, Johnette Howard, Jane Jankowski, Steve Kornacki, Ken Kraemer, Joe Lapointe, John Lowe, Tim Marcinkoski, Mick McCabe, Corky Meinecke, Gene Myers, Tom Opre, Tom Panzenhagen, George Puscas, Janie Reilly, Dave Robinson, Jack Saylor, Steve Schrader, Drew Sharp, Curt Sylvester, Charlie Vincent, Scott Walton

Photographs and illustrations

William Archie: 129, 182
Patricia Beck: 151L
Manny Crisostomo: 32, 33, 34, 36, 54, 97, 111, 131
John Collier: 52, 151R
William DeKay: 56, 57, 118, 119, 128
Hugh Grannum: 13, 69
Daymon J. Hartley: 114, 126, 141, 198
Alan R. Kamuda: 20, 21, 26, 39, 55, 59, 60, 61, 65, 66, 67, 70, 74, 75, 84R, 85, 132, 136R, 174, 186
Pauline Lubens: 5, 14, 15, 16, 17, 96, 121, 137, 146, 166, 167, 168, 172, 193, 195, 196
Dick Mayer: 51, 103, 135
Steven R. Nickerson: 4, 80, 81, 163, 175, 176, 177, 179, 180, 200, 203, 206
Craig Porter: 127, 171, 185, 194, 197, 201, 204
Mary Schroeder: 3, 19, 23, 24, 25, 28, 29, 30, 31, 37, 40, 41, 42, 43, 44, 45, 47, 48, 49, 62, 63, 76, 83, 86, 87, 89, 91, 94, 95, 98, 99, 102, 104, 106, 108, 109, 110, 112, 113, 115, 116, 117, 122, 138, 147, 152, 153, 154, 155, 156, 158, 159, 160, 161, 162, 188, 189, 192
Tim Sharp: 120, 207
Tony Spina: 72, 93, 100, 124, 148, 149
David C. Turnley: 7, 8, 9, 11, 12, 92, 134
George Waldman: 123
AP Wide World: 64, 88, 150, 165, 191
Free Press files: 71, 73, 78, 79, 84L, 107, 136L, 169, 173, 187, 190
Contributors: Nancie Battaglia, Lake Superior State University; Dick Schwarze, Eastern Michigan University; Michigan State

Printing

Gaylord Printing Co., Detroit, Michigan

© 1989 Detroit Free Press
Detroit, Michigan 48231

ISBN 0-937247-14-6

TABLE OF CONTENTS

Guillermo Hernandez, then an ace reliever called Willie, was perhaps the most photographed Tiger in 1984. He was on the mound for all the crucial victories — including the clinching of the American League East, the AL pennant and the World Series. When the Tigers swept Kansas City for the pennant, Alan Trammell and Darrell Evans joined Hernandez for a victory dance. Hernandez later won the Cy Young and Most Valuable Player awards.

◆

ON THE FRONT COVER: Kirk Gibson by Mary Schroeder; Joe Dumars and Isiah Thomas by Pauline Lubens; Glen Rice by Alan R. Kamuda.

ON THE BACK COVER: Bo Schembechler by Manny Crisostomo; Jim Abbott by Pauline Lubens; Jacques Demers and Lorenzo White by Mary Schroeder.

INTRODUCTION

By Mitch Albom

The best way to appreciate a decade, I think, is to try to imagine your life without it. Where we would we be in sports if we never had the '80s?

We would never know how Bo Schembechler reacts when he finally *wins* a Rose Bowl because until the '80s, he never had.

We would never know the glory of a Pistons championship parade because until the '80s, there never was one.

We would never know that Kirk Gibson raises his fists and trots around the bases when he hits home runs in the World Series, or that "Bless You Boys" ever had anything to do with baseball.

We would never know that a single hockey coach, Jacques Demers, could ignite a flame within our city, or that a single hockey player, Bob Probert, could nearly extinguish it, all by himself.

We would never know the feeling when an NCAA championship hangs on a single free throw, and how a state can erupt when that free throw swishes through the net. Michigan wins! Michigan wins!

The faces of the '80s would never be ours to cherish: Billy Sims, wild and explosive; Joe Dumars, a study in concentration; Steve Yzerman, young and apple-cheeked and innocently spectacular; Jack Morris, staring down a batter, 60 feet, six inches and a fastball away.

None of that. Can you imagine? All those posters up in your attic: "Gr-r-reat!" with an unshaven Gibson leaping toward the moon; "NOT BAD, BOYS!" with a champagne-soaked Isiah Thomas kissing the NBA championship trophy. You'd have to give them back. Never existed.

And those ticket stubs: the closed-circuit broadcast of the beautiful war between Thomas Hearns and Sugar Ray Leonard; the Pistons game that was supposed to be played at the Silverdome, until the roof collapsed; the Sunday afternoon when Frank Tanana tossed the final out to Darrell Evans, and leapt into the air, the bubble gum dangling from his mouth, Tigers win the American League East, unbelievable!

It's all part of the stitching, the squares of the pastiche that is the 1980s remembered. It is hard even to think, for those of us with a Michigan address, that Chuck Daly didn't pace the court like a man possessed, or that George Perles wasn't once carried off the field by his Spartans, with roses raining down on the field, or that the Lions didn't once have a punt blocked right back into the arms of the kicker, who caught it and ran for one of the best gains of the day. No Dantley? No Lorenzo? No A.C.?

No need. Here, within these pages, are the headlines and memories of a wonderfully entertaining decade. I think you'll find that the best part of imagining sports without the '80s, quite frankly, is that we don't have to.

Enjoy. ◆

Mark Aguirre and Isiah Thomas shed more than a few tears after the Pistons swept the Los Angeles Lakers to win the 1989 NBA championship.

OLYMPICS

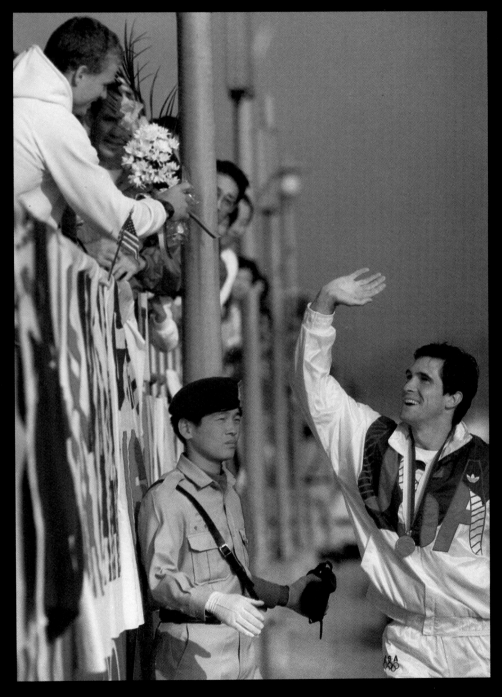

In Seoul, Greg Barton of Homer, Mich., became the first American to wear a kayaking gold medal. Less than 90 minutes later, he was wearing two.

DEPUTY'S BADGE OF GOLD

By Mike Downey

AUG. 1,
1984
◆

Steve Fraser, a deputy sheriff from Washtenaw County, was given little chance of winning a badge of gold. After all, no American ever had won an Olympic medal in Greco-Roman wrestling. And Fraser's draw in Los Angeles included a three-time world champion, Frank Andersson of Sweden. But Fraser stunned Andersson and earned a chance to wrestle with history.

And so, the big, tough wrestler cried. He cried like a baby. He cried like the child that is due Dec. 4 to his wife. He cried because they had draped an Olympic gold medal around his neck, a gold medal that "I'll probably give to the baby, so he'll have something of his own to wrestle with."

He cried because his lovable old coach, Dean Rockwell, was crying himself, a few feet away. He cried because he thought of how many men like Rockwell had made this moment possible for him — men like Tom Minick, Ron Schebil, Dale Bahr — and there was no way ever to thank them properly. There was no million-dollar payday ahead, as with other Olympic champions. There was only that medal.

"If I could cut it up into pieces," Steve Fraser said, cupping the ribboned medallion in his hands, "I'd give each of them one."

Big, tough wrestler. Neighborhood kid from the suburban Detroit streets of Hazel Park and Ferndale. High school football player. College wrestler. Washtenaw County cop. Part of the 198-pound division's hand-to-hand combat in the Summer Olympics. This was the life that Ann Arbor's Steve Fraser flashed back upon the night he became the first American to win an Olympic medal in Greco-Roman wrestling.

He thought about many things after beating Ilie Matei of Romania for the gold. He thought about Frank Stagg, a coach at Webb Junior High, latching onto him one day and not letting go. "He grabbed me in the hallway and put a sleeper hold on me," Fraser said, laughing at the memory. "He's got his arm around my throat and he's saying, 'You're coming to wrestling practice today.' And that's how I became a wrestler. I didn't have a choice. It was either come to practice or pass out."

He thought about his mother and father and stepfather, all of whom were on the scene, all of whom would celebrate with Steve long into the night, all of whom made sacrifices so he could keep doing what he loved best. "It's a different sport than track," he said. "They make a lot of money. Wrestlers scrounge and scrimp for sponsors. I can't tell you how many times we've paid for things out of our own pocket the last two years."

Fraser thought about Leslie, his wife, who was there to watch him win the gold and throw her arms in the air. They worked together at the Washtenaw sheriff's office — he in a community work program, she as an administrative assistant — and for a while there, it looked as if their first child would be twins. An ultrasound scan the other day told otherwise, but Steve said "we're more than happy with just one."

All these things rushed into his head. All these blessings. The men who had encouraged him: Minick, the former sheriff; Schebil, the new administrator; Bahr, the coach at the University of Michigan; Rockwell, the head of the Michigan Wrestling Club. Steve Fraser's mind was abuzz with people to thank and things for which to be thankful.

So when the national anthem was played at the winners' stand, he sang. The tears streaked down his cheeks and he sang as loud as he knew how. "Yeah, I know the words," he said later. "And the ones I don't know, I faked."

There were two three-minute periods in the match, and with 40 seconds remaining in the final one, Fraser was losing, 1-0. Then he got a takedown and tied the score. And it got frantic at that point because a tie was suddenly as good as a win to the American. In Greco-Roman wrestling the last man to score in a tied match wins. "I knew I had it if I just didn't slip or fall or make a stupid mistake," he said.

He did nothing stupid. Forty seconds later, the gold was his. All the work, all the scrounging and scrimping, had led to this, to the point that Steve Fraser was thrown when asked whether this might have been the last match he would wrestle. He had to think about it for a while, think about it until it sank in that this medal, the medal draped from his neck, the neck that the junior high coach once dragged into the sport of wrestling, would probably be the only Olympic medal he would ever get. Steve Fraser cradled the medal, like a single child as opposed to twins, and said he was more than happy with just one. ◆

Steve Fraser proved he was the best in the clutch — literally and figuratively. He won his last two matches by scores of 1-1 and 2-1.

Together, always together. Winners, always winners. Pamela and Paula McGee won two Class A titles at Flint Northern. They won two NCAA titles at Southern California. Then they chased an Olympic dream. Paula was cut during the trials; Pamela went on to win a gold. But at the awards ceremony, the McGees shared the glory.

ME AND PAULA MCGEE

By Charlie Vincent

The gold medal was only part of the reward for Pamela McGee. Tears and smiles and love made the XXIII Olympiad complete for her after the United States crushed Korea, 85-55, in the women's basketball final.

She broke from the awards platform after receiving the gold, along with her teammates, and slipped the medal around the neck of her twin sister, Paula — who was cut from the team during the trials. It was a tearful and emotional expression of love.

"I saw her over there and she was crying and I just thought she'd like it," Pamela said, "so I ran over and put it around her neck."

The twins from Flint were teammates at Southern California and had hoped to play in the Olympics together. But Paula was one of those who didn't make it.

"I think it was harder on me than it was on her, when she was cut," Pam said. "I've always been the stronger twin. If one of us had to be cut, I'd prefer it to be me because I could handle it better.

"When it got down to the final 16, I felt maybe it would be better if I just didn't make the team so I could be with her. But I knew that wasn't right."

Her sister's tears of joy were matched by her mother's smile of pride.

"That," said Pamela, 21, "is what makes it all worthwhile. I don't really get into awards or All-America teams or things like that, but to see my mom smile, for her to feel proud of me, that's the reward.

"We (Pam and Paula) were on a magazine cover once and she carried it around in her purse and showed people and said, 'Those are my babies.' She sacrificed for us and this is the way to pay her back, to show her I love her in some way other than verbally."

In the six Olympic games, McGee's play was overshadowed by Southern Cal teammate Cheryl Miller, who averaged 16.5 points. McGee didn't start a game and her average was just over six points, but in the end she had no complaints about her role. She scored six points in the gold medal game.

"When you get to this echelon of players," she said, "I'm just happy to be among them. I'm just happy to be able to compete and come here and get a gold medal."

And she was happier to be able to give it away. ◆

Forward Pamela McGee averaged about six points in the 1984 Olympics. Credit her with an assist during the medal ceremony, sharing her gold with her twin, Paula.

Despite winning at an unprecedented rate in the ring, the U.S. boxing team was riddled with dissension. Three boxers from Detroit's Kronk Gym — Mark Breland, Steve McCrory and Frank Tate — even left the Olympic camp to train under Emanuel Steward in Santa Monica, Calif. U.S. coach Pat Nappi almost resigned. But somehow the Americans kept beating their opponents to the punch.

Flyweight Steve McCrory, after receiving his gold medal, took time to remember his hometown. "Detroit," he announced, "this is for you."

KRONK'S TRIPLE TRIUMPH

By Mark Kram

For Detroiters Steve McCrory and Frank Tate and the rest of the U.S. Olympic boxing team, it was a day that had long been anticipated and will be long remembered.

With an opportunity to capture an unprecedented 10 gold medals, the United States emerged from the Olympic boxing finals with nine golds and a silver to go with the bronze light-heavyweight Evander Holyfield already had. Of the Americans fighting in the final day of the boxing tournament, only middleweight Virgil Hill had to settle for silver. That by far eclipses the record six gold medals the Cubans won at the 1980 Olympics in Moscow.

"Four hundred boxers start out at the beginning of the Olympics and only 12 win gold medals," said McCrory, the brother of Detroit pro champion Milton McCrory. "This is a big day for me. . . . I know my name will go down in history."

McCrory won his flyweight bout, 4-1, over Redzep Redzepovski of Yugoslavia. Superior in agility, speed and punching power, McCrory carried the bout but was accorded only a slight edge in the scoring, winning 60-58, 59-58, 58-59, 59-58 and 59-59 (he won the tie on secondary criteria). McCrory set the tempo in rounds one and two and scored frequently with right hands, but Redzepovski applied pressure in the third and won the round decisively. He also believed he may have won the bout.

"The Yugoslavian surprised me," McCrory said. "I know I won the first two rounds but I think he probably deserved one round. There was no doubt that I won."

Before the Olympics, McCrory had seen himself as the second coming of Sugar Ray Leonard; after the Olympics, McCrory figured he had arrived. "I wanted to win this gold medal and make $10 million the next two years in television commercials," McCrory said. "I knew I have the ability to do that."

Tate beat Canadian light-middleweight Shawn O'Sullivan, 5-0, but had a predictably difficult bout, winning 58-57, 59-57, 59-58, 59-58 and 59-58. O'Sullivan, who had split two career bouts with Tate, applied pressure from start to finish and had Tate in trouble in the second round. Tate took two standing eight-counts in the second, but rallied back and won the third. The capacity crowd at the Sports Arena registered an angry and protracted protest, but Tate had no doubt that he had won.

"When I came here, I told people we could win 12 gold medals and we won nine, a record," Tate said. "I have never been afraid of Shawn O'Sullivan. I won the first round, but I have to admit he hurt me in the second round. Fortunately, I recovered. I don't think Canada's ever won a gold medal in boxing, and I couldn't be the first American to let them win one. Now me and my teammate Steve McCrory get to go home to see Detroit City."

Highly celebrated Mark Breland, like McCrory and Tate trained by Kronk Gym's Emanuel Steward, won his welterweight bout easily. Plagued by a painful hand injury, Breland relied on his left and had South Korean Young-Sun An in range from beginning to end. He was not the dazzling or destructive force the public has come to expect, but he was in control and unraveled the Korean skillfully.

"Breland was tall and had a long reach," the Korean said. "I tried to get inside, but he had an excellent left jab. I thought I could win, especially in the second round when I landed a right hook to his head, but by the end of the round I started to lose hope."

Breland suffered "torn or strained tendons" in his right hand in his semifinal bout. Perhaps still not fully healed from surgery to that hand a year ago, Breland entered the Olympics conscious of hurting it, and his performances showed it. He won five bouts to reach the finals but did not look especially sharp in the first three and got indifferent reviews. Breland said that he was "feeling the pressure."

"The hand has been bothering me," he said. "When I pulled the gloves on today it was sore again, but I told myself not to let it get in the way of winning the gold medal."

And not to let it get in the way of boxing history. ◆

In 1981 a drunken driver nearly killed Ann Arbor diver Bruce Kimball. He needed 24 hours of surgery. Every bone in his face was broken. His spleen was removed. But he came back. A silver medal at the 1982 National Sports Festival. A silver at the 1984 Olympics. Then Kimball mixed drinking and driving with tragic results. His Mazda RX-7, traveling, by police estimates, at 70 to 90 m.p.h., slammed into a crowd of 30 to 40 teenagers on a dead-end road in Brandon, Fla., dubbed "The Spot." Despite a public outcry, Kimball tried for the Olympic team. The outcry wouldn't subside until he was sentenced in 1989 to 17 years in a Florida prison.

Bruce Kimball was flying high as diving's "Comeback Kid" when he won a silver medal at the Los Angeles Olympics. His career-long nemesis, Greg Louganis, took the gold.

HITTING BOTTOM
By Johnette Howard

This was the final day of Bruce Kimball's hellish week-long chase to make the U.S. Olympic team. And on the little warm-up-mat area the former University of Michigan diver had staked out for himself beforehand were a pack of Marlboros and some Rolaids. Two rolls of Rolaids.

Kimball went on to dive well. But Ohio State senior Pat Jeffrey edged him out on the 10th and last round to join Greg Louganis on the Olympic 10-meter platform diving team. As he collected his things and left the natatorium quickly, Kimball — who slipped to fourth behind Mike Wantuck of Bloomfield Hills, Mich. — told his father and coach, Dick Kimball: "I did all I could."

The defeat climaxed a controversial three-week stay in the spotlight for Bruce Kimball, who faces an Aug. 29 arraignment on five drunken-driving charges, including two counts of manslaughter. Two days ago, Kimball, 25, also was named a defendant in a

wrongful-death suit filed by the parents of one of the two boys killed when Kimball's car struck several persons in a crowd in Brandon, Fla. Six were injured, four seriously.

Dick Kimball, also U-M's diving coach, had said he didn't expect Bruce to pull out if he made the Olympic team because "it's been hell." U.S. Diving Federation spokesmen had repeatedly said no existing rules would bar Kimball from the Olympic team because of the pending charges. But Baaron Pittenger, U.S. Olympic Committee executive director, left the door slightly ajar for the first time during the preliminaries. The seven Brandon residents who drove to Indianapolis to protest Kimball's participation were happy it never came to that. When Kimball — diving two spots after Jeffrey — had finished and his final score was flashed on the scoreboard, the friends of the crash victims leapt to their feet and began clapping and hugging en masse. Several wiped away tears. "I came here 17 and I feel like I'm 77," said Jennifer Beck, who is organizing a fundraiser for the victims. "I'm so glad it's over. When he got those three 10s (on his second dive) I could just feel the tears welling up. I thought he was going to make the team."

After his final dive, Kimball climbed the steps slowly to poolside, where his father was waiting to give him a long hug. Later, in a back room where Kimball packed his things, his dad asked whether he wanted to talk to the press. But Bruce, disappearing into a hallway, gently said no. "I'd just rather go home now, Dad. OK?" ♦

TECHNICAL KNOCKOUT

By Mitch Albom

SEPT. 19,
1988
♦

Anthony Hembrick learned to fight while surviving Detroit's streets and learned to box in the Army. He made the Olympic team but never threw a punch in Seoul, South Korea, suffering the most painful knockout of his life: The U.S. coaching staff blundered in reading the schedule, and Hembrick, a middleweight, arrived too late for his fight.

He sat on a bench in a dimly lit waiting room, a hood pulled over his head, tears streaming down his cheeks. It was all coming apart, his entire Olympic dream, and there was nothing he could do about it but sit and wait, the cruelest punishment you can dish out to a boxer.

Anthony Hembrick is a Detroit kid with a Detroit story — up from the streets, joined the Army, became a champion, made the Olympic team — and he had overcome a lot of things in his life. But he could not overcome stupidity, not this time, because it was not his stupidity, it was his coach's. And now, as Hembrick sat there, paralyzed, crying, the coach, Ken Adams, was trying desperately to explain.

He had read the schedule wrong, he said. He thought the bout was later, much later, maybe the 11th bout of the day, sometime around 12:45 p.m. He and Hembrick had tried to take the 10 o'clock bus from the athletes' village, which would have reached the Chamsil boxing arena about 10:20. The bus was full. It was raining. They waited for the next one. By the time they arrived, the U.S. boxing people were at the door, screaming and waving, while Ha Jong Ho of South Korea, whose coach apparently had no problem reading the schedule, was sitting on a stool inside the ring, counting down the seconds to the easiest victory he would ever have.

They tried to dress Hembrick. Too late. Tried to tape him up. Too late. Tried to argue, appeal, stop the clock. They were frantic, yelling, please! Too late. The bout was declared a walkover about 10:50, a victory by absence, and Ha raised his hands and grinned, which must have been the most physical exertion he had all day.

A small mistake. A huge injustice. And suddenly, Anthony Hembrick was history. The wrong kind.

"Inexcusable!" screamed Ferdie Pacheco, the NBC fight analyst, in a crowd of people who were all screaming similar things. "The coach has a list. Check it, for bleep's sake! The guy's a military man. He can read schedules, can't he? Thirty years in the Army! How can you not check the thing over and over?"

Exactly. How can anything this stupid happen in something this big? Why didn't they have a team bus? Why didn't they have a meeting? There are four boxing coaches in the village and none of them could read the schedule? Come on. Athletes don't give up half their lives so coaches can take the small details lightly.

A small mistake. A huge injustice. ♦

His hopes for a medal dashed, Anthony Hembrick could only admire the taekwondo gold won by fellow Detroiter Lynnette Love.

FLINT'S ONE-HANDED HERO

By Joe Lapointe

Here were the young Americans, jogging around the green grass in the bright sunlight, waving their red, white and blue flags to celebrate a gold-medal victory over Japan in Olympic baseball.

Star-spangled banners in hand, they charged up the pitcher's mound like the Marines at Iwo Jima. Jim Abbott, the University of Michigan pitcher from Flint who got the victory with a complete game, shouted with joy and hugged everyone as the pile grew on top of him and pretty soon knocked him flat.

"My face was buried in the dirt," Abbott said after the 5-3 victory. "It was great. The greatest feeling in the world. I hurt now. My arm, my wrist. Everybody hugging. Guys lying in the dirt, looking up at the sky."

Abbott, a left-hander who has signed with the California Angels and is about to turn pro, savored his last game as an amateur.

"This is a heck of a way to go out," Abbott said as he touched the gold medal on his chest. "Winning a gold medal in a team sport is a great feeling. You hug all the guys and you slap hands. You know how good you feel, and 19 other guys feel that way, too. The feeling is increased 20-fold. It's an incredible moment."

Tino Martinez hit two home runs and knocked in four runs. Abbott went the distance, giving up seven hits and three walks. His only difficult inning was the sixth, when he gave up two runs and his lead was trimmed to 4-3.

It's only a demonstration sport, but these were hardly exhibition games. The victory avenged a 6-3 loss to Japan in the championship game of the 1984 Olympics. For the U.S. fans in the crowd of 18,000, it restored a little bit of sports pride for the United States, especially considering the timing. For this came just three hours after the Soviet basketball team had stunned the U.S. team in the semifinals.

Both basketball and baseball were invented in the United States. Both are played with increasing ability by people from other nations. If you don't think the baseball competition meant as much as the basketball, you probably are right, but you weren't there when a Korean brass band struck up "Stars and Stripes Forever" or when those American fans behind first base — including a man in an Uncle Sam hat — stood and sang "Take Me Out To The Ball Game" during the seventh-inning stretch. Another group of fans behind the backstop sang "Happy Birthday" to Abbott, who turned 21 Sept. 19. ◆

Jim Abbott quarterbacked his high school, Flint Central, in the playoffs. He won the 1987 Sullivan Award pitching for the University of Michigan and Team USA. He carried the flag in the 1987 Pan American Games. That he did it all despite being born without a right hand was a big deal to many people but not to him. But even Abbott was impressed with his star-spangled performance on a mound in Seoul.

With Jim Abbott on the mound, the United States avenged its 1984 Olympic defeat to Japan. Flowers and flag waving followed.

Greg Barton was unbeatable at 1,000
meters — in singles and in doubles.
Class salutatorian at Homer High,
Barton put his mechanical engineering
degree to practical use — designing
and constructing his paddles.

AN EPIC JOURNEY

By Joe Lapointe

Raised on a Homer pig farm, Greg Barton made a journey of epic proportions. In 1984 he became the first American to win a kayak sprint medal. Four years later in Seoul, he became the first to strike gold — twice within 90 minutes.

If time were measured as water, you could say Greg Barton won one gold medal by a tiny drop and another by a bigger drip.

Whatever the measure, Barton won two kayak races — the singles 1,000 meters by himself and the doubles 1,000 meters with Norman Bellingham.

Barton's singles victory marked the first time an American had won an Olympic kayak race. And his doubles gold made for the most successful single day for a Michigan athlete in these Summer Games of Seoul. "I've been kayaking for 18 years; I've worked for a long time for this," said Barton, 28, a native of Homer, Mich., southwest of Jackson, and a University of Michigan engineering graduate who lives in Newport Beach, Calif.

The victory in the first race was as confusing as it was close. Barton, the world champion, appeared to cross the finish line ahead of Grant Davies of Australia. But his supporters' celebration was cut short by a stunning message on the electronic scoreboard. It said Davies had finished ahead of Barton.

"I looked at the scoreboard," Barton said, "and I said, 'Oh, man, I hope someone is up in the photo finish room.'"

Somebody was checking. Using freeze-frame film for a photo finish, the judges — 10 minutes later — awarded a gold to Barton and a silver to Davies. The times:

Barton, 3:55.27.

Davies, 3:55.28.

Charles Dambach, chairman of the U.S. canoe and kayak team, said the finish might have been closer than that. "It was 5-1,000ths of a second," he said, "but the official results don't go that far. They actually considered awarding two gold medals."

In the second race, less than 90 minutes later, Barton and Bellingham spurted ahead in the last quarter-mile and finished .29 ahead of Ian Ferguson and Paul MacDonald of New Zealand. The winning time was 3:32.42.

"Winning the two golds is just icing on the cake," Barton said. "I'm kind of basking in the glory." ♦

The first U.S. kayaking gold went to a versatile athlete born with clubfeet. But Greg Barton developed a perfect body for his sport — Sylvester Stallone chest and arms, tapering off to a slim waist and legs.

BY THE NUMBERS

1980 Winter Olympics (Lake Placid, N.Y.)

ATHLETE	MICHIGAN CONNECTION	SPORT	EVENT	MEDAL
Ken Morrow	Davison	Ice hockey	Hockey (defenseman)	Gold
Mark Wells	St. Clair Shores	Ice hockey	Hockey (center)	Gold

1984 Summer Olympics (Los Angeles)

ATHLETE	MICHIGAN CONNECTION	SPORT	EVENT	MEDAL
Greg Barton	Homer	Kayaking	1,000-meter singles	Bronze
Mark Breland	Detroit's Kronk Gym	Boxing	Welterweight	Gold
Judi Brown	East Lansing (Michigan State)	Track and field	400-meter hurdles	Silver
Brian Diemer	Grand Rapids (University of Michigan)	Track and field	3,000-meter steeplechase	Bronze
Laurie Flachmeier	Detroit	Volleyball	Women's volleyball (blocker)	Silver
Steve Fraser	Ann Arbor (University of Michigan)	Wrestling	198-pound Greco-Roman	Gold
Doug Herland	Ann Arbor	Rowing	Pairs with coxswain	Bronze
Earl Jones	Inkster (Eastern Michigan)	Track	800-meter run	Bronze
Bruce Kimball	Ann Arbor (University of Michigan)	Diving	Men's platform	Silver
Barry Larkin	University of Michigan	Baseball*	Baseball (infielder)	Silver
Steve McCrory	Detroit (Kronk Gym)	Boxing	Flyweight	Gold
Pamela McGee	Flint (Flint Northern)	Basketball	Women's basketball (forward)	Gold
Ron Merriott	Ann Arbor (University of Michigan)	Diving	Men's springboard	Bronze
Chris Seufert	Chelsea (University of Michigan)	Diving	Women's springboard	Bronze
Frank Tate	Detroit (Kronk Gym)	Boxing	Light-middleweight	Gold
Kim Turner	Detroit (Detroit Mumford)	Track and field	100-meter hurdles	Bronze

1988 Winter Olympics (Calgary, Alberta)

ATHLETE	MICHIGAN CONNECTION	SPORT	EVENT	MEDAL
Peter Oppegard	Bloomfield Hills (Birmingham Ice Arena)	Figure skating	Pairs	Bronze
Jill Watson	Bloomfield Hills (Birmingham Ice Arena)	Figure skating	Pairs	Bronze

1988 Summer Olympics (Seoul, South Korea)

ATHLETE	MICHIGAN CONNECTION	SPORT	EVENT	MEDAL
Jim Abbott	Flint (University of Michigan)	Baseball*	Baseball (left-handed pitcher)	Gold
Greg Barton	Homer	Kayaking	1,000-meter singles, pairs	Two golds
Matt Cetlinski	Grosse Pointe/Warren	Swimming	800 freestyle relay	Gold
Jeff Grayer	Flint (Flint Northwestern)	Basketball	Men's basketball (guard)	Bronze
Brent Lang	University of Michigan	Swimming	400 freestyle relay**	Gold
Han Won Lee	Ann Arbor	Taekwondo*	Bantamweight	Bronze
Lynnette Love	Detroit	Taekwondo*	Heavyweight	Gold
Dan Majerle	Traverse City (Central Michigan)	Basketball	Men's basketball (small forward)	Bronze
Debbie Ochs	Howell	Archery	Women's team	Bronze
Connie Paraskevin-Young	Detroit	Cycling	Match sprint	Bronze

Demonstration sport
** Swam in preliminary heat, replaced in final.*

COLLEGE FOOTBALL

Lineman Tony Mandarich provided the
protection and quarterback Bobby
McAllister the action as Michigan
State won the 1987 Big Ten title.

Bo's First Bouquet

By Mick McCabe

JAN. 1,
1981
◆

Five times in his first 11 seasons, Bo Schembechler's Wolverines played in the Rose Bowl. Five times the Wolverines lost. When the University of Michigan fell to 1-2 in 1980 — Schembechler's worst start at the time — another run for the roses seemed remote. But the Wolverines won eight straight and, against 16th-ranked Washington, Schembechler had another chance for redemption, Pasadena-style.

As their fight song boasts, the University of Michigan Wolverines are returning to Ann Arbor as true "Champions of the West" for the first time under Bo Schembechler. And it was a passing attack that brought the usually running-minded Schembechler his first Rose Bowl victory.

Michigan quarterback John Wangler and All-America wide receiver Anthony Carter hooked up just enough to complement the power running of tailback Butch Woolfolk and another strong defensive performance to lead U-M to a 23-6 victory over Washington (9-3). It gave the fifth-ranked Wolverines (10-2) their first victory in Pasadena, Calif., since 1965 and the first after five frustrating losses under Schembechler.

"I've been here five times and five times I sat here with my head between my legs," Schembechler said. "Now I can smoke a cigar and enjoy it."

It was the first time a Schembechler-coached U-M team finished the season with a victory and the ninth straight victory for this U-M team. Don't forget: This was the same team that started the season 1-2. And, for the last 22 quarters, no team scored a touchdown against a U-M defense that returned only three starters from last season.

The Wolverines led, 7-6, at the half on Woolfolk's six-yard run. Carter, a sophomore, had not caught a pass and had carried the ball once for two yards. "John Wangler just hadn't gone to him," Schembechler said. "John felt if he did he would be forcing the ball. At halftime we told him to force it into him." After the half, Carter caught five passes for 68 yards and a touchdown and carried the ball three times for 31 yards.

Carter caught a 27-yard Wangler pass to put the ball on Washington's 11-yard line on U-M's first possession of the third quarter. Four plays later, Ali Haji-Sheikh kicked a 25-yard field goal for a 10-6 lead. The Wolverines scored again on their next possession. Wangler passed 10 yards to Chuck Christian, 17 yards to Alan Mitchell and 14 yards to Carter to set up a seven-yard touchdown pass to Carter. Woolfolk finished with 182 yards in 26 attempts and won the game's most valuable player award.

Schembechler, who suffered a heart attack the night before his first Rose Bowl in 1970, was mobbed after the game. He received a bloody nose from one of his players during the celebration.

"By the time I got pounded out there I could hardly breathe," he said with a smile. "And I don't have the best of hearts." ◆

Bo Schembechler got carried away after winning his first Rose Bowl. The Wolverines hadn't won in Pasadena since beating Oregon State, 34-7, in 1965. Bubba Paris, a 6-foot-6½, 270-pound behemoth on the offensive line, certainly could appreciate it.

◆

Hillsdale College of the Great Lakes Conference won 11 football games in 1985. But the Chargers most cherish a 10-10 tie with Central Arkansas. It gave Hillsdale a share of the NAIA national championship for the first time.

THE NAIA TIES THAT BIND

By Steve Crowe

To Hillsdale College, the final chapter in its longest football season was a touch of Pasadena without the roses, Miami sans oranges and New Orleans minus the sugar. But sweet, nonetheless.

Amid all the pomp and circumstance that a 1,000-student college could hope to be afforded, the Chargers' Mike Gatt found Scott Sugg alone down the sideline for a 58-yard touchdown with 3:04 left that forged a 10-10 tie with co-defending champion Central Arkansas and gave Hillsdale a share of its first NAIA national championship. Before 4,174 at Central Arkansas' Estes Stadium in Conway, the Bears (10-2-1) took a 10-0 halftime lead and appeared to have erased the memory of last season's 19-19 tie with Carson-Newman (Tenn.) in the title game, until, for the second week in a row, Gatt provided a fantastic finish. In the semifinals, Gatt led Hillsdale from a 21-0 fourth-quarter

That co-championship season. Hillsdale and Central Arkansas had to take turns posing with the championship banner and trophy.

deficit against Mesa (Colo.) to a 24-21, double-overtime victory.

Trailing 10-3 at his 42 with a little more than three minutes left, Gatt scrambled to his right and then back to his left before spotting Sugg waving his arms at the Hillsdale 45. Sugg needed just one block, supplied by Dave Mifsud, to make it to the end zone.

"That actually was a broken play," said Hillsdale coach Dick Lowry, whose team (11-1-1) had won 10 straight. "Our receivers always break back toward the quarterback on those, and Scott did what he was supposed to do and then made a nice run."

Mark Baker's extra point tied the score, and both teams seemed content to share the title in the final three minutes. "Win or tie," Lowry said, "we still go home as national champions. I think right now we might be a little down. But once we get on the plane, what we've accomplished will sink in."

Said Central Arkansas coach Harold Horton: "Last year I thought Carson-Newman was a better football team than us. This time, I think we were the better team, not taking anything away from Hillsdale."

But the Chargers outgained the Bears, 340 yards to 145, and swept the most valuable player awards. Linebacker Kurt Norman, the defensive MVP, had 10 tackles and two sacks. Tim Grote, the offensive MVP, caught nine passes for 90 yards. ◆

ANOTHER CLOSE SHAVE

By Tommy George

OCT. 18,
1986
◆

No. 1 Iowa and No. 2 Michigan played for the top of the charts on a dark and rainy October 1985 afternoon in Kinnick Stadium. On the final play, Rob Houghtlin kicked a 29-yard field goal to defeat Michigan, 12-10. One year later, the Hawkeyes had to come to Ann Arbor, where a hungry group of undefeated Wolverines were waiting.

It was as if he were home again in St. Joseph, Mich., in his backyard, booting Campbell's soup cans and pretending the game was on the line. Oh, how many times as a child had Mike Gillette played game-winning scenarios over and over with his cans? And, finally, he found make-believe can become ecstatic reality.

Gillette's 34-yard field goal as time expired lifted fourth-ranked Michigan to a heart-thumping, 20-17 victory over eighth-ranked Iowa before 105,879 at Michigan Stadium. It was redemption for Michigan. Redemption for Gillette.

This time it was the Wolverines' fans who swarmed the field in wild celebration. This time it was kicker Rob Houghtlin and coach Hayden Fry and the rest of the Hawkeyes who walked off the field with that sickened feeling, with the shock and trauma of losing as — on the game's last play — the ball sailed cleanly between the uprights. "We're even now," said Fry, who later sat alone in the first row of Iowa's team bus and, behind those dark glasses, pensively contemplated this one that slipped away.

For Gillette, it was the final, giant leap back from an up-and-down freshman season in 1985. He set the Michigan season record for field goals (16) only to lose his starting job to Pat Moons when Gillette was suspended for the Ohio State game for disciplinary reasons. He kicked a school-record 53-yard field goal in the first quarter against Iowa and then punched the winning kick that made Michigan 6-0 (3-0 in the Big Ten).

"What a day, huh?" Gillette said. "I didn't think about anything but hitting the ball like an extra point. All I had to do was hit the ball straight."

After U-M called a time-out with five seconds left, the ball at the Iowa 17, and summoned Gillette, Iowa (5-1, 2-1) called another time-out. In addition, there was a television time-out.

It's good! Blocker Gerald White, kicker Mike Gillette and holder Monte Robbins watch the winning field goal split the uprights. The Wolverines started their final drive with 1:47 left, after Iowa fumbled in U-M territory.

"He came over," U-M coach Bo Schembechler said, "and I said, 'They're trying to psych you out. They're trying to ice you.' He said, 'Yeah, yeah, yeah. . . .' This is the last guy that would be flustered. He's the cockiest guy that ever lived."

And grateful he got another chance.

"It was a long time coming," Gillette said. "I couldn't ask for more."

Nor could the Wolverines. ◆

Michigan quarterback Jim Harbaugh, the quiet but confident son of a football coach, stepped out of character the week of the Ohio State game. He publicly guaranteed a victory. With a Rose Bowl berth on the line, the Wolverines and Buckeyes clashed in a tug-of-war that, arguably, was the Big Ten's best game of the decade.

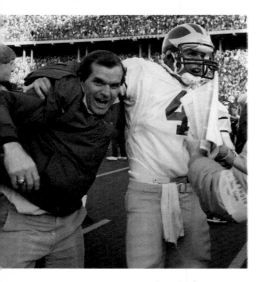

It was the best and worst of weeks for Jack and Jim Harbaugh. Jack, head coach at Western Michigan, was fired on Monday after a 3-8 season. Michigan coach Bo Schembecher, Jack's boss from 1973 to 1979, called the firing "one of the tragedies of sport" and the Western position "the worst job in America." Jim, also on Monday, guaranteed a victory over Ohio State. He delivered and celebrated with his dad.

A MICHIGAN CLASSIC

By Tommy George

Michigan had been there before — no, not in quite the same setting or for such tremendous stakes, but this scenario was all too familiar. Precious seconds left. The ball floating toward the goalposts on a game-deciding field goal.

For Michigan, the Big Ten co-championship appeared to be slipping away. The roses were wilting. But in the five seconds it took Ohio State's Matt Frantz to attempt a 45-yard field goal that drifted left with 61 seconds left, several Wolverines experienced memories both sweet and sour. Oh, how sweet the recollection will be for Michigan, which beat Ohio State, 26-24, before an Ohio Stadium record crowd of 90,674.

Michigan (10-1) and Ohio State (9-3) share the Big Ten championship with 7-1 records, but the Wolverines will go to the Rose Bowl against Arizona State in Pasadena, Calif., on New Year's Day because they won this classic battle. Ohio State accepted a Cotton Bowl berth in Dallas. In the end, U-M's destiny was decided by one kick. Again for the Wolverines, in the final seconds. Hit or miss? They had been there before.

"I've been there a lot in 24 years of coaching," said Michigan coach Bo Schembechler, who got the game ball after becoming U-M's all-time leader in coaching victories with 166, passing Fielding H. Yost. Schembechler, of course, vividly remembers Michigan's recent games decided by late kicks, beginning with the game-ending loss by a field goal, 12-10, at Iowa last season and the game-ending miss by Chris White that left U-M and Illinois tied, 3-3, at Champaign. Then came Notre Dame's last-minute miss by John Carney in this year's season opener, a 24-23 U-M victory; the last-second boot that beat Iowa, 20-17, at Michigan Stadium; and Minnesota's game-ending kick last weekend, which ruined U-M's perfect season, 20-17.

"We have been there before," quarterback Jim Harbaugh said. "We've seen it happen against us and for us. I was getting ready over there, if it went through, to try and drive us to get a field goal to win it."

Cornerback Garland Rivers was on the field during Frantz's kick, lining up deep and running and leaping for the block. "I tried not to think about all the times before this has happened to us, but just tried to knock the ball down," Rivers said. "I dove and looked back. And what did I see? I saw victory."

The game started as an Ohio State rout. The Buckeyes covered 125 yards in 13 plays on their first two possessions for a 14-3 lead. But Michigan closed the gap to 14-6 by the half and built a 26-17 lead by early in the fourth quarter. U-M finished with 529 yards (268 rushing and 261 passing) and 27 first downs, averaging 6.5 yards a play and leading in possession time, 35:39 to 24:21.

Harbaugh and tailback Jamie Morris were the catalysts. Harbaugh backed his guarantee of victory by completing 19 of 29 passes for 261 yards. Morris ran all over the Buckeyes with 210 yards on 29 carries and two touchdowns.

"Bo told us Thursday that he wanted us to run and play our best game ever, to play like we never have before, and then he came to my room last night and said there would be some creases and holes," Morris said. "We just had to find them."

Morris did.

But Frantz knew he could make up for Morris and all of Michigan's punch. The Buckeyes had pulled to 26-24 with 9:42 left on a 17-yard Jim Karsatos-to-Cris Carter touchdown pass — their second of the game. After the teams traded punts, U-M tailback Thomas Wilcher fumbled at OSU's 37 with 3:17 left, setting up the potential game-winning drive. Ohio State reached Michigan's 28, and on fourth-and-two coach Earle Bruce sent in Frantz.

"It was a tough decision," Bruce said. "You have to take that chance."

Frantz couldn't question it.

"I thought it would be good," Frantz said. "I just knew it would be good. It felt good when I kicked it. I can't believe it." ◆

Down 14-6 at the half, the Wolverines scored their first touchdown midway through the third quarter on Jamie Morris' four-yard run. He would score the go-ahead points on an eight-yard run, set up by his 52-yard out-of-control, across-the-field rush.

Duffy Daugherty became so popular nationally that Time magazine once pictured him on its cover. But Michigan State was Daugherty's life. He coached the Spartans for 19 seasons (109-69-5) but will be remembered best for his '65 and '66 teams, which went 19-1-1 overall and 14-0 in the Big Ten. Each team finished second in the final Associated Press rankings.

ALWAYS DUFFY

By George Puscas

Nobody ever called him Hugh. Maybe his mother, occasionally his coal-miner father. To all others, he was Duffy. Always Duffy.

Some people wear their nicknames well, but nobody ever wore one better than Hugh Daugherty, 72, the former Michigan State football coach who died in Santa Barbara, Calif. There was little formality about him. He was publicly the Irish pixie, short and stocky, a man of endearing charm, with smiles and jokes that seemed constant. For years, he regaled banquet crowds around the country and made college football seem like a game filled always with fun for all.

It's an exaggeration, of course, to say that it was all fun and everybody loved Duffy Daugherty. There were notable exceptions. But he made it close.

On the football staff at MSU are two men who were Daugherty disciples when they were with top Detroit high school teams. One is George Perles, the head coach, out of Western High. The other is Ed Rutherford, from Denby, who is Perles' administrative assistant. They had been Daugherty's pipeline into the fertile city football fields, and both later were hired by him. Daugherty could inspire deep loyalty, perhaps because he had it.

Several times in the midst of his long reign at MSU, he had opportunities to move to another school at far greater pay. In 1962, at a Big Ten meeting in Chicago, word came that Texas A&M, which had tried to hire him earlier, was offering $75,000 a year — more than double his MSU pay — and other blandishments, to come there and coach. Daugherty sat at a hotel bar talking about it, and finally, he said: "Thanks for drinking with me. I've decided not to take that job, you know."

It led to the line that Duffy Daugherty had joined health and happiness as things money cannot buy. But a day later, he called. "That's not true," he said, laughing. "I can be had."

Nobody ever had him, not in the sense that they could take him away from Michigan State. When he left in 1972, the decision was his; the well had gone dry at MSU, and perhaps, at age 57, so had he.

In Daugherty's final game in the 5-5-1 1972 season, the Spartans beat Northwestern, 24-14. His players carried Duffy from the field on their shoulders. Those who loved him are left today with one last, sadder march. ◆

Duffy Daugherty gave Michigan State fans and athletic director Doug Weaver plenty of reasons to applaud. Daugherty was inducted into the College Football Hall of Fame in 1984.

Warriors of the Road

By Mick McCabe

Eastern Michigan and Jim Harkema had faced longer odds. In 1982 Eastern had the nation's longest losing streak — 27 games. In 1984 the Mid-American Conference tried to expel Eastern because of small crowds. And Harkema, a highly successful coach at Grand Valley State, won only once in 1983, his first season, and twice in 1984. But the program and Harkema survived. In 1987 he led the Hurons to their first MAC title and California Bowl, only to face a 16½-point favorite.

I t was the perfect ending to a fairy tale. That is what happened when Eastern Michigan upset heavily favored San Jose State, 30-27, in a classic California Bowl in Fresno. Ron Adams' 31-yard touchdown pass to Craig Ostrander with 3:59 remaining won the game. Gary Patton had runs of 12 and 35 yards in the winning drive.

"Ostrander kept telling me all day he could get it," said Eastern coach Jim Harkema, "so we went for it."

So this Eastern Michigan team — which commissioner Jim Lessig tried to kick out of the Mid-American Conference before the 1984 season — may have saved the MAC's affiliation with this bowl and the Pacific Coast Athletic Association, whose champion had blown out the MAC's in the three previous Cal Bowls. Northern Illinois was the last MAC team to win it; the Huskies beat Cal State-Fullerton, 20-13, in 1983. Even in '87, the deck seemed stacked against the Hurons before they played their first game. Eastern was the only MAC team with five conference road games. But Harkema began calling his team the "Road Warriors" — and they did more than anyone hoped when they dumped 16½-point favorite San Jose State (10-2).

"It's just a great achievement, football-wise," Harkema said. "But we take it with a great deal of humility because San Jose is a great football team. I told our players at halftime they were playing big-time football."

The Hurons had the ball almost 37 of the 60 minutes, which kept San Jose's highly touted quarterback, Mike Perez, on the sidelines. He completed 26 of 39 passes for 290 yards, but he also threw some very bad passes.

The Eastern offense had quite a feel for the game. Patton rushed for 130 yards on 21 carries. Although Adams threw for only 100 yards (7-of-12 with two interceptions), he made several key completions and ran for 43 yards on 14 carries. After the Hurons regained possession with just over two minutes left, Adams got the first down they needed. It came on a seven-yard bootleg on third-and-four, and San Jose never touched the ball again.

"There is a real deep satisfaction," Harkema said. "We're 10-2, and we're bowl champs. It's like you've climbed a mountain." ◆

A California Bowl victory brought hugs and kisses for Eastern Michigan linebacker Tom Kiefer.

The '80s brought plenty of turmoil and few victories to Michigan State's football program. Darryl Rogers bolted for Arizona State, leaving in a comedy of lies and bitter feelings. Muddy Waters, a small college coaching giant, mustered only 10 victories in three seasons. Next came George Perles, hired away from the new USFL three months before he was scheduled to coach his first game. In four seasons, Perles' best was 7-5 in 1985. Fans were grumbling when the Spartans opened 1-2 in 1987. But then came the magic. A 7-0-1 Big Ten season. A Top-10 ranking. And a date in Pasadena.

Defensive end Joe Bergin got a grip on Todd Krumm after the senior safety recovered a Southern California fumble with 1:37 left in the game. "The way they were moving the ball," Krumm said, "we needed something." Something else Michigan State got: its first Rose Bowl victory since a Duffy Daugherty-coached team beat UCLA, 17-14, in 1956.

A CROWN OF ROSES

By Mitch Albom

They had the ball! They had the ball! Todd Krumm was cradling it, dancing with it, raising it above his head and leaping into the arms of teammate Kurt Larson, and only gravity kept them from flying off into space. All the waiting, all the lean years, all the talk of Rose Bowl jinx — it was all crushed down and squeezed inside this little brown football, and now, Michigan State had it. At last.

"It was awesome! It was a relief!" Krumm would yell outside the locker room after Michigan State had stunned the disbelievers with a nail-biting, 20-17 victory over Southern California in the Rose Bowl — the first time a Big Ten team had won it in seven years. Awesome? Relief? Tell us about it. Until that point — when Krumm recovered a Rodney Peete fumble with 1:37 left — destiny seemed sure to slip the Spartans a mickey.

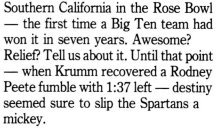

They had played a powerful first half — an arresting display of rushing and defense — but like a tired runner, the Spartans' energy seemed to fade. A 14-3 halftime lead slipped to 20-17, and USC was a dragon down the stretch. Hot? Ho, boy. Peete was directing the Trojans to a heroic finish, as surely as if a Hollywood screenwriter had called for it.

And then, the most miraculous thing: With USC on the MSU 30, Peete called for the snap — and never got it. The ball bounced, players fell on it, Larson kicked it, and on two bounces it landed in Krumm's waiting grasp, and he was never going to let it go.

"Kurt was hugging me, but I wanted to hug him," Krumm would say. And in the stands, MSU faithful were hugging one another. Was this incredible or what? They had the lead. They had one minute left. And they had the ball! They had the ball!

"I'm still nervous — can you believe that?" coach George Perles said after it was all over, after his Spartans had survived one final threat by USC, and had watched the clock turn to 0:00 and ring in the New Year better than it ever did in Times Square. "This feels great. For us, for the Big Ten, for everybody."

Raise your hand if you weren't at least a little moved by this fairy tale. That way we know who the dead people are. How long had all the parties waited for this? MSU hadn't been to Pasadena in 22 years. The conference hadn't won out there since 1981.

"What do you think about breaking the Big Ten jinx?" a reporter asked Perles. ➡

Michigan State's dream season
started with a 27-13 victory over USC
in East Lansing and ended with a 20-
17 victory over USC in the Rose Bowl.
Senior tailback Lorenzo White rushed
for 111 yards and two touchdowns in
the first game, 113 yards and two
touchdowns in the rematch.

"You've got to ask those other teams about the jinx," he answered. "I like the Rose Bowl."

I like the Rose Bowl? Too much. But then, this whole adventure was like that, this whole week of Spartans In Paradise. Here was the most unlikely of teams — nobody picked them to get this far — a group of nice, quiet, muscular guys coached by a ruddy-faced, basso-voiced man who said, "Hey, I don't care how Michigan and Ohio State did it. We're going to Disneyland and we're going to enjoy the hell out of it."

Yeah.

And the game? Oh, my. This was a lifetime in one afternoon. Sunlight to darkness, warmth to cold, a lead to a tie to a glorious victory that was not assured until the final snap. How much older was everyone when this thing ended? Ten years?

"It felt like the second half went on forever," admitted quarterback Bobby McAllister, who provided the most acrobatic play of the afternoon, scrambling to the sidelines, directing traffic, then leaping as he reached out of bounds and connecting on a 36-yard miracle to Andre Rison — a play that led to the winning field goal. He leapt. He threw it in mid-air.

"What do you call that?" he was asked.

"I call it . . . "

He laughed.

"I call it 'make something happen.' "

Perfect. Because that's what MSU needed. That pass — and another earlier bomb to Rison of 55 yards — kept the otherwise slow-grinding MSU offense from running out of steam. It was just one of countless memories for an MSU scrapbook:

Here was a brilliant display of labor by Lorenzo White, who carried 24 times in the first half alone for 89 yards and two touchdowns. The quiet senior tailback, who had failed to win the Heisman Trophy, played those first 30 minutes as if they might cast the award in his image next year. He finished with 113 yards, and more important, a victory in his last game. "We won; I'm done," he said. A pretty and effective final rhyme.

Even though George Perles had lost his first two bowls, he demanded that the Spartans concentrate on having a good time in California. Perles even taped his weekly TV show at Disneyland, with help from potential MSU recruits Donald Duck and Mickey Mouse. The good times kept rolling for holder Greg Montgomery and kicker John Langeloh after Langeloh, a redshirt freshman, broke a 17-17 tie with a 36-yard field goal with 4:14 left. He had earlier kicked a 40-yarder.

And from the rhyme to the reason: defense. Percy Snow, sophomore linebacker, 17 tackles, 15 unassisted. If you're looking for a single reason for victory this day, you can start with his number. Despite its third-quarter drowsiness, the MSU defense — its forte all year — was a steel drum when it had to be. That's how you win big games.

What else? Lord. Who can remember it all? There were fake field goals — two by USC — and interceptions and a long punt return and a USC touchdown pass, Peete to Ken Henry, in which only a centimeter of shoe kissed the fair territory of the end zone. Thrills, chills, spills. A sellout crowd split down the middle, half green and white, half red and gold. The fans were so loyal that when one side began the wave, the other refused to carry it. A Rose Bowl worthy of its tradition, for sure.

And finally, an MSU victory. This is one for the also-rans, the co-stars, the teams that live in the shadows of more famous programs. Listen up: Sometimes the underdog gets a shot. And sometimes the underdog wins. How fitting that the long, lamented Big Ten hex is broken by Michigan State.

"I know we usually have the 24-hour rule," Perles said after the game — reverting to his 24 hours of celebration or mourning he allows his team following games, "but I'm waiving that. They can celebrate from now until next spring for all I care."

Minutes after the game was over and the TV cameras had taken you to a commercial break, the MSU players began jogging off the field, then suddenly turned and headed back the other way, to the far corner, where sat thousands of Michigan State fans, who had waited — what, forever? — for this. And the marching band rose, and marched into the Michigan State fight song, and everybody, players, fans, joined in — "FIGHT! FIGHT! FIGHT!" — their voices crashing into the cool California darkness.

Beautiful. Here was the final scene of the dream; players and fans singing in unison, some of them crying, after a game that finally, finally, put an end to the old and a sparkle to the new. They had the ball. They had it all. ◆

1989

◆

FINALLY, IT'S BO'S SHOW

By Mitch Albom

He was running for all of them, for this Michigan team, and for every Michigan team that has ever come to Pasadena and had its face smeared with California egg. Someone grabbed his feet. He broke free. Someone wrapped around his thigh. He yanked loose. He ran through the linemen and through the linebackers and through the hands and arms and bodies, breaking free as the ghosts of Wolverines past screamed in a collective voice: "GO! GO! NEVER STOP!"

Leroy Hoard was charging downfield, and he was taking Michigan with him. A 61-yard run that would ensure a Michigan victory in this traditionally haunted stadium. And when he sprinted over the goal line on a gutsy fourth-and-goal call for the winning touchdown, and the Michigan fans showered the field with plastic seat cushions — "SIT ON IT, USC!" — well, you could hear the sigh of relief all the way out in Pasadena.

"I can hardly even remember, it happened so fast!" gushed Hoard after Michigan beat the Trojans, 22-14, in the 75th Rose Bowl. "They say when worst comes to worst take the ball and run — and that's what I did!"

Wake up and smell the roses, U-M. This was not only a great Michigan victory, a great comeback, and a tribute to the spirit of a team that had to come back from the very first game of the season — but it was also long overdue. Bo Schembechler has brought too many good teams out West too many times and gone home empty.

Not this time. Against the No. 5 team in the country, which featured Mr. Charisma, Rodney Peete, at quarterback, the 11th-ranked Wolverines (9-2-1) did it the way they have all year, as a team — a suddenly choking defense, a suddenly gambling offense. And when the gun sounded, they banded together for one final team effort: carrying Schembechler off on their shoulders.

Happy New Year, Bo.

Smell the roses.

"ON BEHALF OF SOME GREAT WOLVERINES, I ACCEPT THIS TROPHY!" yelled Schembechler when they handed him the victor's trophy. And why not? In his 20 years as U-M coach, he had suffered through seven Rose Bowl defeats and only one victory before this one. Finally, in the dying sunlight of Pasadena, a Schembechler dream came true. And it was just the way he likes it. Here was a game that ran the gamut of emotion.

Pick it up at halftime, the score Trojans 14, Wolverines 3. The Michigan offense had fallen asleep. Receivers were dropping passes. The Wolverines failed to gain a first down in the second quarter. They were getting beaten up and beaten down, and Peete had scrambled through their defense twice for touchdowns. The jokes were hatching again. Good ol' Michigan. Nice team. Just can't beat the Pac-10.

And then, the second half.

"Bo told us to forget the score at halftime, just forget it," said defensive tackle Mark Messner. "He said if we stopped beating ourselves (a fumble, overthrown passes, a missed 34-yard field goal in the end of the first half), then we could beat this team."

And he was right. In that second half, it seemed as if the voices from Wolverines past joined in a singular chorus that screamed "No more! Enough of this embarrassment!" And suddenly the 1988 Wolverines began to rise, from the mountain of dirt on their Rose Bowl reputation, from the unforgivable errors they had committed earlier in the game. And they rolled. A touchdown drive to close it to 14-9. A snake-tight defense. Another drive featuring Hoard's running and a clutch pass from Demetrius Brown to tight end Derrick Walker. Another touchdown. More defense. And that final drive, the undying legs of Hoard carrying them to Pasadena heaven.

"HAIL TO THE VICTORS VALIANT . . . " the outnumbered U-M fans sang in ➡

Defensive tackle Brent White found himself in the center of Michigan's post-game celebration. White had five tackles, including the lone sack of USC quarterback Rodney Peete.

Michigan receiver John Kolesar
couldn't corral this pass from
Demetrius Brown but did grab three
for 49 yards.

Michigan fullback Leroy Hoard stretched his way to 142 yards and two touchdowns. Hoard, a redshirt sophomore from New Orleans, gained more yards against the Trojans than nine of their first 11 opponents. Southern Cal (10-2) had been second in the nation in rushing defense, allowing 76.6 yards a game.

the stands. For here was a comeback performance led by comeback kids. Remember Brown, the shy quarterback who was demoted in preseason for iffy grades and a lackadaisical attitude? All he did was rifle a touchdown pass, direct the offense, scramble when necessary, and yes, not throw a single interception, thank you.

And how about Hoard? He had been suspended at midseason because he cut two classes. Schembechler doesn't bend the rules. Not for walk-ons. Not for stars. Hoard had justifiably won the Rose Bowl MVP trophy with 19 carries, 142 yards and two touchdowns.

And what of Schembechler, the coach who refuses to bend, keeps his team under the same strict principles as always — and had to lug around that lousy bowl record year after year? How long had he been at this? Long enough that one of his assistants in his first Rose Bowl (1970) was coaching against him across the sidelines. Larry Smith, USC's head man, once baby-sat for

Schembechler's kids. Now he was trying to do unto him what the other Pac-10 coaches had done seven of eight times.

Sorry, Larry.

"There is a world of difference between winning and losing," admitted Schembechler, who had lost five of these Rose Bowls in the '70s, and two since his only previous victory (1981, a 23-6 victory over Washington). "Losing tears the heart out of you." He grinned. "And I don't have a real good heart to begin with."

His cardiologist might agree; his team might object. They end the 1988 season with only two defeats — to the No. 1 and No. 2 teams in the country, Notre Dame and Miami (Fla.), by a combined three points. And

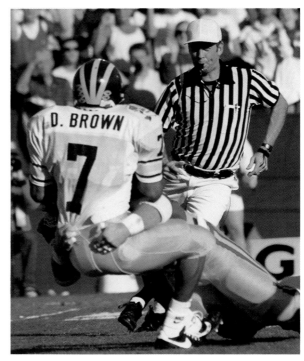

they played this last game as much for their coach as for themselves. With 50 seconds left, when John Milligan stepped in front of a Peete pass in USC's final desperation drive, intercepted it, fell on the ground and was smothered by wildly cheering teammates, well, they had delivered.

"A dream come true," said Messner. "A dream come true," said Hoard. What else can you say at a moment like that?

An hour after the victory, with the stadium empty and the night sky dark and cold, Schembechler sat in the yellow coaches' room, reclining in a chair, his fingers wrapped around an empty Diet Pepsi can.

"That how you celebrate?" he was asked.

"Nope." He smiled. "Look here. I wanna show you something."

He got up, reached for his sports coat, and pulled out a long, plastic-wrapped cigar.

"See this?" he said. "I quit smoking how long ago? But I promised myself I'm gonna smoke one of these after every Rose Bowl we win."

He broke into a howling laugh.

"And that probably ain't gonna be too many!"

Light 'em if you got 'em. Michigan wins — in January. On the feet of a once-suspended fullback, the arm of a once-demoted quarterback, the hits of a once-defeated defense, and the resiliency of a team that believes in its coach, and therefore, believes in itself. Happy New Year, Michigan. Wake up and smell the roses.

Or in Bo's case, the smoke. ◆

Demetrius Brown, who had thrown seven interceptions against MSU the year before, kept his cool and kept the Wolverines hot. He missed on 13 of 24 passes but none were intercepted. He threw a six-yard TD pass — set up by his 22-yard scramble.

After a 0-7 bowl record in the '70s, Michigan coach Bo Schembechler won two Rose Bowls, a Bluebonnet, a Fiesta and a Hall of Fame in the '80s.

BY THE NUMBERS

College football

1980 SEASON	RECORDS	FINISH	PASSING	RUSHING	RECEIVING
Central Michigan (MAC)	9-2-0 (7-2-0)	1st, 1 GA Western Michigan	Northup (1,011)	Todd (695)	Mike Hirn (388)
Eastern Michigan (MAC)	1-9-0 (1-7-0)	10th, 5½ GB Central Michigan	Davis (1,143)	Williams (456)	Dackin (363)
Michigan (Big Ten)	10-2-0 (8-0-0)	1st, 1 GA Ohio State, Purdue	Wangler (1,522)	Woolfolk (1,042)	Carter (818)
Michigan State (Big Ten)	3-8-0 (2-6-0)	9th, 6 GB Michigan	Leister (1,559)	Smith (667)	Jones (568)
Western Michigan (MAC)	7-4-0 (6-3-0)	2nd, 1 GB Central Michigan	George (644)	Morrow (778)	Hinton (429)

1981 SEASON	RECORDS	FINISH	PASSING	RUSHING	RECEIVING
Central Michigan (MAC)	7-4-0 (7-2-0)	3rd, 1 GB Toledo	DeMarco (1,159)	Mitchell (1,068)	Hirn (295)
Eastern Michigan (MAC)	0-11-0 (0-9-0)	10th, 8 GB Toledo	Green (1,391)	Calhoun (971)	Dackin (440)
Michigan (Big Ten)	9-3-0 (6-3-0)	T-3rd, ½ GB Iowa, Ohio State	Smith (1,661)	Woolfolk (1,459)	Carter (952)
Michigan State (Big Ten)	5-6-0 (4-5-0)	T-6th, 2½ GB Iowa, Ohio State	Clark (1,521)	Roberts (461)	Jones (624)
Western Michigan (MAC)	6-5-0 (5-4-0)	5th, 3 GB Toledo	George (1,419)	Faulkner (701)	Phillips (809)

1982 SEASON	RECORDS	FINISH	PASSING	RUSHING	RECEIVING
Central Michigan (MAC)	6-4-1 (5-3-1)	4th, 1½ GB Bowling Green	DeMarco (1,113)	Adams (1,090)	Jackson (412)
Eastern Michigan (MAC)	1-9-1 (1-7-1)	9th, 5½ GB Bowling Green	Coulter (1,415)	Calhoun (656)	Simpson (385)
Michigan (Big Ten)	8-4-0 (8-1-0)	1st, ½ GA Ohio State	Smith (1,735)	Ricks (1,388)	Carter (844)
Michigan State (Big Ten)	2-9-0 (2-7-0)	T-8th, 6 GB Michigan	Leister (1,321)	Ellis (671)	Grant (547)
Western Michigan (MAC)	7-2-2 (5-2-2)	2nd, 1 GB Bowling Green	Conklin (851)	Faulkner (910)	Phillips (577)

1983 SEASON	RECORDS	FINISH	PASSING	RUSHING	RECEIVING
Central Michigan (MAC)	8-3-0 (7-2-0)	T-2nd, 1 GB Northern Illinois	Fillmore (915)	Adams (1,431)	DeBoer (540)
Eastern Michigan (MAC)	1-10-0 (0-9-0)	10th, 8 GB Northern Illinois	Coulter (1,827)	Calhoun (871)	Powell (582)
Michigan (Big Ten)	9-3-0 (8-1-0)	2nd, 1 GB Illinois	Smith (1,420)	Rogers (1,002)	Nelson (494)
Michigan State (Big Ten)	4-6-1 (2-6-1)	7th, 6½ GB Illinois	Brown (837)	Butler (549)	Turner (549)
Western Michigan (MAC)	6-5-0 (4-5-0)	6th, 4 GB Northern Illinois	Hoffman (1,407)	Faulkner (1,668)	Spielmaker (653)

1984 SEASON	RECORDS	FINISH	PASSING	RUSHING	RECEIVING
Central Michigan (MAC)	8-2-1 (6-2-1)	3rd, 1 GB Toledo	DeMarco (1,427)	Adams (1,204)	DeBoer (831)
Eastern Michigan (MAC)	2-7-2 (2-5-2)	T-8th, 4½ GB Toledo	Gordon (949)	Patton (566)	Powell (261)
Michigan (Big Ten)	6-6-0 (5-4-0)	T-6th, 2 GB Ohio State	Harbaugh (718)	Morris (574)	Nelson (459)
Michigan State (Big Ten)	6-6-0 (5-4-0)	T-6th, 2 GB Ohio State	Yarema (1,477)	White (616)	Ingram (499)
Western Michigan (MAC)	5-6-0 (3-6-0)	T-8th, 4½ GB Toledo	Hoffman (1,732)	Cheatham (778)	Reed (591)

BY THE NUMBERS

College football

1985 SEASON	RECORDS	FINISH	PASSING	RUSHING	RECEIVING
Central Michigan (MAC)	7-3-0 (6-3-0)	3rd, 3 GB Bowling Green	Fillmore (1,191)	Brown (655)	DeBoer (494)
Eastern Michigan (MAC)	4-7-0 (3-6-0)	T-6th, 6 GB Bowling Green	Adams (977)	Patton (631)	Vesling (354)
Michigan (Big Ten)	10-1-1 (6-1-1)	2nd, ½ GB Iowa	Harbaugh (1,976)	Morris (1,030)	Jokisch (681)
Michigan State (Big Ten)	7-5-0 (5-3-0)	T-4th, 2 GB Iowa	Yarema (840)	White (2,066)	Ingram (745)
Western Michigan (MAC)	4-6-1 (4-4-1)	4th, 4½ GB Bowling Green	Conklin (1,574)	Howard (819)	Sorce (567)

1986 SEASON	RECORDS	FINISH	PASSING	RUSHING	RECEIVING
Central Michigan (MAC)	5-5-0 (4-4-0)	T-5th, 2 GB Miami (Ohio)	Carruthers (912)	Stevenson (1,104)	Houston (210)
Eastern Michigan (MAC)	6-5-0 (4-4-0)	T-5th, 2 GB Miami (Ohio)	Adams (1,995)	Patton (1,058)	Vesling (653)
Michigan (Big Ten)	11-2-0 (7-1-0)	T-1st, 0 GA Ohio State*	Harbaugh (2,729)	Morris (1,086)	Higgins (621)
Michigan State (Big Ten)	6-5-0 (4-4-0)	5th, 3 GB Michigan, Ohio State	Yarema (2,581)	White (633)	Rison (966)
Western Michigan (MAC)	3-8-0 (3-5-0)	8th, 3 GB Miami (Ohio)	Conklin (1,668)	Glenn (602)	Spielmaker (575)

1987 SEASON	RECORDS	FINISH	PASSING	RUSHING	RECEIVING
Central Michigan (MAC)	5-5-1 (3-4-1)	T-6th, 3½ GB Eastern Michigan	Carruthers (1,323)	Hood (1,121)	Reed (652)
Eastern Michigan (MAC)	10-2-0 (7-1-0)	1st, 2 GA three teams**	Adams (1,527)	Patton (1,242)	Ziegler (486)
Michigan (Big Ten)	8-4-0 (5-3-0)	4th, 2½ GB Michigan State	Brown (1,251)	Morris (1,703)	McMurtry (474)
Michigan State (Big Ten)	9-2-1 (7-0-1)	1st, 1½ GA Indiana, Iowa	McAllister (1,171)	White (1,572)	Rison (785)
Western Michigan (MAC)	5-6-0 (4-4-0)	5th, 3 GB Eastern Michigan	Kruse (1,592)	Davis (477)	Hence (858)

1988 SEASON	RECORDS	FINISH	PASSING	RUSHING	RECEIVING
Central Michigan (MAC)	7-4-0 (5-3-0)	T-3rd, 2 GB Western Michigan	Bender (1,309)	Riley (1,238)	Hopkins (433)
Eastern Michigan (MAC)	6-3-1 (5-2-1)	2nd, 1½ GB Western Michigan	Sullivan (1,664)	B. Foster (762)	Ostrander (676)
Michigan (Big Ten)	9-2-1 (7-0-1)	1st, 1 GA Michigan State	Taylor (957)	Boles (1,408)	McMurtry (470)
Michigan State (Big Ten)	6-5-1 (6-1-1)	2nd, 1 GB Michigan	McAllister (1,406)	Ezor (1,496)	Rison (961)
Western Michigan (MAC)	9-3-0 (7-1-0)	1st, 1½ GA Eastern Michigan	Kimbrough (2,465)	Davis (1,054)	Agema (486)

Michigan and Ohio State finished at 7-1, two games ahead of Iowa and Minnesota. Michigan went to the Rose Bowl because it beat Ohio State.
**Bowling Green, Kent State and Miami (Ohio) tied for second at 5-3.*

Coaches

Central Michigan: Herb Deromedi (1980-88), 62-32-3 (.655). Total: 62-32-3 (.655).
Eastern Michigan: Mike Stock (1980-82), 1-23-0 (.042); Bob LaPointe (1982), 1-6-1 (.188); Jim Harkema (1983-88), 29-34-3 (.462). Total: 31-63-4 (.337).
Michigan: Bo Schembechler (1980-88), 80-27-2 (.743). Total: 80-27-2 (.743).
Michigan State: Muddy Waters (1980-82), 10-23-0 (.303); George Perles (1983-88), 38-29-3 (.564). Total: 48-52-3 (.481).
Western Michigan: Elliot Uzelac (1980-81), 13-9-0 (.591); Jack Harbaugh (1982-86), 25-27-3 (.482); Al Molde (1987-88), 14-9-0 (.609). Total: 52-45-3 (.535).

Bowls

Eastern Michigan: 1987 California: Beat San Jose State, 30-27.
Michigan: 1981 Rose: Beat Washington, 23-6. 1981 Bluebonnet: Beat UCLA, 33-14. 1983 Rose: Lost to UCLA, 24-14. 1984 Sugar: Lost to Auburn, 9-7. 1984 Holiday: Lost to Brigham Young, 24-17. 1986 Fiesta: Beat Nebraska, 27-23. 1987 Rose: Lost to Arizona State, 22-15. 1988 Hall of Fame: Beat Alabama, 28-24. 1989 Rose: Beat Southern California, 22-14.
Michigan State: 1984 Cherry: Lost to Army, 10-6. 1985 All American: Lost to Georgia Tech, 17-14. 1988 Rose: Beat Southern California, 20-17. 1989 Gator: Lost to Georgia, 34-27.
Western Michigan: 1988 California: Lost to Fresno State, 35-30.

Final Associated Press rankings

Michigan: 1980: Fourth. 1981: 12th. 1983: Eighth. 1985: Second. 1986: Eighth. 1987: 19th. 1988: Fourth.
Michigan State: 1987: Eighth.

Michigan state colleges

Great Lakes Conference champions: 1980: Hillsdale (5-1). 1981: Grand Valley State (6-0). 1982: Hillsdale (6-0). 1983: Saginaw Valley State (6-0). 1984: Saginaw Valley State (6-0). 1985: Hillsdale (5-1). 1986: Hillsdale (5-0). 1987: Northern Michigan (4-0). 1988: Hillsdale (5-0).
Michigan Intercollegiate Athletic Association champions: 1980: Adrian (5-0). 1981: Hope (5-0). 1982: Hope (5-0). 1983: Adrian (5-0). 1984: Hope (5-0). 1985: Albion (4-0-1). 1986: Hope (4-0-1). 1987: Hope (5-0). 1988: Adrian, Alma (4-1).

PRO FOOTBALL

Despite playing for fewer than five
seasons, Billy Sims ran for more yards
than any other Lion and added an
exciting dimension to a hapless team

The Lions' reward for finishing 2-14 — tied with San Francisco as the NFL's worst — was no booby prize. They used the No. 1 pick in the 1980 draft to selected Billy Sims, a flashy 25-year-old halfback from Oklahoma. He made an immediate impact. "I promise," he said on draft day, "we won't have a 2-14 season." Then he backed it up on the field, rushing for 153 yards in his debut against the Rams. The Sims Era had begun.

After their 4-0 start, Billy Sims and Co. got turned upside down. Losing seven of the next 10 games dashed their playoff chances. Still, Sims rushed for 1,303 yards — nearly 300 more than Steve Owens' club record — and the Lions won more often than they lost (9-7) — their first winning record in eight seasons.

SIMSENSATIONAL!

By Curt Sylvester

I t must have come as a terrible shock to the Vikings — all of that music and dancing and Lions players blowing kisses to the Silverdome crowd. Most of all, there was an odd look about the scoreboard: Detroit 27, Minnesota 7.

That's the way it was as the undefeated Lions fattened their NFC Central Division lead to two games with their fourth straight victory. And it was all very unlike what the Vikings have come to expect of the Detroit franchise over the last 19 years.

There was Billy Sims, running for 157 yards and blowing kisses to the crowd in the final seconds.

There was quarterback Gary Danielson, recovering from a shaky second quarter to scramble and pass the Lions' offense back to life.

There was James Hunter, coming up with two interceptions, one denying the Vikings a touchdown at the end of the first half.

There was Ray Oldham picking off two more Tommy Kramer passes, taking one of them 29 yards into the end zone for a touchdown.

And there was the sellout crowd of 80,291 — most of them, anyway — standing there after it was all over, cheering and dancing and singing yet another verse of the Lions' theme song, "Another One Bites the Dust."

This could hardly be the same Detroit team which, at one time, contributed 13 consecutive losses to the Vikings' domination of the Central Division.

And it isn't. Just check the standings. The first-place Lions lead Minnesota and Tampa Bay by two games. And check the statistics. In four games, Detroit has outscored its opposition 69-0 in the second half.

Danielson passed for two touchdowns — three yards to tight end David Hill on the opening drive of the game, and five yards to wide receiver Freddie Scott. Rookie Ed Murray kicked field goals of 36 and 24 yards. Detroit's last score came after a 52-yard run by Sims, putting him over 100 for the third time in his four games with the Lions. He spent at last part of the final minutes waving kisses to the crowd.

"That's something I did back in college," he said. "I think they appreciate it. They were beautiful, we need that. It makes us work that much harder. It sort of reminds me of being back in Norman." ◆

OUT OF NOWHERE

By Curt Sylvester

Anybody who doesn't know Eric Hipple by now just isn't paying attention. Or made the mistake of turning off Monday Night Football before its first play.

Hipple, the unheralded second-year quarterback from Utah State, in his first NFL start, threw a 48-yard pass on the first play, then followed it with four touchdown passes and two touchdown runs as he led the Lions to a desperately needed 48-17 victory over the Chicago Bears at the Silverdome.

"I don't know if I feel like a Prince Charming," Hipple said, grinning and rubbing his reddish-blond beard. "I know I don't look like one. And I don't know if it's a fairy tale feeling. In the back of your mind, you always feel you can do the job ... although this game was obviously a little out of the ordinary."

Hipple scored the Lions' first two touchdowns on runs of one and four yards, then went to work on the passing game. He threw a two-yard scoring pass to running back Rick Kane, a 10-yarder to tight end David Hill, a 44-yarder to wide receiver Freddie Scott and a 94-yarder to wide receiver Leonard Thompson. Hipple finished with 336 yards on 14 of 25 passing. In the second half, he was 4 of 4 and his last three passes went for touchdowns.

Hipple didn't waste any time showing what he could do, as he stepped back and lofted a 48-yard pass to Scott on the first play.

"I think that was to show them we were going to open

As a rookie quarterback, he held for field goals and extra points. Never threw a pass. Never handed off. In his second season, he did more of the same. Finally, he played a bit in the second half of a lost cause at Tampa Bay. Two weeks later — with the Lions 2-4, starting quarterback Gary Danielson injured and No. 2 Jeff Komlo bombing — coach Monte Clark decided to start the no-name third-string quarterback from the little-known school.

up the ball, maybe scare Chicago a little bit," Hipple said. "It lifted my confidence quite a bit. After that, I fell right into the tempo of the game."

Two running plays later, Hipple let the Bears know he was a runner, too, pulling the ball down and dashing 12 yards. Hipple had one more completion — a 15-yarder to Thompson — before scoring his first touchdown on a one-yard sneak, putting Detroit up, 7-0, barely eight minutes into the game.

The Lions built a 27-14 halftime lead. Hipple needed two plays and a penalty at the start of the second half to put the game away. He threw to Hill for 19 yards, then tossed a long pass to Scott. An interference penalty against cornerback Leslie Frazier turned it into a 41-yard gain. Hipple completed the drive with a perfectly placed 10-yard scoring pass to Hill in the left corner of the end zone.

By then, the ABC-TV announcers — Frank Gifford, Don Meredith and Fran Tarkenton, who weren't seen in Detroit because of the blackout rule — were tripping over themselves to praise Hipple. "A star," Gifford said, "has been born tonight." ◆

After baffling the Bears with his legs and arm, Eric Hipple nearly led the Lions to their first playoff berth since 1970. They won six of nine games and needed only to beat Tampa Bay in the finale. Alas, Tampa Bay won the game, 20-17, and the Central Division, dashing the Lions' hopes of playing in Super Bowl XVI at the Silverdome.

Two goal-line series made for a Super Sunday for San Francisco. In the first quarter, Joe Montana went up and over the pile for a one-yard touchdown dive and a 7-0 lead. In the third quarter, the 49ers piled up on the Bengals, stopping them four times inches from a touchdown that would have made it 20-14.

SWEET XVI FOR 49ERS

By George Puscas

Forget Bill Walsh, the coach. Never mind Joe Montana, the quarterback.

It took no genius on the sideline to make the San Francisco 49ers champions of the pro football world. No artist on the playing field was needed to beat the Cincinnati Bengals in Super Bowl XVI.

All that was required was the presence of the Bengals themselves. In what could have been their greatest hour — certainly the finest hour of the long season — they were one of the great flops of the football extravaganza. San Francisco won, 26-21.

All week long the Detroit area — indeed, the entire country — had built toward a fever pitch for the Cincinnati-San Francisco confrontation. The Super Bowl came off beautifully, out-of-towners reveling at parties and tolerating the sting of our winter. Nothing says the Silverdome cannot be a regular site for future Super Bowls.

There was a monumental traffic tie-up surrounding the stadium before the game, but once the fans arrived, they roared in anticipation — and kept roaring.

Only the Bengals seemed to lack enthusiasm. They were as cold and sloppy as the weather. They arrived in a deep freeze and played with a perplexing numbness. Maybe a dumbness, too. From the opening moments, the Bengals were a cold team prone to errors that belied their standing as champions of the American Football Conference. Forrest Gregg, their tough-minded coach, would not admit to raising hell with them at halftime, after they had fallen behind 20-0. But he did have a "talk" with them.

"I just told 'em it was about time we played a little football," Gregg said. "And we did for a while in the second half."

In his heart, though, he knew it was too late.

"We have come back in similar situations and won the game," he said, but then he conceded: "You just don't spot a team as fine as the 49ers a 20-0 lead. You can't get away with that."

The Bengals tried. They took the play away from the 49ers in the third period, flashing to one touchdown to cut the 49ers' lead to 20-7, then storming toward another.

The game's pivotal moment followed. It challenged the wisdom of the Bengal bunch, and the muscle of the 49ers' defense. The Bengals banged four times at the 49ers from the 3-yard line. The 49ers won. The final try of the Bengals' huge fullback, Pete Johnson, was the one that raised questions about bench strategy. Johnson was battered down, short of the goal, and the Cincinnati rally was broken.

Quarterback Ken Anderson wondered about the play call, as did many others.

"They decided to run," he said, "and then it was just a question of which play to run and which side we'd run it to."

Having tried the left side — where 49er Jack Reynolds had dropped Johnson, the Bengals decided to go to the right.

"We've scored on that play every time this season," Gregg said.

If the Bengals did not lose all their zip with that failure, they lost a lot of time. Only 10 minutes remained in the game before they closed within striking distance, 20-14, of the 49ers, but that proved their last gasp.

They had given up too much too early, and because they did, they never really got into the game. If they had a game plan, it was not recognizable, once they had tossed away their opportunities.

At the heart of it all was the basic fact that the 49ers were cracking the Bengals heavily, punishing them physically. They are a bold, aggressive team with a heavy portion of young players mixed with veterans. From the outset, they came at Cincinnati with a eagerness that shook the Bengals. And they did not relent.

That usually is what happens when a victim complains of being "flat" in its performance.

Chances are, it has been flattened. ◆

JAN. 24,
1982
◆

All were new to the super-hype of the Super Bowl. The San Francisco 49ers, two years removed from a 2-14 season. The Cincinnati Bengals, two years removed from a 4-12 season. The Pontiac Silverdome, the first northern site for football's extravaganza.

San Francisco's Joe Montana won the MVP award for completing 14 of 22 passes for 157 yards. Cincinnati's Ken Anderson went 25 of 34 for 300 yards.

Anthony Carter provided the speed and Novo Bojovic the foot as the Panthers won the USFL's first title in Denver. After the USFL, A.C. sparked the Minnesota Vikings; Lions fans begrudged management for not signing him. Bojovic helped kick the Detroit Drive to two Arena Football League titles and became a well-liked, fun-loving sports personality. After the USFL title game, he cackled as he read a list of firsts. "Who was the first man to get a penalty in the championship game?" he asked. "Me," he announced proudly. "I kicked the ball out of bounds."

THE BOYS OF SUMMER

By Curt Sylvester

JULY 17,
1983
◆

The United States Football League lasted only three stormy seasons, dying in 1986 after it beat the NFL in court yet received only $3 in damages. But in 1983 spring-and-summer football was new and exciting and successful. The Michigan Panthers began 1-4 but started winning and started drawing fans. More than 60,000 saw their 37-21 semifinal victory over the Oakland Invaders. Thousands stormed the Silverdome field with 25 seconds left, tearing down the goalposts, ripping up the artificial turf and ending the game early. Suddenly, the Panthers had become big-time.

It wasn't the Super Bowl, but don't try to tell the Michigan Panthers they aren't at least a little bit super.

The Panthers completed a storybook first season by defeating the Philadelphia Stars, 24-22, for the USFL's inaugural championship. A crowd of 50,906 at Denver's Mile High Stadium and a national television audience watched. And the Panthers did it the way they have played for the last three months — just about super.

Quarterback Bobby Hebert completed 20 of 39 passes for 314 yards and three touchdowns. Two touchdowns went to wide receiver Derek Holloway; the third was a game-clinching 48-yard play to Anthony Carter. Kicker Novo Bojovic did the rest with a 33-yard field goal and three extra point kicks.

Philadelphia's only scoring until midway through the fourth quarter came on two David Trout field goals.

Then, after the Stars scored on a 21-yard Chuck Fusina-to-Willie Collier touchdown pass and it appeared they might be ready for one of their spectacular fourth-quarter comebacks, Hebert and Carter teamed up to put the game away with three minutes to go. Fusina made it close when he threw a two-yard touchdown pass to Rodney Parker and added a two-point conversion to Scott Fitzkee as time ran out.

As the crowd poured onto the field, tight end Mike Cobb and tackle Ray Pinney hoisted Panthers coach Jim Stanley onto their shoulders, and the Panthers began celebrating Detroit's first major professional team championship since the Tigers won the World Series in 1968.

"We owed it to the fans of Detroit," said club owner Al Taubman in the sweaty, champagne-soaked locker room. "They're the greatest fans in the world."

The players screamed. They shook bottles of champagne and squirted each other. They hammed it up in front of the television cameras. "It feels great," said strong safety David Greenwood, who had been caught on the outskirts of the celebrating. He grinned and said, "Let me get a bottle of champagne, I've got to enjoy this."

Three months ago, the Panthers hardly were thinking celebration.

That's when they were tied with the Washington Federals for the league's worst record, 1-4. After that they won 13 of 15 games to become the USFL's first champion. However, until Carter caught Hebert's final pass of the game, eluded Stars cornerback Antonio Gibson, and went the final 35 yards into the end zone, there was no celebrating.

"I was wondering if the Stars were going to do to us what they did to Chicago," Cobb said. "But I knew the guys were going to dig down and not let that happen." The Stars had qualified for the championship game by whipping George Allen's Blitz, the league's preseason favorite, after trailing by three touchdowns in the last quarter.

The Panthers dug down, all right. Hebert saw a Philadelphia safety getting ready to blitz and knew he had a good chance to get Carter open. "I audibled out the route to A.C. because I knew the cornerback would be playing out there alone," Hebert said. "When the safety blitzes, he has no help so he has to play deep." Hebert had his view blocked on the play . . . until he saw Carter with the ball in his arms, making his cut to the outside of the field. "Hebert told me to take him deep," Carter said. "I did and he got the ball there. I saw Holloway ahead of me, and I knew he'd get the block."

And how did they feel after it was over? "I can't even explain it," said Hebert, earlier voted the season's outstanding quarterback. "It's beyond words, the greatest feeling I ever had." Hebert was voted the game's most valuable player, ahead of Carter, who had nine receptions for 179 yards.

Fusina completed 25 of 47 passes for 192 yards but was sacked four times, twice by linebacker John Corker. Stars running back Kelvin Bryant, the USFL's player of the year, finished with 89 yards in 13 carries.

"We're in the history books," Stanley said. ◆

Rookie Bobby Hebert passed for 295 yards in the Silverdome semifinals. He added 314 more in the Denver finale.

It had been 25 seasons since the Lions had won a division title. And there were plenty of times 1983 looked as if it would be No. 26. Like after the Lions fell to 1-4 and Monte Clark stuck out his hand and grinned at reporters, "See you at the cemetery." But Clark hadn't lost his job and the Lions weren't dead yet. Detroit won seven of its next 10 games. And, on a fittingly bizarre day, the Silverdome goalposts came down and the Lions tasted championship champagne.

Rookie Mike Cofer offered encouragement after Curtis Green sacked Tampa Bay's Jack Thompson. The '83 Lions relied on other rookie standouts — Jeff Chadwick, James Jones, Steve Mott and Rich Strenger.

THE CENTRAL ISSUE

By Curt Sylvester

With a little bit of pride, a lot of excitement and a great deal of relief, the Lions won their first division title in 26 seasons.

They survived the belligerent resistance of the down-and-out Tampa Bay Buccaneers for a 23-20 victory, putting the icing on their NFC Central Division title and playoff berth. The Lions last won a division title in 1957, when there were only 12 teams in the NFL — before expansion, before the AFL and before anybody dreamed of numbering championship games with I's, V's and X's.

And the victory over Tampa Bay lets the Lions go to the playoffs in the relative dignity of a 9-7 record. Last season, because of the players' strike, they made the playoffs at 4-5.

This was neither an impressive nor graceful performance, but it was fitting. The mood was set by running back Billy Sims, whose new five-year contract was revealed shortly before kickoff and stirred as much excitement as the game. Sims rushed for 11 yards on his first carry and eight on his second — giving him more than 1,000 yards for the season — but fumbled before he hit the turf.

It was the way the Lions have played all year — up a little, then down a little.

In the end, there were just enough ups to offset the downs against a Tampa Bay team that is one of the worst in football, a team that won only two of 16 games. The Lions stumbled and fumbled but came from behind twice, even though they knew their title and playoff berth had been assured by Chicago's 23-21 victory over Green Bay earlier in the afternoon.

"We were kind of disgusted," said defensive tackle Doug English. "We said, 'Let's forget about them. Let's win this game.' We didn't want to be an 8-8 team."

Had the Lions lost, they would have been the first division champion in NFL history with a non-winning record.

"Thank God we were able to come back from that bad start," coach Monte Clark said. "It's a great feeling after 26 years to make it. These guys worked hard and they deserve it. . . . I couldn't be happier."

Starting quarterback Eric Hipple went to the bench with a knee injury early in the third quarter, and Gary Danielson came in to avert disaster, rallying the Lions for their final 10 points. Danielson threw a 54-yard pass to Sims to set up the 38-yard Ed Murray field goal that broke a 13-13 tie midway through the fourth quarter. And Danielson completed the scoring with a six-yard touchdown pass to rookie wide receiver Jeff Chadwick. Tampa Bay cut the final margin to three points on Jack Thompson's third touchdown pass, with 1:17 remaining, but the Lions recovered the Bucs' onside kick and ran out the clock.

The game almost became a sidelight to the saga of Sims' contract, signed two days ago. The Lions revealed the $4.5 million contract because Sims' former agent, Jerry Argovitz, announced that he would sue for tampering. Argovitz, a dentist turned agent turned part-owner of the USFL's Houston Gamblers, said Sims signed in July for $3.5 million and would join the Gamblers for the '84 season. During the game, the Lions had legal papers served on Argovitz.

"Both sides are telling the truth," Sims said. "We have to go to court and see where I'll be playing."

Argovitz, a Texan wearing black boots, gold jewelry and a fur coat, paraded through the Silverdome issuing fighting words to Lions owner William Clay Ford. "Either Billy Sims is going to be in a Houston uniform," he said, "or we're going to call it Argovitz Motor Company or the Detroit Gamblers."

For a champions' locker room, the Lions' celebration was subdued. There was plenty of champagne, but also plenty of questions the Lions didn't want asked or to answer about Sims, who gained only 56 yards in 15 carries.

"I'm not gonna play lawyer," Ford said. "I'm gonna play happy owner. It's been a long time." ◆

1983

◆

*The Lions' NFC semifinal
playoff game against San
Francisco was almost a
microcosm of their 1983
season: They fell behind early,
struggled back, then needed a
heroic finish. Placekicker Ed
Murray, who had already
kicked the longest field goal in
playoff history — 54 yards —
earlier in the game, seemed just
the man to be the hero.*

GAME OF INCHES

By Curt Sylvester

The Lions finally know they belong. And they think they know where: in the NFC title game. But they won't be there.

A handful of crucial mistakes spoiled their chance at a stunning upset and left them with a 24-23 loss to the San Francisco 49ers at Candlestick Park. It came down to a 43-yard field goal attempt by Ed Murray with 11 seconds left — and the ball sailed wide to the right.

"It's a shame it had to come down to a missed field goal," said coach Monte Clark. "I jumped up and started to celebrate; I thought it was good."

That's how close it was, but Murray knew as soon as the ball left his foot that the kick was no good. "I was trying to guide it, to make sure I didn't miss it," he said. "And I led it too far to the right. . . . It was a foolish thing I did. I should have done the normal thing I always do — kick the stuff out of it."

The field goal would have won the game, but it wasn't the reason Detroit lost. The Lions lost because they simply made too many mistakes.

Quarterback Gary Danielson, starting for the first time this season in place of injured Eric Hipple, threw five interceptions. Ulysses Norris dropped a pass that could have set up a first-quarter touchdown. Billy Sims was caught from behind at the 49ers' 4-yard line by a player he didn't see. Leonard Thompson slipped trying to change direction when he had a chance to score on a reverse. Cornerback Bobby Watkins let San Francisco wide receiver Freddie Solomon get away from him for the game-tying touchdown pass from Joe Montana. And Murray, who kicked an NFL playoff-record 54-yard field goal in the first half, missed two 43-yarders in the fourth quarter.

So it didn't matter that the Lions outgained the 49ers in first downs, rushing yardage, passing yardage and total offense. Or that their defense all but shut down the 49ers.

"I think we outplayed 'em, but you've got to give them all the credit in the world," said offensive tackle Keith Dorney. "They're going on to the NFC championship game and we're not. It hurts a lot."

The Lions' scoring came on three Murray field goals — 37, 21 and 54 yards — and on touchdown runs of 11 and three yards by Sims. Danielson completed 24 of 38 passes for 236 yards. Sims rushed 20 times for 114 yards as Detroit produced 412 yards; the 49ers 291.

Danielson was more than a little upset with the five interceptions, which helped produce 17 of the 49ers' 24 points. Montana completed 18 of 31 passes for 201 yards. "I read all week about the quarterback was going to be the difference in the game and I didn't want to be the difference," Danielson said. "I told the guys before the game I wouldn't be the weak link — but I made too many mistakes."

With folded hands and a silent prayer, Monte Clark watched placekicker Ed Murray attempt to win the game. Clark jumped in the air to celebrate, just as the kick sailed wide. "It was typical of our year," he said. "But I think with this season we've built an important foundation. This is going to be important to us for a long time."

Much of the Lions' second-half comeback was the result of Danielson's passing. With the 49ers on top, 17-9, late in the third quarter, Danielson completed six straight passes, moving the Lions 73 yards in 10 plays. Sims' 11-yard touchdown run made it 17-16 with 13½ minutes left. An interception and 24-yard return by Watkins led to another Detroit touchdown, and the Lions led, 23-17, with 4:54 left. But it only set up the heart-breaking finish. Montana brought the 49ers back with a 70-yard drive and his 14-yard touchdown pass to Solomon. Ray Wersching added the extra point.

Danielson completed four of five passes, including two for 25 yards to Freddie Scott, to move the Lions to the San Francisco 24 with 11 seconds left. The teams lined up, the ball was snapped, Danielson spotted it on the 33 and Murray kicked. The ball sailed wide, and the 1983 season — that championship season — had ended for the Lions. ◆

Ed Murray could only kick the San Francisco ground in disgust after he kicked away a chance at a game-winning, 43-yard field goal. "I'm sure everybody on the team is feeling what I'm feeling," he said. "Unfortunately, they don't have everybody around their locker asking them about it."

Almost as quickly as it started, Billy Sims' career was over, cut short by a 1984 knee injury.

The end came only a few months after the Lions beat the USFL in a court fight to keep Sims. He retired after less than five seasons, but Sims left his name in the Lions' record book for yards gained in a career (5,106) and season (1,437).

A CAREER CUT SHORT

By Mitch Albom

The end came with a gentle squeeze. Billy Sims sat on the table, stuck out his right leg, and felt five fingers ease around the knee. "Does it hurt?" asked Dr. David Collon, who knew the answer but squeezed anyhow.

"Uh-huh," breathed Sims.

And it was over. This is where football careers die, not on the goal line but in the sterile silence of a rehab room. Twenty minutes and a few X-rays later, Collon would dictate the note that everyone knew was coming, the one that included the words "unfit for football." It would be sent to the Detroit Lions. And after 21 months of waiting, the greatest running back the Lions had ever seen would officially be history.

Who was Billy Sims, you ask? He was a thunderclap on the football sky, rolling in suddenly and shaking the heavens and then disappearing. And since the day he went down almost two years ago, Detroit has waited for the thunder to roll again. It never did.

And so now came the official retirement press conference, and Sims, dressed in resiliency and a charcoal gray suit, stepped up to a microphone to say good-bye.

"I must say it's been a fabulous career . . ." he began. The cameras whirred. He said what was expected. He said he would miss the game, the players, the thrills.

"Having been just a football player for so long . . ." someone began.

"Uh, I was never just a football player," he said.

And no, he was not. Billy Sims was more like a project from the gods, meant to straddle glory and tragedy his whole life. When he was 12, he left his mother's home in the St. Louis projects to live with his grandmother in Hooks, Texas. His decision. He would bale hay and pump gas. Yet, he would also go to Oklahoma and win a Heisman Trophy.

The week he signed with the Lions, he lost his great-grandmother and his half-brother, who drowned in a swimming pool accident. The day before his fateful injury he predicted he would break the Lions' all-time rushing mark on his first run.

And he did. And he never played again.

He didn't want the ball on the play that crippled him. "Call somebody else," he panted at the quarterback. He got it anyway, because he was the star. Glory and tragedy, No. 20.

"Do you feel empty now?" someone asked him at his farewell gathering.

"I guess," he said. "I feel I had some more running to do around here. But then again, I had my rookie year. I had some good games. . . ."

Oh, yes. Good games. Electrifying games. He was compact and muscular, a cutback runner — a bull's-eye for injuries — but he ran as if he knew his time was limited.

Who was Billy Sims, you ask? He was a bona fide Detroit star. A dash of flash in cowboy boots, who kept insisting he was "a regular guy" while all the time glittering like neon. Even his contract negotiations — a lurid assortment of big numbers and big accusations — were front-page news. Why not? This is a fuel-injected town that likes things fast and fluid, and Billy Sims was both. "We're losing our matinee idol," said one Lions staffer, and that was a fair statement.

And a final one. Sims — who turned pro at 25 and retired at 30 — will be more than fine financially, thanks to the $1.94 million he'll collect from Lloyd's of London. Then again, he still has pain when he walks. By age 50, he'll likely have trouble getting around. He knew as early as last fall he would not be back in this game. But he kept trying. Kept rehabilitating. Kept going back for another checkup. Another disappointment.

"What if you had passed your physical this morning?" someone asked.

Sims paused. "I wouldn't have told anybody," he said. And the room broke up laughing.

So shed no tears for Billy Sims. He played a bone-breaking game in bone-breaking fashion. And like much of the rest of his life, his peaks were both brief and magnificent.

Who was he? A thunderclap that has now rolled onto quieter skies. Officially retired. Yes. But remember him not for how he left the game. Remember him for how he played it.

Because, man, he could play. ◆

Billy Sims won the Heisman Trophy as a junior at Oklahoma. The first player drafted in 1980, Sims became an instant success with the Lions, rushing for 153 yards and three touchdowns in his debut against the Rams. He went on to a club-record 1,303 yards. He broke the record the next year with 1,437 yards and added a third 1,000-yard season in 1983. Sims was on his way to perhaps his best season before a tackle by Minnesota linebacker Walker Lee Ashley ended his career Oct. 21, 1984.

Bobby Layne liked to be the middle of social activities — this time flanked by Joe Schmidt and Paul Hornung during a 1980 NFL charity golf outing. "If I wanted a quarterback to handle my team in the final two minutes," said George Halas of the Chicago Bears, "I'd send for Layne." Halas had traded Layne after the 1948 season, because he had Sid Luckman and Johnny Lujack at quarterback.

LIFE AS A TWO-MINUTE DRILL

By George Puscas

DEC. 1,
1986

♦

Bobby Layne, a swaggering, ruddy-faced Texan, left his personal mark on every game he played — and on the hours that followed it. He was the leader of the Lions in the 1950s, the brightest era in club history. Detroit claimed four division and three world championships during the decade. And a legend.

Time ran out on Bobby Layne. The former great quarterback of the Lions is dead. He was, in his time, bigger than life, certainly bigger than the game he played. The Lions, and perhaps the National Football League, never have known anyone quite like him. "There's no question that he was a legendary figure," said Lions general manager Russ Thomas, a scout and assistant coach then. "No one ever led a team as he did."

Layne was 59. Weakened by a three-year battle with throat cancer and cirrhosis of the liver, he succumbed in Lubbock, Texas. Three weeks earlier, he had collapsed following a reunion of former Lions in Detroit.

It's difficult to separate the off-field Layne from the man who made the Lions the dominant force of his time. Stories of his adventures abound. He was not shy about them. He neither hid nor alibied.

On the chill, dreary afternoons immediately following practices at Tiger Stadium, Layne's day would begin when he led his troops to a nearby bar. The Lions were known as roustabouts in the NFL. If not older, they were more distinguished, loaded with all-pro players such as Doak Walker, Leon Hart, Les Bingaman, Lou Creekmur, Thurm McGraw, Jack Christiansen, Jimmy David, Dorne Dibble, Cloyce Box and Dick Stanfel.

At the bars, they would gossip and carouse, eventually to go their way.

"You can call it cornball," Layne said, "but it's effective. Football is a team game and the guys have to belong. This is a feeling you can get just in one day on the field."

But Layne, so the stories go, seldom retired early. He was a nightlife regular. He thrived on it. He seemed to require late-hour drinking and entertainment for refueling. "I don't know what it is," he explained in his late years. "But I've always been a guy who requires only four, five hours' sleep."

Alex Karras, only briefly a teammate, had an explanation. He said that Layne's father had died in the crash of his pickup truck, and Bobby, then 7, was trapped in the cab with the body for two days before he was found. "He hasn't been able to sleep right since," Karras said.

Some said Layne never played without a hangover, or never played sober and wouldn't be effective otherwise. It's probably an exaggeration, but Layne never bothered to deny it back then. Layne's epitaph was written years ago by his childhood friend Walker, who declared, "Bobby never lost a game in his life. Time simply ran out on him."

Layne's style was to hold the Lions in close contention — they seldom routed anyone, even in their best years — and then win dramatically in a race with the clock through the final two minutes. Even now, nearly a quarter-century after his last game, he is remembered as the master of the heart-pounding, clock-stopping drive to a winning score.

The 1953 NFL title game was exemplary. The Lions trailed the Browns, 16-10, with three minutes left and had the ball at their 20. "Aw right, fellas," Layne said in a nasal twang with a touch of whiskey on his lips. "Y'all block and ol' Bobby'll pass you raht to the championship." The Browns expected Layne to pass to Walker or Dibble because Jim Doran, subbing for the injured Hart, had caught only six passes all season. Layne passed twice to Doran to work out of danger. Then Doran suggested another pass. Layne floated the ball to him for the touchdown, Walker kicked the point, and the Lions won, 17-16.

Layne was with the Lions from 1950 through the second game of the 1958 season, when he was traded without explanation to the Pittsburgh Steelers. At the time, rumors of gambling (Layne was a frequent poker visitor in Las Vegas) and Layne's discontent circulated about town. But neither Layne nor the Lions' owners ever explained his sudden departure. He stayed with the Steelers until 1962, when he retired.

He remained close to the Lions and was a frequent guest at the Michigan Sports Hall of Fame banquets. He led the parties there, too.

Always the leader, always Bobby. ♦

Wayne Fontes' enthusiasm won over William Clay Ford's heart and wallet. Fontes figured to be the final coach hired during Russ Thomas' long reign as general manager, a position held since 1967. He was scheduled to retire after the 1989 season. Fontes quickly decided to rely primarily on the run 'n' shoot offense, an NFL first. The offense, based on three- and four-receiver sets, was renamed the silver stretch. Fontes used the third pick in the draft for tailback Barry Sanders, a Heisman Trophy winner from Oklahoma State, and a sixth-round pick for quarterback Rodney Peete, the Heisman runner-up from Southern California.

AN INTERIM SUCCESS

By Corky Meinecke

Three times in the five seasons after their division title, the Lions won only four games. Attendance dwindled from 553,595 in 1983 to 296,607 in 1988. Monte Clark was gone after the '84 season. Darryl Rogers didn't finish his fourth season. With five weeks to go in '88, Rogers' defensive coordinator got an interim title and a longshot chance to make a lasting impression.

The players spoke.

The owner listened.

The coach stays.

"I think it's just beautiful," Lions fullback James Jones said after learning that owner William Clay Ford had decided to drop the "interim" from coach Wayne Fontes' title and given him a three-year contract. "Usually," Jones said, "the owner says, 'Well, I don't care what the players think.' But this time, William Clay Ford looked beyond all that and said, 'This once, I better listen to them. They could be right this one time.' "

Fontes, 48, thinks so.

"When the three years of my contract are up," he said, "I hope I'll be standing in front of you again saying, 'Yeah, I've just been renewed for a long time.' That's my goal now. I want to stand up here again in three years and say, 'Guys, we got it going here.' "

That wasn't the case when Fontes inherited the job from Darryl Rogers after a 23-20 loss to the Tampa Bay Bucs Nov. 13 at the Silverdome. The Lions were 2-9. In the final five weeks, the Lions twice beat Green Bay and nearly upset Chicago, the Central Division champion. They went 2-3 under Fontes and finished 4-12. Along the way, Fontes laid down new rules designed to instill more discipline. And although the Lions were out of contention, he hired two offensive coaches — Lynn Dickey and Mouse Davis. "He took a team that was probably as low as you can get and revitalized it," said Ford, who never interviewed anyone else. "He gave them an interest and a desire to play the last five games."

Still, when Fontes drove over to Ford's office in Dearborn for a meeting, he had no idea which way his boss was leaning.

"You're my head football coach," Ford

said moments after Fontes had sat down in the owner's office. "How about three years?"

Upon which Fontes hugged him.

"I certainly did," Fontes said. "And when he walked in the building this morning, I grabbed him again. I went for his wallet. . . .

"We're in the entertaining business, and I'm going to try to make the offense as entertaining as we can. If you make it entertaining and open it up, we'll get the crowd back. And when you start winning, more people will come back."◆

Before Wayne Fontes faced the zebras and the Cleveland Browns in his first exhibition game in 1989, he received a two-year contract extension. Why? Owner William Clay Ford said he was impressed by the veteran coaching staff Fontes had assembled.

◆

Billing itself as the "Indoor War," the Arena Football League hit town in 1988. This scaled-down version of football featured 50-yard fields and nets behind the end zones. Each team used eight players at a time, seven of whom had to play offense and defense. The Detroit Drive and its cast of no-names proved adept at the fast-paced game. They won the 1988 ArenaBowl in Chicago. A dispute between the owners and the league founder nearly killed the league in 1989. Eventually, a five-team league played a mini-season. Again the Drive was in high gear.

George LaFrance, a double MVP, had a tougher time lifting the trophy than beating the Gladiators. Like most of the Drive, LaFrance attended an obscure college, Baker (Kan.). Teammate Anthony Corvino attended Southern Connecticut State. During the game, lineman Rodney Beachum chased after Pittsburgh's Alvin Williams. Beachum had five tackles.

DRIVE AND OVERDRIVE

By Perry A. Farrell

Tim Marcum's salt-and-pepper hair was drenched with beer and champagne as he tried to expound on what he and his team had just accomplished.

He had thought of a threepeat — three straight ArenaBowl championships — "but that got that other guy in trouble," he said, referring to Los Angeles Lakers coach Pat Riley. Marcum had etched his name in Michigan history and captured the hearts of 12,046 fans who came to Joe Louis Arena to watch the Drive claim its second straight Arena Football League championship. It was a resounding 39-26 victory over the Pittsburgh Gladiators.

The 1980s ended with three straight league champions for Marcum — two in Detroit. Marcum also coached the Denver Dynamite to the inaugural Arena Football title in 1987.

The Drive will be remembered as the last professional team in the 1980s to win a championship in Detroit. The first had been the Detroit Express of the American Soccer League in 1982.

As league and ArenaBowl most valuable player George LaFrance struggled to lift the Little Caesars Cup, Marcum thanked Detroit. "We got the greatest sports fans in the U.S.," he said in his Texas twang. The crowd cheered.

From the opening series the Drive, who went four consecutive quarters without allowing a touchdown in the playoffs, hounded Gladiators quarterback Willie Totten. On the second play, he fumbled after being rushed by Alvin Rettig. The ball rolled out of the end zone for a safety. The Drive's stingy defense did not give up a first down until 48 seconds were left in the first half.

Detroit's offense scored on its first three possessions — a one-yard plunge by quarterback Tony Burris, a 17-yard run by Lynn Bradford and a 50-yard field goal by Novo Bojovic to take a 19-3 lead with 11:51 left in the first half. Burris was 12 of 26 for 176 yards and five interceptions.

The Drive built a seemingly safe 26-6 lead, but in 52 seconds Pittsburgh cut it to 26-19. The Gladiators scored 10 seconds before the half and 42 seconds into the third quarter. But, six minutes later, LaFrance ran a post pattern and beat Cornelius Ross to the left corner of the end zone for a 32-yard touchdown, extending the lead to 32-19.

"That," Marcum said, "was the biggest play of this game."

"We'll look back on this," Bojovic said, "and look at our rings and realize this was a team effort."

For Marcum, it was threepeat. ◆

Little Caesars

DETROIT DRIVE
Arenabowl
Champions
1988

OWNER-PRES. MIKE ILITCH
GEN. MGR. GARY VITTO
ASST. COACH JIM BATES
ASST. COACH STEVE TRIMBLE

EXEC. V.P. JIM LITES
HEAD COACH TIM MARCUM
ASST. COACH SKIP STRESS
ASST. COACH DAVE WHINHAM

BY THE NUMBERS

Detroit Lions (NFL)

YEAR	W-L-T	FINISH	SCORING	PASSING	RUSHING	RECEIVING	TACKLES
1980	9-7-0	2nd, 0 GB Minnesota	Murray (116)*	Danielson (3,223)	Sims (1,303)	Scott (834)	Fantetti (85)
1981	8-8-0	T-2nd, 1 GB Tampa Bay	Murray (121)	Hipple (2,358)	Sims (1,437)	Scott (1,022)	Fantetti (148)
1982	4-5-0	4th, 1½ GB Green Bay	Murray (49)	Danielson (1,343)	Sims (639)	Sims (342)	Fantetti (54)
1983	9-7-0	1st, 1 GA G.B., Minn., Chi.	Murray (113)	Hipple (2,577)	Sims (1,040)	Jones (467)	Fantetti (132)
1984	4-11-1	4th, 5½ GB Chicago	Murray (91)	Danielson (3,076)	Sims (687)	Jones (662)	Hall (147)
1985	7-9-0	T-3rd, 8 GB Chicago	Murray (109)	Hipple (2,952)	Jones (886)	Thompson (736)	Graham (113)
1986	5-11-0	3rd, 9 GB Chicago	Murray (85)	Hipple (1,919)	Jones (903)	Chadwick (995)	Johnson (112)
1987	4-11-0	T-4th, 7 GB Chicago	Murray (81)	Long (2,598)	Jones (342)	Mandley (720)	Gibson (82)
1988	4-12-0	T-4th, 8 GB Chicago	Murray (82)	Hilger (1,558)	James (552)	Mandley (617)	Spielman (153)

Led National Football Conference

Coaches: Monte Clark (1980-84), 34-38-1 (.473); Darryl Rogers (1985-88), 18-40-0 (.310); Wayne Fontes (1988), 2-3-0 (.400). Total: 54-81-1 (.401).

Post-season: Lost to Washington, 31-7, in 1982 first round; lost to San Francisco, 24-23, in 1983 NFC semifinals.

Award winners: Jim Arnold (punter), All-NFL (1987, 1988); Jerry Ball (defensive tackle), All-Rookie (1987); Lomas Brown (offensive tackle), All-Rookie (1985); Jeff Chadwick (wide receiver), All-Rookie (1983); Doug English (defensive tackle), All-NFL (1983); Tom Ginn (center), All-Rookie (1980); Curtis Green (defensive end), All-Rookie (1981); Devon Mitchell (safety), All-Rookie (1986); Ed Murray (placekicker), All-NFL, All-Rookie (1980); Billy Sims (running back), Rookie of the Year, All-Rookie (1980), All-NFL (1981); Chris Spielman (linebacker), All-Rookie (1988); Bobby Watkins (cornerback), All-Rookie (1982). (All awards selected by the Professional Football Writers Association.)

Pro Bowl representatives: 1980 (Al Baker, Ed Murray, Billy Sims); 1981 (Doug English, Tom Skladany, Sims); 1982 (Keith Dorney, English, Sims); 1983 (William Gay, English); 1987 (Jim Arnold); 1988 (Michael Cofer, Arnold).

Hall of Fame inductees: Frank Gatski, center (1985); John Henry Johnson, fullback (1987); Doak Walker, halfback (1986).

Notable deaths: Mike Rodak (no position available), (1981); Buddy Parker, coach (1982); Jim Steen, tackle (1983); Regis Monahan, back (1983); Raymond Whyte, co-owner/director (1985); Jack Christiansen, defensive back (1986); Bobby Layne, quarterback (1986); Aid Kushner, trainer, (1987); Frank Szymanski, center (1987); Bill Callihan, back (1987); Nick Pietrosante, running back (1988); Joe Don Looney, running back (1988).

Michigan Panthers (United States Football League)

YEAR	W-L-T	FINISH	SCORING	PASSING	RUSHING	RECEIVING	TACKLES
1983	12-6-0	1st, 0 GA Chicago	Bojovic (103)	Hebert (3,568)	Lacy (1,180)	Carter (1,181)	Pennywell (88)
1984	10-8-0	2nd, 3 GB Houston	Bojovic (112)	Hebert (3,758)	Williams (984)	Holloway (1,219)	NA

Coach: Jim Stanley (1983-84), 22-14-0 (.611). Total: 22-14-0 (.611).

Post-season: Beat Oakland, 37-21, in 1983 semifinals; beat Philadelphia, 24-22, in 1983 championship game; lost to Los Angeles, 27-21, in triple overtime in 1984 first round.

Award winners: John Corker (linebacker), All-USFL, Defensive Player (1983); Thom Dornbrook (guard), All-USFL (1983); Bobby Hebert (quarterback), All-USFL, Outstanding Quarterback, Championship Game MVP (1983); Ray Pinney (offensive tackle), All-USFL (1983).

Detroit Drive (Arena Football League)

YEAR	W-L-T	FINISH	SCORING	PASSING	RUSHING	RECEIVING	TACKLES
1988	9-3-0	2nd, 1½ GB Chicago	Dixon (124)	Ingold (2,246)	Holman (148)	Dixon (1,007)*	Dixon (50)
1989	3-1-0	T-1st, Denver, Pittsburgh	LaFrance (66)*	Trigg (522)	Bradford (86)*	LaFrance (335)**	Evans (21)

Led the league
**Tied for league lead*

Coach: Tim Marcum (1988-89), 12-4-0 (.750). Total: 12-4-0 (.750).

Post-season: Beat Pittsburgh, 34-25, in 1988 semifinals; beat Chicago, 24-13, in 1988 ArenaBowl; beat Chicago, 46-10, in 1989 semifinals; beat Pittsburgh, 39-26, in 1989 ArenaBowl.

Award winners: Lynn Bradford (running back/linebacker), All-Arena (1989); Dwayne Dixon (wide receiver/defensive back), Ironman, All-Arena (1988); Steve Griffin (wide receiver/defensive back), ArenaBowl MVP (1988); Walter Holman (running back/linebacker), All-Arena (1988); George LaFrance (wide receiver/defensive back), MVP, ArenaBowl MVP, All-Arena (1989); Reggie Mathis (lineman), All-Arena (1989).

GOLF/TENNIS

Betsy King blew a four-shot lead late
in the third round but still ruled the
1989 U.S. Women's Open at
Indianwood Golf and Country Club.

1981

♦

In the first of three major golf events in Michigan in the '80s, a just-turned-senior delighted his army in the U.S. Senior Open at Oakland Hills Country Club.

ARNIE COMES OF AGE

By Jack Saylor

The USGA didn't plan it that way, but there was a "sudden death" playoff in the U.S. Senior Open anyway.

It came abruptly at Oakland Hills' famed 16th hole in the 18-hole playoff among Arnold Palmer, Billy Casper and "unknown" Bob Stone. Palmer, fighting back from a huge early deficit, crept into a one-stroke lead over Stone. Casper was three back. Then the curtain fell. Stone and Casper dumped their second shots into the water that guards the green at the picturesque 400-yard, par-four hole. Palmer watched this turn of events, pulled out a seven-iron and safely laid his approach deep into the green.

"You knew I wasn't going to be short," he said.

Casper splashed another shot into the lake before reaching the green. Result? Par for Palmer, bogey for Stone and a disheartening quadruple-bogey eight for Casper. The tournament was over.

Arnie parred in to capture the title with an even-par 70 (36-34) to Stone's 74 (34-40) and Casper's 77 (36-41). Palmer pocketed $26,000; Stone and Casper earned $9,586 each. The three players had tied with nine-over 289 totals for the regulation 72 holes.

Palmer, 51, heads for this week's British Open as King of the Golden Oldies — he's reigning champion of the PGA and USGA Seniors. "It's one of the best tournaments I've ever played in," Palmer said. "The field was good and the course is one of the real challenges of golf."

Palmer turned his playoff venture into a challenge, too. The 82nd victory of his legendary career — 61 on tour and 21 others — didn't come nearly as easily as the score might suggest. Palmer got off to a shaky start and found himself six shots behind Stone in the first six holes.

Unawed by his world-famous playmates, Stone, a 51-year-old club pro from Independence, Mo., surged in front with a birdie on the second hole. Then Stone, eager to get home "for some hunting," stunned his rivals by holing a 170-yard seven-iron shot for an eagle on the 424-yard fifth hole. It put him three under. The announced crowd of 2,762, almost all dues-paying members of Arnie's Army, nearly defected to Bob's Battalion. But suddenly Stone's production dried up.

"I just tried to keep playing the golf course," he said. "But I missed a couple short putts and never got it going again."

Stone's rapid start didn't concern Palmer as much as his own game did. "My charge, if you wish, was a charge back to par," he said. "This golf course will level you out. I was worried about par — not Bob. There's not a birdie hole on this golf course."

Still, he extracted four of them.

"I made a minor adjustment on my putter last night," Palmer said. "It's just an old flange putter that Jerry Barber gave me, but this is the first tournament in five years I've used the same putter all week."

It began to work miracles with 20-foot birdie putts on the eighth and ninth holes. At the 12th, he tapped in a 10-footer. He fell back with a bogey at the 13th. But at No. 15 he drained a 40-footer for his fourth birdie and surged in front by himself for the first time.

That set the stage for Casper and Stone to become water-logged at the 16th.

Stone headed back to his Independence pro shop. "I'll be there at daylight," he said. Casper headed for his San Diego golf camp, greatly encouraged by his performance. And, of course, Arnie jetted to Latrobe, Pa., then on to Washington to catch a 9 p.m. Concorde to Britain. ♦

Arnold Palmer missed two crucial putts on the 18th hole — a birdie try that would have broken a three-way deadlock in the third round and a 10-footer for par that would have prevented a three-way playoff. But Palmer said he won the trophy because of newfound confidence in his hand-me-down putter.

An amazing bunker shot on the 17th hole — to within two inches of the cup — all but clinched the U.S. Open for Andy North. After North's shot, Dave Barr, co-leader at the time, and T.C. Chen, one down at the time, each bogeyed the 201-yard, par-three hole.

An Open Survivor

By Jack Saylor

The tournament would be remembered for Tze-Chung Chen's double-eagle in the first round and his double-hit in the finale. But Andy North, the winner of this U.S. Open at Oakland Hills Country Club, made history, too.

Just when it looked as if nobody would — or could — win the 85th U.S. Open, Andy North hung around and accepted the title.

North survived with a one-stroke victory as the noose of pressure strangled his rivals at Oakland Hills Country Club. North struggled to a four-over-par 74 and wound up the only player under par for four rounds, claiming his second Open championship and first victory of any kind since the 1978 Open at Cherry Hills in Colorado. His 72-hole total of 279 (70-65-70-74) bettered par by one stroke and earned him $103,000 from the $660,000 purse. He made history, too. North became only the 13th person to win two Open titles.

The fairways were paved for North's victory when Tze-Chung Chen suffered a quadruple-bogey, including a penalty stroke for double-hitting a shot, at a time when he was leading the field by four strokes.

Chen, a third-year pro from Taiwan, rode a historic first-round double-eagle to threaten a runaway, then folded at the par-four fifth hole in the final round. He proceeded to lose seven shots in a four-hole stretch.

"It was a freaky thing," North said. "T.C. opened the door for a lot of us."

Chen managed a smile. "I can't complain," he said. "I just played bad — the double-hit. . . . I never play golf like that."

Chen, who shot a 41 on the front nine, courageously pulled himself together, tying Canadian Dave Barr and South African Denis Watson for second place.

The course — called the Monster — took its revenge. Chen slumped from opening rounds of 65-69-69 to a 77. Barr shot a 72 and Watson a 73. All finished at even-par 280.

It might have been the capricious 6,996-yard golf course, which had hoodwinked everyone by yielding a record 24 subpar rounds the second day, that was the real winner. Consider: Only four rounds under par were shot the final day as the pressure cooker heated up before 37,330 fans on the mostly overcast and windy afternoon.

North made five bogeys — and he won. Chen had five bogeys in addition to the disaster hole.

Barr had five bogeys, including the last two holes.

Payne Stewart bogeyed three of the last six holes and finished at 281.

Monster, indeed.

Chen admitted the fifth hole triggered his downfall. "It upset me a lot," he said. "Everything gone, my putt fading. I think everybody has pressure — some a lot, some just a little. But I don't really think I had a lot."

North, seemingly on the ropes after bogeying the ninth, 10th and 11th holes, regrouped with an eight-foot birdie putt at the 12th that put his foundering ship in order. North then played par golf the last seven holes.

It was similar to his 1978 Open victory.

"I had a four- or five-shot lead there and bogeyed three in a row," he said. "It's nice to have been there. You know if you keep it on track you still have a chance. I've been out here 13 years and been in position a few times. The experience helps."

North didn't get the lead for good until the 17th hole, a 201-yard par-three.

Barr's three-iron shot was long and he chipped poorly, leaving a 35-foot putt. He bogeyed, then bogeyed No. 18 after he couldn't reach the green from a fairway bunker.

North hit his tee shot at 17 into a deep bunker to the right. Chen, one shot back, was on the green but facing a long putt.

North hit an excellent sand shot within two inches for a tap-in par. Chen had neither line nor distance on his putt, and he three-putted for a bogey.

After hitting a fat four-iron short of the 18th green, North was told by USGA president Jim Hand that he had a two-stroke lead. "Knowing you only need bogey to win," North said, "is a great feeling." ◆

T.C. Chen landed in precarious places in the final round. But the first day, on the second hole, a 527-yard par-five, Chen made the first double-eagle in U.S. Open history. After his drive, Chen had 255 yards to the pin. He chose a three-wood. "I thought it would be close but never thought it would go in," he said. Few spectators saw the shot; no photos of it exist.

In 1983, a month past his 16th birthday, Aaron Krickstein of Grosse Pointe Woods became tennis' latest whiz kid, rallying from a two-set deficit to beat 15th-seeded Vitas Gerulaitis. That made him the youngest male to reach the third round of the U.S. Open. But a torturous, four-year string of stress fractures to his feet and left leg pushed Krickstein from the forefront of tennis' youth movement. He moved back into the spotlight at 21 — again at the U.S. Open — by defeating the Wimbledon champion in a memorable five-setter.

KRICKSTEIN TAKES THE FIFTH

By Steve Crowe

Wimbledon champion Stefan Edberg offered plenty of excuses for his five-set loss to Aaron Krickstein of Grosse Pointe Woods in the U.S. Open round of 16. But Edberg neglected to mention the most important one — the inspired play of Krickstein, who impressed the New York crowd of 17,732 time and again with brilliant passing shots and deep lobs.

Krickstein's reward is his first appearance in a Grand Slam quarterfinal, against Darren Cahill of Australia in a featured, center-court match.

"This is probably the highest point right now in my career," Krickstein said. "You have to experience this to really know how it feels."

Edberg, seeded third, complained about being the only player to compete in two night matches — two in three nights — and blustering winds that intensified as the evening progressed. And he used the naughtiest of words in referring to the paper that swirled around the stadium and onto the court in the fifth set. "It's ridiculous," he said, "playing in this stadium with all those ------ papers flying around."

But it was Krickstein, 2-0 lifetime against Edberg, who blew into the quarterfinals with a 5-7, 7-6 (7-4), 7-6 (7-2), 4-6, 7-5 victory. Krickstein raised his record to 6-0 in five-set Open matches and stayed undefeated overall in his last seven five-setters. His first Open match — back in 1983 — went five sets, a victory over the Wimbledon junior champion, a 17-year-old Swede named Stefan Edberg.

This 60-game match, which lasted three hours and 52 minutes, turned in Krickstein's favor when he broke Edberg for a 5-4 lead in the fifth set. Edberg responded with a service break, but another break by Krickstein and a love game on his serve finished Edberg.

"This is the biggest tournament of the year as far as I'm concerned," Krickstein said. "If I had only one tournament each year to play, this would be it." ◆

Aaron Krickstein leaped up and down six times after nailing a backhand volley to finish off Stefan Edberg in the round of 16. Krickstein wasn't too upset when he lost in the quarterfinals to Darren Cahill of Australia, 6-2, 5-7, 7-6 (7-2), 5-7, 6-3. "Maybe it's better I didn't win," he said. "I've been trying to do everything really gradually."

Her Royal Coolness

By Charlie Vincent

JULY 16,

1989

◆

There was a Scottish flavor to the U.S. Women's Open at Indianwood Golf and Country Club in Lake Orion, Mich. — the heather alongside the fairways, the deep bunkers, even a Scottish band at the closing ceremonies. But the King was a no-nonsense American named Betsy.

Sunday, Betsy King knew where the booby traps were.

Sunday, she walked the same path that had blown her game to bits on Saturday. But this time she did what she had to do to win the 44th U.S. Women's Open Golf Championship. This time she played the game of a champion — straight and true and with rock-solid nerves.

King, who had not shot less than 288 in her 14 previous U.S. Women's Open appearances, left the rest of the field far behind with a closing round of 68 to finish at 278. She could have removed most doubt about who would win this tournament on Saturday. But her four-stroke lead evaporated on the final four holes — bogey, par, double-bogey, bogey — and left her tied with Patty Sheehan.

So they spent Sunday afternoon together, in a twosome at the back of the pack. There were others who could win this tournament, but for either of these women to win it, she would have to beat the other — at least. It was head-to-head. The same, almost, as sudden death. They had played a sudden-death playoff two years ago in the Dinah Shore — King's only previous victory in a major tournament — and Sheehan was beaten after two holes.

Sunday, she was beaten after eight, the result of a disastrous triple-bogey that left her at even par while King, with four birdies on the front side, had gone to six under. By the time the day was over, King had beaten Sheehan by 11 strokes.

And by the time she reached the 15th tee, King was five strokes ahead of her nearest rivals, Nancy Lopez, Pat Bradley and Penny Hammel. It was at the 15th, though, that trouble had struck on Saturday. And for King it was like returning to the scene of a horrible accident. "I thought about it when I got on the tee," she said. "I felt doubt a little bit."

She hit her tee shot straight and long and in the middle of the fairway. It was such a perfect shot that it might have brought a smile to her face. But it did not. Betsy King is not an emotional player. Or an emotional person.

She had won more than $500,000 this year — more than any player had won before in a full LPGA season. That's nice, she says. "But I guess I get more excited when I play board games . . . or pickup basketball."

She hit her second shot as perfectly as her first, to the middle of the fairway, chipped beyond the cup and with two conservative putts parred the 15th.

Whereas she had parred the 16th Saturday, she took a birdie Sunday. Whereas she had double-bogeyed the 17th, she took a bogey. And now she was all but home free.

As she walked the final yards in the late afternoon sunshine toward the enormous closing green, now encircled by 20,000 spectators, the applause washed down upon her. And Betsy King, the woman with the emotions of a rock, felt something stir within her.

"It's something you always wish you could experience," she said. "I tried to respond the best I could. When I go to plays and things like that and people get standing ovations, I always cry. Now here I was getting one, and as I got close to the green, I told myself: 'Hey, I've got to compose myself.' "

So Betsy King didn't cry. She just stepped front and center and won the biggest tournament of her life. ◆

Even in victory, Betsy King held her emotions in check. After holing out, she threw her golf ball to the crowd, and it barely reached them.

BY THE NUMBERS

The Dream 18

The idea sounded simple enough: Select the best 18 golf holes in Michigan. The Free Press did just that in 1986. But it wasn't easy. A selection committee spent hours whittling down an original list of 120 holes. The Free Press wanted the best 18 — not necessarily the toughest.

NO	COURSE	LOCATION	HOLE	YARDS	PAR
1	Indianwood	Lake Orion	17	194	3
2	Warwick Hills	Grand Blanc	2	431	4
3	Michaywe	Gaylord	5	414	4
4	Boyne Highlands	Harbor Springs	10	420	4
5	The Legend	Shanty Creek, Bellaire	7	501	5
6	Schuss Mountain	Mancelona	18	397	4
7	The Bear	Grand Traverse, Acme	3	539	5
8	The Bear	Grand Traverse, Acme	12	417	4
9	Pointe O'Woods	Benton Harbor	9	203	3

Out: 3,516 yards, par 36

NO	COURSE	LOCATION	HOLE	YARDS	PAR
10	Katke-Cousins	Rochester	4	472	4
11	Oakland Hills South	Birmingham	16	409	4
12	Bay Pointe	West Bloomfield	15	368	4
13	Meadowbrook	Northville	2	567	5
14	Radrick Farms	Ann Arbor	15	185	3
15	Travis Pointe	Ann Arbor	4	588	5
16	Plum Hollow	Southfield	12	223	3
17	Detroit Golf Club North	Detroit	18	416	4
18	Country Club of Detroit	Grosse Pointe Farms	18	420	4

In: 3,648 yards, par 36

Total: 7,164 yards, par 72

Major tournaments in Michigan

YEAR	EVENT	COURSE	WINNER	SCORE
1981	U.S. Senior Open	Oakland Hills Country Club	Arnold Palmer*	289 (9-over)
1985	U.S. Open	Oakland Hills Country Club	Andy North	279 (1-under)
1989	U.S. Women's Open	Indianwood Golf & CC	Betsy King	278 (6-under)

*Won 18-hole playoff with Billy Casper and Bob Stone.

Buick Open

A PGA Tour event at Warwick Hills Country Club in Grand Blanc, Mich.

YEAR	WINNER	SCORE
1980	Peter Jacobsen	276 (12-under)
1981	Hale Irwin*	277 (11-under)
1982	Lanny Wadkins	273 (15-under)
1983	Wayne Levi	272 (16-under)
1984	Denis Watson	271 (17-under)
1985	Ken Green	268 (20-under)
1986	Ben Crenshaw	270 (18-under)
1987	Robert Wrenn	262 (26-under)
1988	Scott Verplank	268 (20-under)
1989	Leonard Thompson	273 (15-under)

*Won sudden-death playoff with Bobby Clampett, Peter Jacobsen and Gil Morgan.

Greater Grand Rapids Open

A Senior PGA Tour event at Elks Country Club in Grand Rapids, Mich.

YEAR	WINNER	SCORE
1986	Jim Ferree*	204 (9-under)
1987	Billy Casper	200 (13-under)
1988	Orville Moody	203 (10-under)
1989	John Paul Cain	203 (10-under)

*Won sudden-death playoff with Gene Littler and Chi Chi Rodriguez.

Nancy Lopez birdied four of the last seven holes in the 1989 U.S. Women's Open — which still left her four shots behind champion Betsy King. Lopez, in pursuing the only women's major title to elude her, finished second.

Detroiter Thomas Hearns had plenty
of practice dressing like a champion.
The Hit Man became the first boxer to
win titles in five weight classifications.

As the 1980s were born, so was a new boxing awareness in the city that claimed Joe Louis, Sugar Ray Robinson and a rich ring tradition. Emerging were trainer Emanuel Steward and his Kronk Recreation Center team, notably a long-armed Detroiter, Thomas Hearns; a tough Downriver kid, Mickey Goodwin; and a slim Columbus, Ohio, fighter, Hilmer Kenty. Kenty got the first title shot.

KRONK'S KRUNCH

By George Puscas

Hilmer James Kenty finally escaped the shadow of his buddy, the sleek Thomas Hearns, to find his own place in the boxing sun. But you wonder who was in darkness — Kenty, or the rest of us?

The kid always knew he was good, plenty good. It never bothered him that everybody talked about Hearns and gave him little notice at all, because he knew his day would come. And now finally it has, and people are wondering who is this unknown slicker who could step into the ring and batter a world champion so severely nobody will believe it.

Ernesto Espana, having yielded his World Boxing Association lightweight championship to Kenty, could not believe it happened to him, not the way it happened. Kenty simply whupped him from here to Caracas. He did it to poor Ernesto just about as beautifully as one boxer can do it to another in a magnificent display that stunned 13,172 at Joe Louis Arena. "I don't think Kenty has ever fought like that before," said Nick Acosta, the manager-trainer of now ex-champion Espana. "He surprised us. I never expected him to be like that."

Espana's surprise was showing all over his face as he sat stunned, hurt and unbelieving with Acosta tenderly placing ice packs on the sore spots. Espana's right cheek was cut, his nose and lips swollen grotesquely. His cheekbones were puffed and reddened from the smashing of countless stinging jabs and exploding rights from Kenty.

"Kenty was great; he is a great fighter," said Acosta, who brought in two of the world's finest fighters only to have them thoroughly beaten by Kenty and Hearns. Hearns had destroyed Angel Espada, the former welterweight champion, in a fourth-round knockout that disgusted Acosta so thoroughly that the manager would not talk to his man.

"He looked like he was still knocked out from his fight last December," Acosta said.

It was a typical Hearns showing, the kind Detroit fight fans have come to expect. Hearns suspected before the first punch was thrown that Espada already was thoroughly intimidated, and it was just a matter of time before he made him his 24th knockout victim in 26 fights. He had taken all the will from Espada with a brutal right-left-right pounding to the gut in the second round, and then in the fourth, he cracked him with another right just below the rib cage and Espada sat down.

Having seen that, Espana was more intent than ever to put it to Hilmer Kenty and save something for the Latin world. Looking over at Espada in the far corner of their dressing room, Espana, awaiting his turn in the ring, muttered something in Spanish. "He says he's ready now for the killing," said Acosta, smiling meaningfully. Little did they suspect a near-killing would be Espana's.

Kenty was that strong and unrelenting and convincing. He showed Espana the fastest hands he has ever seen, laying 'em right on his nose and eyeballs so often and with such precision poor Ernesto was bewildered and frustrated. As the punishment mounted, you sensed the hopelessness of the Venezuelan's plight and finally, in the ninth round, Kenty caught him with one right hand, then another, and another, then a gruesome series of at least five more blows to the head. Espana reeled crazily along the ropes and at last referee Larry Rozadilla jumped between the fighters, grabbed Espana and led him stumbling back to his corner.

It was an extraordinary day in every way for manager Emanuel Steward, for not only did Kenty reach the top of his game and Hearns moved onward in his title quest, but Mickey Goodwin, the Kronk middleweight, "came of age" as they say. Goodwin battered Baltimore's Leo Saenz into a 10th-round knockout in the opening fight of the program.

Steward dreams of having all three as world champions, and indeed, they make a rather awesome trio — Kenty, whose record is 17-0, Hearns 26-0, Goodwin 21-1. Together they are 64-1 with their fists, and it is why they are talking today about the Kronk Krunch. ◆

Hilmer Kenty and Thomas Hearns were a mean team for Kronk. "It's the greatest feeling in the world, winning a world championship," Kenty said after beating Ernesto Espana. "As soon as Thomas Hearns gets a chance, we're going to have two of 'em and we're going to keep 'em — right here in Detroit." But Kenty lost his title 13 months later, suffered a detached retina and left Kronk in a contract dispute. He eventually returned but retired before getting another title shot. Mickey Goodwin also left Kronk in a contract dispute.

AUG. 2,
1980
♦

Despite winning national AAU and Golden Gloves championships as an amateur, Thomas Hearns was little known in fight circles when he turned pro. But a reputation quickly emerged; his glaring eyes and furious punching captivated an ever-larger following. He was unbeaten in 28 fights — and had 26 knockouts — when he got his first chance at a championship.

THE HIT MAN

By George Puscas

True to his boast, Thomas Hearns unleashed a stunning barrage on defenseless Pipino Cuevas, then knocked the Mexican out with an awesome right to the head in the second round to win the World Boxing Association's welterweight championship.

The end came with Cuevas struggling to his knees, looking blankly at an electrified crowd of 14,000 at Joe Louis Arena as referee Stanley Christodoulou began to count him out. He never completed the formality. Cuevas' manager, Lupe Sanchez, recognizing instantly that his fighter was finished, climbed through the ring ropes, signaled an end to the fight and reached out to help Cuevas.

Pandemonium seized the crowd. Dozens stormed into the ring. Hearns, the unbeaten Detroit Hit Man, had completed an odyssey that in just 2½ years took him from the city's east side ghetto to the top of his game.

"That's exactly the way we planned it," said an ecstatic Emanuel Steward, manager of Hearns and lightweight champion Hilmer Kenty, who successfully defended his title with a ninth-round TKO over Korea's Yung Ho Oh.

There can be no doubting Hearns now. The lanky kid did everything that had been asked, if not expected, of him as he simply destroyed Cuevas — a champion since 1976 — and placed himself alongside Roberto Duran as the world's top-ranking welterweight. Hearns fought the perfect fight, right down to the finest detail. He set out to take advantage of his extraordinary height and reach advantage, and he employed it to the fullest from the opening bell. He popped Cuevas repeatedly with long lefts to the head.

"Hearns is a very good fighter," Cuevas said, "and I hope he will be as good a champion as I was."

The knockout came after Cuevas at last retaliated, catching Hearns with a strong right that momentarily caused him to back off. But then it was as if Hearns had paused to catch his breath. He came back with a left that jarred Cuevas, then caught him with a thundering right. Cuevas was dropping to the canvas, but halfway down, he caught another murderous right hand from Hearns.

He fell flat on his face. He lay unmoving for a moment, but already two among the thousands sensed it was all over. The two were Hearns and Cuevas' manager. ♦

After a mob scene in the Joe Louis Arena ring, Thomas Hearns celebrated his first pro title moderately with close friends. "He's felt for some time that he's the champion," said his manager, Emanuel Steward. "He sat with his tennis shoes and watched television. He didn't want a big celebration with champagne."

WHY LOUIS WAS A LEGEND

By George Puscas

APRIL 12,
1981
◆

Joe Louis ruled the heavyweight division longer than any other man before or since. He held boxing's most prestigious title from 1937 to 1949, for 12 years and 25 successful defenses. Despite all his accomplishments and all the money he made, however, in his later years he was poor and sickly, working as a greeter in a Las Vegas nightclub.

The city hushed. An eerie silence gripped the neighborhoods, from the Black Bottom on the fringe of downtown Detroit to the Jewish sector out Dexter Avenue and into the enclaves of ethnics on the city's north and west sides. It was as if a plague or deadly gas was slipping over the town, sending citizens fleeing for cover or leaving streets deserted to the night.

Several times a year it happened — not only in Detroit, but in cities throughout the United States. Whenever Joe Louis fought on the radio, the cities stopped and listened. No single performer before or since captured the attention of the nation as did Louis, the legendary Brown Bomber of the Depression years of the 1930s. Louis, a Detroiter who grew up to be the among the most famous men in the world, died after collapsing at home in Las Vegas from a cardiac arrest. He was 66.

Strangely, biographies of the man many call the greatest heavyweight fighter ever either fail to mention the phenomenon of a nation stilled when he swung into action, or make little of it. Strange, because it remains one of the more peculiar mass reactions to any sports happening.

Joe Louis was special, a special man in a distinct period of history, and he has become legend for that as much as his superb boxing skills.

Much of his life story has been distorted over the years, or at least is different from what was known of him in the 1930s and 1940s, when his every fight captured the attention of millions and pulled them in huddles around the radio to listen to the blow-by-blow descriptions.

He has been characterized, for instance, as a crusader for black America. He was not that at all, and he was the first to deny it. Rather, he was a simple young man with no discernible complaints or aggressions outside the boxing ring. Content with his role as a prizefighter, he neither prodded nor offended anyone, by manner or speech, and so he was universally popular and admired.

Race did play a significant part, however, in the building of the Joe Louis

Detroiters celebrated in the streets after yet another Joe Louis victory in 1935. In Chicago, Louis had knocked out King Levinsky in the first round.

legend. Adolf Hitler created the circumstances in 1938 when he personally delegated Max Schmeling to prove the superiority of his white master race. When Schmeling beat Louis, Hitler danced, or so it was said.

Several years ago, before he fell ill, Louis recalled the circumstances of the first Schmeling bout and the rematch two years later. After the first bout, staged before Louis kayoed James Braddock to win the heavyweight championship in 1937, great controversy arose over Schmeling's victory. It was claimed the German had won with a foul blow, a shot to the kidneys.

Louis remembered only that it had been a rugged fight, that he had been hit hard and often, and that later his back did indeed hurt. But he never personally claimed a foul.

As for the celebrated rematch in 1938, when the world was kindling a war, Louis insisted: "I never thought about any race thing. The papers were filled with stuff about ➡

Hitler talking, and I met once with President Roosevelt, who said he hoped I would win. But I had nothing personally against Max. I liked him, and we're friends even now. In my mind, I wasn't champion until I beat him.

"The rest of it — blacks against whites — was somebody's talk. I had nothing against the man, except I had to beat him for myself."

He destroyed Schmeling in the first round. In two minutes and four seconds, he threw about 40 punches and knocked Schmeling down four times. The story goes that Hitler shuddered and cursed just as he had when Jesse Owens, another black American, ruled the 1936 Olympics in Berlin.

In Detroit, the streets exploded with Louis' victory. It was perhaps the most joyous celebration the city has seen for one man, one athlete. We had plenty of practice from his earlier fights, for the Bomber was already a hero in a period that knew few.

He had been stamped as a champion of all Americans at that time, and it was almost tradition that, whenever he fought, the cities would fall silent, the populace listening to radios. When he won, whether by knockout, as was mostly the case, or by decision, the neighborhoods erupted all around, everywhere, acclaiming him and their own triumph.

Not in our time has there been any other like him. If Muhammad Ali was beautiful and if, as some believe, Ali was a better fighter, Joe Louis was something significantly more: A cultural phenomenon.

The celebrations were wild and joyous, street dancing developing spontaneously, the partying often carrying into the early morning hours with old men and tired ladies, with toddlers and house pets romping and raising hell in the streets over, of all things, a man who had won a prizefight.

Reports of similar demonstrations came from around the country, but Detroit's own outpouring seemed more significant. Joe Louis had, after all, sprung from our midst, out of the old Brewster gym behind the Stroh's Brewery near downtown. He was a kid who discarded his violin and skipped his lessons to excel at a less delicate art.

He had gained his first recognition in the Free Press Golden Gloves tournament. This economically battered town was proclaiming itself the "City of Champions" — the Tigers, the Lions, the Red Wings and basketball Eagles all claimed world titles in 1935.

His title finally came two years later, but it is not odd that he is the best remembered from that era. ◆

Joe Louis' first fame came as the outstanding novice in the 1933 Free Press Golden Gloves tournament. One of his many pro victims was Bob Pastor, in a 1939 Detroit bout that earned Louis $118,400. He retained his heavyweight title with an 11th-round knockout. For his 18-year career, Louis made about $4.7 million, part of which went for his Springhill Farms in Utica, Mich.

1981

◆

It was the first heavyweight title fight in Detroit since 1970, when Joe Frazier successfully defended his title in Cobo Arena against Bob Foster. This bout pitted quiet Larry Holmes, the champion for three years, against colorful, controversial Leon Spinks, a 1976 Olympic gold medalist who had won the title from Muhammad Ali in 1978, then lost it back on a decision the same year.

Leon Spinks probably felt like throwing in the towel often during the decade. He moved to Detroit as champion and found almost as much trouble as in his native St. Louis. In 1980, he told police that after leaving a bar he was robbed of a full-length fox coat, jewelry and his gold teeth — worth $45,000 together. In 1985, a week after Michael Spinks took Larry Holmes' title, Leon lost many of his personal belongings and ring mementos in an auction because of a dispute with a moving company. In 1988, his boxing skills long gone, he became a bartender downtown.

Heavyweight Mismatch

By George Puscas

Champion Larry Holmes need search and beg for respect no longer. Finally, it is his. He earned it with a smashing, third-round technical knockout of ex-champion Leon Spinks, retaining the World Boxing Council heavyweight title before a roaring crowd of 15,000 at Joe Louis Arena.

The 31-year-old Holmes, unbeaten in 38 straight fights but previously denied acceptance as a class champion, did all that could be expected of him as he hammered out his victory in classic style. He was fully in control, never wavering or halting. He dropped Spinks, who attempted to force the fight, for a nine-count midway through the first round. Then, early in the fateful third round, Holmes lashed out with a right that shook Spinks. A moment later, he connected with a stiff jab followed by another left hook that dumped Spinks to the floor. Spinks went down on his knees, trying to push himself up with his hands. With referee Richard Steele tolling over him watchfully, Spinks finally made it to his feet.

"I knew he was really hurt then," Holmes said, "and the fight should have been stopped right then. I don't care to kill anybody."

But Steele waved the fighters back into action, and Holmes stepped forward, keeping

Spinks trapped in the corner and banging him at will — left, rights, then simply solid right-hand blasts that rocked Spinks' head back and from side to side.

Spinks' brother, Michael, a ranking light-heavyweight contender, leaped onto the ring apron, urging the referee to stop the fight before Leon was seriously injured. Steele looked, realized Spinks could not defend against the battering, and waved off Holmes after two minutes and 34 seconds of the round. "Holmes is no slouch," Michael said. "He knows how to finish a guy."

There was no questioning the referee's decision. Spinks had been consistently and thoroughly beaten. Holmes' greater size, speed and strength, which were expected to be decisive, proved too much for Spinks.

"I shot my best shot," Spinks said. "I thought I had him."

Poor Leon. He tried mightily, but he simply did not have the equipment or the talent to threaten Holmes, and his bid to regain the heavyweight title he had won from Muhammad Ali collapsed almost before it began. ◆

SUGAR AND THE SLUGGER

By George Puscas

SEPT. 16,
1981

♦

Sugar Ray Leonard, in a strange role reversal, turned slugger and battered Thomas (Hit Man) Hearns into a 14th-round technical knockout in a raging struggle for the undisputed world welterweight boxing championship. A sellout throng of 24,083 at the Caesars Palace Sports Pavilion in Las Vegas, and millions more on television outlets around the world, saw Hearns suffer his first defeat even as he led significantly on all three judges' cards.

Hearns and Leonard, at a post-fight press conference, exchanged compliments and hoisted each others' arms. Leonard wore dark glasses over his puffy left eye.

"In my book," Leonard said, "we are both champions."

Hearns had a message for fans back home. "Detroit," he said, "I shall return."

The end came after Leonard caught Hearns flush on the jaw with a looping right, sending him staggering and falling along the ropes. Leonard, sensing the chance, leaped after Hearns and hammered him with heavy blows to the body as the Detroiter sagged, stunned, on the ropes.

A stunning left sent Hearns, now desperately trying to cover up, along the ropes leading away from his corner. He was plainly in deep trouble. Referee Davey Pearl leaped forward to signal an end to the fight at 1:45 of the round.

Hearns said Leonard hurt him in the sixth round, but he thought he had recovered. He apparently was right, as he began to win rounds on the judges' cards. But Hearns made an error in the 13th round, and Leonard capitalized on it. Leonard connected with a left hook and then a combination to the head. That was the beginning of the end for Hearns. He went down once in the 13th and it was ruled a push, although he seemed helpless, draped on the ropes. The second time he went through in almost the same spot. Pearl went to a nine-count before Hearns struggled back into the ring.

It was a remarkable performance by Leonard, who proved that he is the finest craftsman in the ring today. He had survived his own moments of peril, changed his style, and changed again to wither Hearns.

"There were just two champions," Hearns said, "and one had to be eliminated. Of course I want a rematch. I think I deserve one." ♦

In a world of fragmented boxing titles, this was for the championship everyone would recognize: Thomas Hearns, the grim, taciturn basher from Detroit, against Sugar Ray Leonard, the stylish, fresh-faced Olympic hero. Each held half the title. Hearns was unbeaten. Leonard, defeated only by Roberto Duran, already had avenged that loss.

Although leading with the judges, Thomas Hearns was clearly on the ropes in the final two rounds.

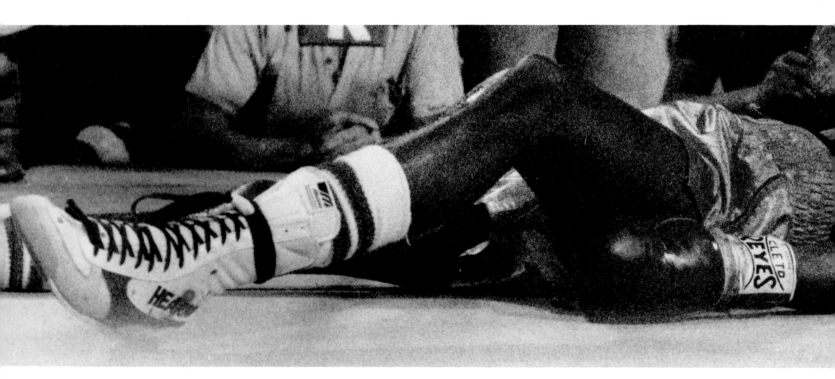

Thomas Hearns predicted he would knock out Marvin Hagler in the third round. Instead, it was Hearns on the canvas in the third. "This is not the end for me," Hearns vowed. "I'm a winner. I don't take defeat easily."

MARVELOUS AND MERCILESS

By Mike Downey

APRIL 15,
1985

◆

M an, did Thomas (Hit Man) Hearns get hit. Marvelous Marvin Hagler knocked out Detroit's favorite son in the third round of their middleweight championship fight at Caesars Palace in Las Vegas.

Even with a face that was a mask of blood, Hagler kept coming. Hearns had belted him early in the first round and opened a serious cut, and he tried desperately to put Hagler away in a wild and vicious three minutes.

Much to Thomas Hearns' dismay, Sugar Ray Leonard retired 14 months after their 1981 showdown. He had a detached retina, at least partially caused by Hearns' punches. Hearns kept fighting, when his chronically sore right hand would allow. After knocking out Roberto Duran in two rounds in 1984, he pursued Marvelous Marvin Hagler, the undisputed middleweight champion and universally recognized successor to Leonard as boxing's best.

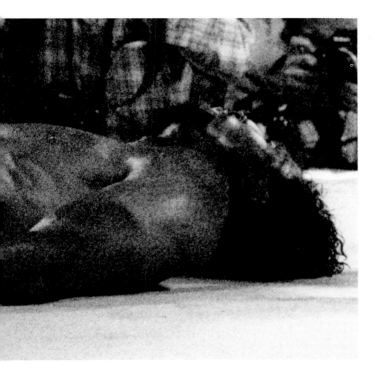

The two men stood toe-to-toe, landing punch after punch in one another's face. There was no way the boxers would be able to keep dishing out and taking such punishment for 12 rounds.

Less than 30 seconds before the end of the fight, Hagler's face was so bloody that the referee halted hostilities and took Hagler into a corner to be examined by a physician. As soon as the fight resumed, though, Hagler started pounding Hearns without mercy.

Floored by a vicious right hand, Hearns staggered to his feet just before the count of 10, but referee Richard Steele took one look at Hearns and immediately stopped the fight, two minutes and one second into the round. "I wanted to show the world I was the greatest," Hagler crowed afterward. "I hope everybody got their money's worth."

Even with his face bloodied by the first-round barrage, Hagler (61-2-2) would not be denied. "This is what you call a complete victory!" he shouted. "This was war!"

In that first round, Hearns hit Hagler with punches that would have sent lesser men into a deep sleep. He hit him with the same right hand that had dropped Roberto Duran like a rock in a pond. But as the round was ending, Hearns got hit with one himself and staggered backward. Two of the three judges gave the round to Marvelous Marvin, even though he was a bloody mess.

Hearns was a changed man in Round 2, not nearly as forceful with his punches and moving on rubbery legs. By the end of the round, the Hit Man was in serious trouble. In desperation, Hearns (40-2) did exactly what he did in his other loss — to Sugar Ray Leonard — when the momentum in that fight changed. He got on his bicycle and started backpedaling. The slugger became the boxer. The brief rest he got while Hagler's cut was inspected gave Hearns a few moments to catch his breath. But the end was near. Hagler clubbed him with a big right, then clubbed him again. Hearns toppled backward. As the count neared 10, the wobbly Hit Man managed to stand, but it was obvious he did not have all his faculties. The referee called it a night.

"I do have to give Marvin his proper respect for being a great champion," Hearns said half an hour later. "The man has not held the title for seven years for nothing. The man showed me his greatness. He fought one great fight. . . . Even the greatest lose sometimes." ◆

In 1942, Sugar Ray Robinson fought
Harvey Dubs in Detroit — his second
of 12 bouts in his hometown. Robinson
kayoed Dubs in the sixth round.
Robinson's only Detroit loss was a
1943 bout with Jake LaMotta.

THE SWEETEST SCIENTIST

By George Puscas

APRIL 12,
1989

◆

Eight years to the day after Joe Louis died, Detroit and the boxing world lost another of their greatest legends, Sugar Ray Robinson. How good was Robinson? As the phrase starts: pound for pound ...

Long before Sugar Ray Robinson first stepped into a professional ring nearly a half-century ago, boxing was known among poets and romantics as the sweet science.

It was, at best, a facetious name for such a cruel sport.

And then came Sugar Ray Robinson.

Pound for pound, as others put it, he was the sweetest scientist, the greatest fighter who ever lived. No one in his time disputed it, and even now, few would doubt it.

Sugar Ray Robinson, 67, who died in Culver City, Calif., after a lengthy illness, was the classic fighter, the grandest practitioner of the toughest of all sports.

We have been blessed with great fighting men in Detroit. Joe Louis, the late former heavyweight champion, and Robinson, former welterweight champion and five-time winner of the middleweight title, were Detroiters.

"The way I think of them," said Ben Greene, a former fight manager-writer in New York, "is that Louis was boxing's Babe Ruth, and Robinson was Ty Cobb. They were both that great."

Louis, the famed Brown Bomber, once modestly agreed he was the best of all heavyweights. But, he insisted, the finest fighter of all — pound for pound at 160 or thereabouts — was Robinson, an incomparable boxing stylist.

In 1961, Robinson, whose retinue included a barber, hairdresser, tailor, butler and chauffeur, came to Detroit to meet Wilf Greaves. It was his last of 12 fights in town. He trained at J.L. Hudson's Northland Center. We would meet before his daily sessions in a mobile trailer that served as his dressing room. No fighter, before or since, dressed quite the way Robinson did. One of his aides removed his shoes and socks, another took off his pants, a third removed his shirt. Then in order, they would dress him, donning his socks, his ring gear, lacing and tying his shoes and gloves. Frequently, he would interrupt them, demanding that his hair be combed.

He was a handsome, vain man; the aura of a star hung over him, perhaps because he placed it there. But he was friendly and generous. In recent years, Robinson had been a recreation director in the Los Angeles area.

Because he left Detroit before his 11th birthday, Robinson (born Walker Smith Jr.) frequently is considered a New Yorker. He lived most of his life in the East, but he always insisted his roots were in Detroit, only a mile or so from the Paradise Valley area where Louis lived. In a career that spanned 25 years, Robinson won 174 of 201 fights, more than half of the losses coming after his 40th birthday.

Robinson and Jake LaMotta — who fought six times — met twice at the old Olympia in February 1943. On Feb. 5, LaMotta upset Robinson, avenging an Oct. 2, 1942, loss in New York. On Feb. 26, Robinson beat LaMotta again.

The Robinson-LaMotta duels during World War II fed Detroit's hunger for boxing. Not long before, Louis had risen to world acclaim, and now, here was Robinson. The sport reached its zenith in Detroit in those years, with even Louis coming home from the Army to box exhibitions at Olympia.

When the war ended, Robinson, who operated a nightclub in New York's Harlem district, was in need of money. So he organized a dance troupe to tour the United States and Europe. He was a hit in Paris, where he paraded in a pink Cadillac convertible with collections of women aboard. His finest fighting came during the 1950s. He won the middleweight title from LaMotta, then lost and regained it four more times. Among his rivals in boxing's golden decade of 160-pounders were Randy Turpin, Carl (Bobo) Olson, Gene Fullmer and Carmen Basilio. ◆

Sugar Ray Robinson's arm went up 174 times during his 26-year career. He officially retired in 1965, at 44.

Thomas Hearns towered over Sugar Ray Leonard in the third and 11th rounds. But in the end, the judges scored the bout a wash.

No SATISFACTION

By George Puscas

JUNE 12,
1989
◆

Sugar Ray Leonard was 33 now, an elder statesman of the fight game, a familiar figure as a TV commentator, and a man who had announced his retirement in 1982 amid much fanfare. He had boldly returned in 1987 and taken Marvin Hagler's title. He was a solid favorite in the long-awaited rematch with Thomas Hearns, 30, whose skills were thought to have diminished.

Deep in Thomas Hearns' corner, the men who guide him during fights seethed in the aftermath of his latest. They were not alone — Hearns, manager-trainer Emanuel Steward, cornermen Prentiss Byrd, Walter Smith and Ralph Citro. The crowd of 15,400 in the Caesars Palace Stadium in Las Vegas took up a thunderous chant in the dark desert air: "Bull----! Bull----!"

All of it was in protest of the 12-round draw that deprived Hearns, in his finest hour in recent years, of a clear victory over Sugar Ray Leonard. The memory of his 1981 loss to Leonard, Hearns repeatedly had said, haunted his life, and he ached to remove the monster that taunted him. The draw enabled Leonard to keep his World Boxing Council super-middleweight title.

Despite their immediate disappointment at ringside, Hearns and Steward refused to protest. "Certainly I think I was ahead and should have won," Hearns said. "I thought I had put a few rounds in the bank."

Indeed, Hearns was ahead until the 12th round. Leonard won the round on all three judges' cards, but one of the judges scored it 10-8, whereas the other two made it 10-9. The two-point difference on one card was just enough to erase Hearns' lead.

Hearns (46-3-1) had banged Leonard (35-1-1) smartly early in the final round, but Leonard came back and appeared to batter Hearns in a closing rush. "He hit me a couple times," Hearns said, "but he didn't hurt me. I was just too exhausted to do much except try to avoid him."

Steward similarly refused to be drawn into a hot feud with the judges.

"My fighters never complain," Steward said, "no matter what happens with the judges. They learn that as amateurs. I thought Hearns was a clear winner, but we can't do anything about that, can we?"

No. Judging fights is subjective, so protests are frequent. Larry Holmes, the former heavyweight champion, took a protest to civil court in Las Vegas after he was deprived of victory in his second bout with Michael Spinks, in 1986. He lost there, too.

"I thought 10-8 was a method of saving Leonard for another day," Steward said. "What bothers me is that when we look back in the books years from now, we'll still see that Tommy didn't win. That's all people will know."

It was a great fight, better than their classic 1981 encounter — which Leonard won on a 14th-round knockout — because Hearns spent most of this one on a cannonading attack. After a slow start, the fight raged a half-dozen times toward a sudden finish, turning one way then the other as Hearns, then Leonard, took charge.

Hearns' best rounds were the third and the 11th, when he knocked down Leonard, and the seventh and eighth, when his right hand wobbled Leonard. Nevertheless, Leonard won the seventh on two cards.

From Hearns' corner, Steward frequently exhorted his fighter to "Let it go! Let it go!" — meaning to use his powerful right to hammer Leonard.

"You'll notice," Steward said, "that Tommy's best rounds came when he used that right. It was our plan."

Leonard's best round was the fifth, when he staggered and dazed Hearns with a left hook. Hearns grabbed him, but Leonard broke away and bounced a sequence of blows off Hearns' head.

"When that round ended," Steward said, "I told Tommy everything he had done in boxing was on the line. It woke him up."

Leonard — like Hearns the only boxer with titles in five weight classes — was gracious afterward, conceding that Hearns was far more effective than Leonard expected.

"I never got into the rhythm and flow of the fight," complained Leonard, his eyes still puffy from Hearns' pounding. "But I'm gonna have to study the films — I'm not sure my age was to blame, or whether it was Tommy Hearns. He fought a damned good fight." ◆

After the fight, Thomas Hearns huddled with his daughter. Earlier in the day, Hearns' brother Henry was arraigned on a first-degree murder charge in Southfield, Mich.

BY THE NUMBERS
Major title fights involving Michigan boxers

DATE	MICHIGAN BOXER	SITE	OPPONENT	OUTCOME
3/2/80	Hilmer Kenty (Detroit)	Detroit	Ernesto Espana	KO 2:53 9th (won WBA lightweight title)
8/2/80	Thomas Hearns (Detroit)	Detroit	Pipino Cuevas	KO 2:39 2nd (won WBA welterweight)
4/12/81	Hilmer Kenty (Detroit)	Atlantic City, N.J.	Sean O'Grady	Lost decision 15 (lost WBA lightweight)
6/12/81	Leon Spinks (Detroit)	Detroit	Larry Holmes	KO'd 2:34 3rd (Holmes retained WBC heavyweight)
9/16/81	Thomas Hearns (Detroit)	Las Vegas, Nev.	Sugar Ray Leonard	KO'd 1:45 14th (lost world welterweight unification)
11/14/81	Dujuan Johnson (Detroit)	Cleveland	Aaron Pryor	KO'd 1:49 7th (Pryor retained WBA junior-welterweight)
3/7/82	Caveman Lee (Detroit)	Atlantic City, N.J.	Marvin Hagler	KO'd 1:07 1st (Hagler retained world middleweight)
12/3/82	Thomas Hearns (Detroit)	New Orleans	Wilfred Benitez	Decision 15 (won WBC super-welterweight)
3/19/83	Milton McCrory (Detroit)	Reno, Nev.	Colin Jones	Draw 12 (WBC welterweight remained vacant)
8/13/83	Milton McCrory (Detroit)	Las Vegas, Nev.	Colin Jones	Split decision 12 (won vacant WBC welterweight)
2/26/84	Roger Mayweather (Grand Rapids)	Beaumont, Texas	Rocky Lockridge	KO'd 1:59 1st (lost WBA junior lightweight title)
6/15/84	Thomas Hearns (Detroit)	Las Vegas, Nev.	Roberto Duran	KO 1:07 2nd (retained WBC super-welterweight)
8/31/84	Pinklon Thomas (Pontiac)	Las Vegas, Nev.	Tim Witherspoon	Majority decision 12 (won WBC heavyweight)
4/6/85	Jimmy Paul (Detroit)	Atlantic City, N.J.	Harry Arroyo	Decision 15 (won IBF lightweight)
4/15/85	Thomas Hearns (Detroit)	Las Vegas, Nev.	Marvin Hagler	KO'd 2:01 3rd (Hagler retained world middleweight)
12/6/85	Milton McCrory (Detroit)	Las Vegas, Nev.	Donald Curry	KO'd 1:53 2nd (Curry won world welterweight unification)
12/21/85	Eddie Mustafa Muhammad (Detroit)	Pesaro, Italy	Slobodan Kacar	Lost split decision 15 (Kacar won vacant IBF light-heavyweight)
3/22/86	Leon Spinks (Detroit)	Reno, Nev.	Dwight Muhammad Qawi	KO'd 2:56 6th (Qawi retained WBA cruiserweight)
3/22/86	Pinklon Thomas (Pontiac)	Las Vegas, Nev.	Trevor Berbick	Lost decision 12 (lost WBC heavyweight)
10/30/86	Joe Louis Manley (Detroit)	Hartford, Conn.	Gary Hinton	KO 2:14 10th (won IBF junior-welterweight)
12/5/86	Jimmy Paul (Detroit)	Las Vegas, Nev.	Greg Haugen	Lost majority decision 15 (lost IBF lightweight)
12/5/86	Duane Thomas (Detroit)	Las Vegas, Nev.	John Mugabi	KO 0:56 3rd (won WBC super-welterweight)
3/7/87	Thomas Hearns (Detroit)	Detroit	Dennis Andries	KO 1:26 10th (won WBC light-heavyweight)
4/19/87	Milton McCrory (Detroit)	Phoenix, Ariz.	Mike McCallum	KO'd 2:20 10th (McCallum retained WBA junior middleweight)
5/30/87	Pinklon Thomas (Pontiac)	Las Vegas, Nev.	Mike Tyson	KO'd 2:00 6th (Tyson retained WBC, WBA heavyweight)
5/30/87	Tony Tucker (Gr. Rapids)	Las Vegas, Nev.	Buster Douglas	KO 1:36 10th (won IBF heavyweight)
8/1/87	Tony Tucker (Gr. Rapids)	Las Vegas, Nev.	Mike Tyson	Lost decision 12 (Tyson won world heavyweight unification)
10/10/87	Frank Tate (Detroit)	Las Vegas, Nev.	Michael Olajide	Decision 15 (won vacant IBF middleweight)
10/29/87	Thomas Hearns (Detroit)	Las Vegas, Nev.	Juan Roldan	KO 2:01 4th (won WBC middleweight)
11/13/87	Roger Mayweather (Grand Rapids)	Los Angeles	Rene Arredondo	KO 2:00 6th (won WBC super-lightweight)
6/6/88	Thomas Hearns (Detroit)	Las Vegas, Nev.	Iran Barkley	KO'd 2:34 3rd (lost WBC middleweight)
7/28/88	Frank Tate (Detroit)	Las Vegas, Nev.	Michael Nunn	KO'd 0:40 9th (lost IBF middleweight)
11/4/88	Thomas Hearns (Detroit)	Las Vegas, Nev.	James Kinchen	Majority decision 12 (won NABF super-middleweight)
12/8/88	John David Jackson (Detroit)	Detroit	Lupe Aquino	KO 8th (won vacant WBO junior middleweight title)
6/12/89	Thomas Hearns (Detroit)	Las Vegas, Nev.	Sugar Ray Leonard	Draw 12 (Leonard retained WBC super-middleweight)

BASEBALL

Catcher Lance Parrish toasted the
Tiger Stadium crowd after Detroit
polished off the Padres in five games
to win the 1984 World Series.

In 22 years of professional baseball, Al Kaline never played a day for any team but the Detroit Tigers. Two weeks after his Hall of Fame induction, the Tigers retired a uniform number for the first time: Kaline's No. 6.

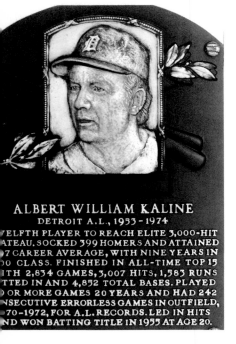

ALBERT WILLIAM KALINE
DETROIT A.L., 1953-1974
ELFTH PLAYER TO REACH ELITE 3,000-HIT
ATEAU. SOCKED 399 HOMERS AND ATTAINED
7 CAREER AVERAGE, WITH NINE YEARS IN
0 CLASS. FINISHED IN ALL-TIME TOP 15
TH 2,834 GAMES, 3,007 HITS, 1,583 RUNS
TTED IN AND 4,852 TOTAL BASES. PLAYED
OR MORE GAMES 20 YEARS AND HAD 242
NSECUTIVE ERRORLESS GAMES IN OUTFIELD,
70-1972, FOR A.L. RECORDS. LED IN HITS
ND WON BATTING TITLE IN 1955 AT AGE 20.

Al Kaline flew to New York in January 1980 after his election to the Baseball Hall of Fame. Upon his return to Detroit the next day, several hundred fans mobbed Kaline, the 10th player elected in his first year of eligibility. "I don't like the word superstar," he said on the flight back. "I think I was a quality player. Not as good as a few, but better than most." In 22 seasons, Kaline batted .297, hit 399 home runs, drove in 1,583 runs, won 10 Gold Gloves and captured a batting crown (.340 in 1955).

AL'S DAY IN THE SUN

By Joe Lapointe

The skies of Cooperstown, N.Y., were gray and rainy for much of Al Kaline's day in the sun. Then, as he prepared to officially and ceremoniously enter the Hall of Fame, the clouds parted as if by script. As Kaline stood with his bronze plaque on the back porch of the National Baseball Library, the sun shone brightly in the blue sky.

Kaline told everyone how happy he was to take his place among the immortals of the national pastime. He spoke with his own kind of solemn joy, and only once did his voice crack and tears come to his eyes — when he told the gathering how much he wanted to thank his parents for their "love and hard work." Then he acknowledged all other members of his family and Tigers management before he turned to the hundreds of Detroit sports fans on hand.

"Most of all," he said, "I'd like to particularly thank Tiger fans everywhere."

The crowd cheered.

"But especially," Kaline said, "those who supported me my entire career in Detroit. We've had our highs and some lows. But through it all, Detroit fans have stuck with the Tigers to prove they are the best in baseball."

They were lucky fans, too, fortunate to watch Kaline get 3,007 base hits and play a splendid version of

rightfield for 22 years as the greatest Tiger of the post-war era. He felt the same way.

"Sometimes," Kaline said, "I feel I am one of the luckiest people in the world."

As usual, he looked fit and handsome, wearing a light summer suit, blue shirt and tie, with his hair neat and in place. He sat next to Brooklyn Dodgers great Duke Snider, who also was inducted, along with posthumous inductions for Chuck Klein, an old-time National League star, and Tom Yawkey, who owned the Boston Red Sox.

Kaline broke into the majors in 1953 without ever having played a minor league game. He was only the 10th man to be chosen for the Hall of Fame in his first year of eligibility.

In his speech, Kaline cited two other members of the Hall, Stan Musial and Ted Williams, who sat with him on the rostrum. He called them his boyhood idols when he was growing up in Baltimore.

"When I was a youngster," Kaline said, "life was a baseball game." ◆

Because Ty Cobb's remarkable career ended before numbers were added to uniforms, the Tigers had never retired a player's number. But rightfielder Al Kaline had been so good for so long that the tradition ended Aug. 17, 1980. Kaline's No. 6 was retired between games of a doubleheader with Texas. "Many players take their uniforms for granted," he said. "I never did. Every time I put on the Tiger uniform, I did it with pride."

The 50-day strike that interrupted the 1981 baseball season kept the Tigers in the race until the last weekend. If they could win the final Saturday and Sunday at Milwaukee, under the strike year-only format, the Tigers would be the second-half champions of the AL East.

Milwaukee reliever Rollie Fingers got the cigar; Tigers pitcher Milt Wilcox got the seat. Wilcox, scheduled to start the season's final game, expected to pitch for a division title.

Fingers later won the American League's MVP and Cy Young awards — the first time a pitcher won both since Detroit's Denny McLain in 1968.

A STRIKING CONCLUSION

By Brian Bragg

The Tigers' pennant dreams and the hopes of their fans were drowned in a sea of Milwaukee champagne Saturday afternoon as the Brewers battled from behind to clinch the American League East title for Season II with a 2-1 victory.

The usually powerful Brewers finessed their way into the East playoffs with two eighth-inning bunt plays that confused and frustrated the Tigers. The rally beat Tigers ace Jack Morris, who was bidding for his 15th victory and carried a 1-0 lead into the eighth.

The teams have one more game to play, but the Brewers hold an insurmountable 2½-game lead and will play the New York Yankees, first-half champions, in next week's East playoffs. The Tigers, who held the East lead for most of the past six weeks, lost their third game in a row.

"We could've gone out in a blaze of glory," Morris said. "Now it's just another year. I'm sure I'm going to feel worse in two or three days than I do right now. But, heck, I made some good pitches today, and if we get three runs we're going to win the game."

Manager Sparky Anderson echoed those sentiments.

"Jack had super stuff," he said. "He was going to win the game, 1-0. But we haven't hit the ball all year, and the way we lost it was just one of those things."

Anderson sat back in his chair and reflected a moment after making a congratulatory phone call to Milwaukee manager Buck Rodgers.

"I feel bad for the people at home in Detroit," Anderson said. "They put so much of their heart into these players. If only the players could realize how much. They really care."

The Brewers' biggest crowd of the stretch run — 28,330 — showed up for the victory party, and they weren't disappointed.

The Tigers had scored off Pete Vuckovich in the sixth inning, and it seemed the Season II fight would go down to the last day. But Morris walked Paul Molitor to begin the Brewers' eighth. Morris thought two of the pitches were strikes, but umpire Mike Reilly didn't agree.

Then hot-hitting Robin Yount dropped a bunt to the right side. First baseman Ron Jackson called Morris off the ball and wheeled as if to fire to second for the force play. But he thought Morris was in his way. Jackson hesitated, took a few steps and hesitated again before throwing to first base. Too late, and the Brewers had two runners on.

"I knew I could have fielded the ball and had a play at first," Morris said, "but Ronnie called me off it. He thought he could make the play at second."

Cecil Cooper followed with another bunt, this one to the left side. Morris pounced on the ball and looked at third base for a force. Such a play was impossible, and by that time so was the throw to first, so the bases were loaded with Brewers. Ted Simmons then lined one through the middle. Morris got a glove on it, but couldn't hold on, and Molitor raced home with the tying run as shortstop Alan Trammell threw out Simmons.

"If I'd have got it in my glove," Morris said, "it might have become a double play, and we're out of a jam."

The Tigers walked Ben Oglivie intentionally to set up a possible force play, but Gorman Thomas lifted a long fly to right-center, and Yount tagged and scored the deciding run.

"This is a terrible way to end it," Trammell said. "Those bunt plays . . . "

Milwaukee relief ace Rollie Fingers, who had entered the game in the top of the eighth, breezed through a 1-2-3 ninth inning, and the celebration was on. Fans poured onto the field. The Brewers mobbed Fingers, who has allowed only one earned run at County Stadium all season. After 15 minutes the field was cleared and the Brewers took a curtain call.

The Tigers simply sat in their dugout, watching in envy. ♦

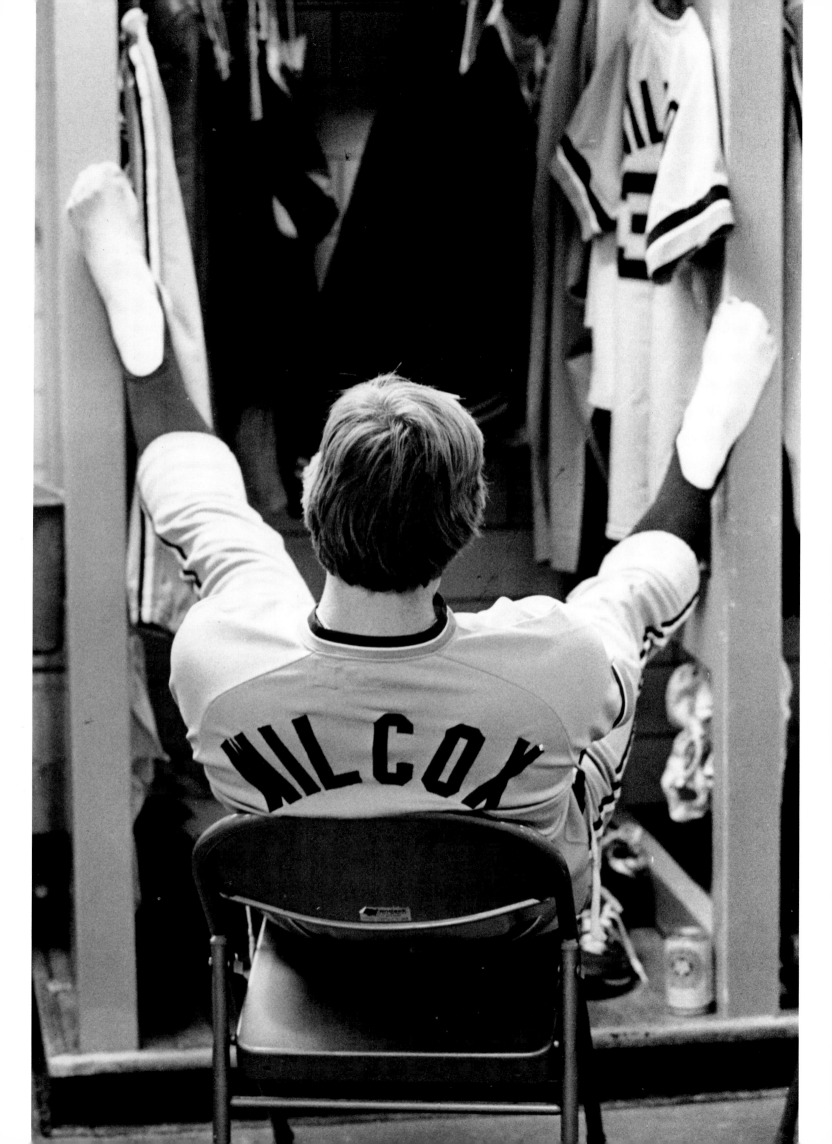

APRIL 15,

1983

◆

Milt Wilcox was a 32-year-old journeyman, a .500 pitcher with a history of arm trouble who had been dumped by three major league teams. But on a chilly spring night in Chicago, in a 6-0 victory, he threw what his catcher, Lance Parrish, would call "the best ballgame I've ever caught — or seen."

ONE PITCH FROM PERFECTION

By Mike Downey

Dawn was breaking when it dawned on Milt Wilcox what he had done, or had almost done. It was 6 a.m., April 16, 1983, the morning after. He was wandering aimlessly along Michigan Avenue in Chicago, eyes still red from one hour's sleep, and had just passed the only surviving landmark of the Great Chicago Fire, the stately Water Tower. That's when it hit him — the second thing to hit him all night.

"God," he said as it finally sank in. "Just how close was I?"

As close as it gets. He was one out away from a perfect game, which would have been the 13th pitched, when Jerry Hairston of the Chicago White Sox drove a single through the middle like a stake through Dracula's heart. A cry of anguish could be heard as near as the Comiskey Park boxes and as far away as a living room in suburban Detroit, where Winifred Wilcox, watching her son on TV, saw Hairston's single and broke down crying.

One hit was all there was, and Wilcox waved to the cheering Chicagoans after knocking their Sox off. He walked only as far as the first-base coach's box, where microphones were thrust at him like harpoons. Kirk Gibson eventually intercepted him and told him he owed the 24 other Tigers a buck apiece for messing up an otherwise perfect game.

It took quite a while for the clubhouse commotion to settle down. Teammates stood in front of a television, watching Johnny Carson do Carnac the Magnificent, and answers were improvised with Wilcox the subject of every question. At long last, the pitcher slumped in front of his locker in peace. "Let's have breakfast tomorrow," one last remaining reporter said. "What time will you get up in the morning?"

"I won't sleep," Wilcox said.

"Not at all?"

"Not tonight."

He couldn't stop thinking of the game. "What did I do?" he would ask later, sitting in a hotel restaurant. "I've been thinking about it. A one-hitter is great and winning itself is satisfying, but there's sort of an empty feeling, too. I keep thinking about that pitch to Hairston. I probably rushed it. I probably should have taken my time.

"I spent the whole game knowing they were going to get a hit sooner or later, but when I finally thought I had a chance, that's when I let it get away. It was like a big bubble bursting right in front of my face." ◆

One pitch after pinch-hitter Jerry Hairston ruined Milt Wilcox's perfect game, Rudy Law hit a grounder directly to first baseman Rick Leach, who made the unassisted play to end the game and then embraced Wilcox near the bag in sympathy. Wilcox struck out eight White Sox; only five hit the ball out of the infield.

ONE FRANCHISE TO GO

By Mike Downey

OCT. 10,
1983
◆

In the front office and in the boardroom, the Tigers had been a model of stability. But John Fetzer, who had headed a syndicate that purchased the team from the Briggs estate in 1956, was 82 years old and quietly seeking a buyer. The price was nearly 10 times the $5.5 million he and his partners had paid.

Now that Detroit has more pizza men in charge than the Hill Street police precinct, we can all sit back and place our orders. Pennants and Stanley Cups all around. Because anyone who figured Old Man Fetzer would own the Tigers' bats, balls and resin bags until he was 182 years old was in for a jolt when Thomas Monaghan ordered a franchise to go.

You thought Mike Ilitch checking the Norrises off the ice was a slice? Man, this was peppers and mushrooms. This topped it. No more than a whisper had passed that the Motor City's baseball team might be for sale, and even at that, there had been assumptions all around that someone else would make the bid. Monaghan was never mentioned. Ilitch already owned the hockey Red Wings and the arena in which they played but had hinted he might fork over another 30 mil for the Tigers. Somebody should have deduced the common denominator. Fast, fast food, baby. Mr. Ilitch owns the Little Caesars pizza chain. Mr. Monaghan owns Domino's, the Ann Arbor-based pizza chain.

The sports business obviously appeals to these businessmen, and by the same token,

the hurry-up food biz must rake in money hand over fist. If only someone had alerted Jim Campbell not to spend all those decades in the baseball business and instead put his bread into all that pizza dough out there, he might have had the bucks to buy out John Fetzer himself. As it is, Campbell finds himself stepping up from his general manager's level to a three-man executive dais with the outgoing owner, Mr. Fetzer, and the incoming one, the surprising Mr. Monaghan.

Half his life ago, Monaghan stopped ordering pizzas and started selling them. Now, at 46, he is all grown up and ultra-wealthy, but he feels like a kid again. When he took a bow before the public as the newest boss of one of baseball's oldest teams, Monaghan said there was only one better job. That one, he said, already belongs to Alan Trammell.

A word should be said for the ownership of John Fetzer. Let's see . . . OK, here's a word: Admired. Fans and sports writers might not have admired Old Man Fetzer, relating a shortage of World Series appearances to a shortage of smarts. But his peers did. Most of the lords of baseball seemed to be fond of Fetzer, even if they had crossed swords at times.

But if Thomas Monaghan can do for Detroit what Detroit would like him to do, the city will be his. And just wait'll you see this guy and Lou Whitaker turn the double play. ◆

Eleven months after the Tigers were sold, executives Jim Campbell, John Fetzer and Thomas Monaghan were dodging division-clinching champagne.

The Tigers began the 1984 season with more than the usual spring optimism, buoyed by a strong finish the year before. "I hate to run my mouth off and say we're going to do this or that," pitcher Jack Morris said before beating Minnesota on Opening Day. "But potentially, I think we can be very good." The team won its first three, then took on Chicago on a Saturday afternoon.

NO RUNS, NO HITS, NO LOSSES

By Bill McGraw and Gene Myers

Two down in the ninth inning. Ron Kittle at bat. Jack Morris on the mound.

The national cameras of NBC and 24,616 oohing and ahhing fans at Comiskey Park, home turf of the Chicago White Sox.

Morris' wife, Carol, has stopped waxing the kitchen floor. The Morrises' close friends, Jan and Eric Hipple, the Detroit Lions quarterback, are documenting the action on videotape.

The crowd at the downtown Lindell AC, and hundreds of other Michigan bars, roars on every pitch. Crowds surround the TV displays in malls and stores.

Jack Morris, a 28-year-old right-hander and ace of the Tigers' staff, stands one batter from a no-hitter, something no Tiger has accomplished since Jim Bunning in 1958.

With the count one ball, two strikes, and Detroit leading, 4-0, Morris releases his 120th pitch of the day. It tails to the outside of the plate, but Kittle goes for it with a confused swing. He misses.

As the fans break into wild applause, the Tigers rush to surround Morris on the mound. Catcher Lance Parrish gives his longtime teammate a ferocious hug. Players are leaping up and down, slapping each other — and Morris — with high-five handshakes.

"I'm so excited, I can hardly talk," Morris said. "I'm just excited. . . . I've had better stuff before, but anytime you throw a no-hitter or even a shutout, you have to have luck."

"I'm a nervous wreck," Carol Morris said an hour after the game. "I'm still shaking."

"You have to give the man credit," Kittle said. "He was going after us and challenging us throughout the game. I don't think we hit many decent foul balls all day."

The White Sox last season were American League West champions after winning 99 games and scoring 800 runs. But Morris, who won 20 games last season for the first time in his seven-year career, sailed through the lineup with hardly a hitch. He struck out eight and walked six, and there were only three hard-hit balls all day, including one sharp grounder and a mean line drive that were scooped up nicely by first baseman Dave Bergman, a late-inning defensive replacement.

"It wasn't a Picasso," said plate umpire Durwood Merrill, "but it might have been a Rockwell."

In the ninth inning, facing four of the top five batters in Chicago's lineup, Morris retired Carlton Fisk and Harold Baines on weak ground balls. Greg Luzinski walked on a close 3-2 pitch, and the crowd booed Merrill's call. Then Kittle ended the game with his strikeout.

Morris became the fourth Tiger to pitch a no-hitter in the 84th season of the franchise. Besides Bunning, Virgil Trucks did it twice in 1952 (but he lost 19 times that season), and George Mullin did it in 1912 (he lost 17 times that season).

"Some people think it's a great thing to be part of a no-hitter," Sox manager Tony La Russa said, "but the club that gets no-hit suffers some embarrassment."

Morris' toughest inning was the fourth, when he walked the first three batters. Next up were Luzinski and Kittle, who totaled 67 home runs and 195 RBIs last season. Luzinski checked his swing, but tapped a grounder to Morris, who threw to Parrish to start a double play. Kittle struck out, ending the inning.

Back in Detroit at the Lindell AC, a bar frequented by sports fans and sports figures, a crowd of 75 gathered to watch the TV screens by the time Morris took the mound for the final inning. The applause built to a roar on each pitch in the ninth. Hamburgers got cold, and waitresses stopped serving. When Kittle struck out, the standing ovation matched the one at Comiskey Park in length if not volume.

The crowd grew larger at the television displays at Sears at Oakland Mall in Troy as the game progressed.

"We often get folks watching the games, mostly men standing around while their wives shop," salesman Jerry Carr said. "This time we got the women, too. When it was over, everybody was jumping around, screaming and hollering. It was great." ◆

Jack Morris got a defensive hand from first baseman Dave Bergman and the right pitch requests from catcher Lance Parrish. Although Morris finished 19-11 with 3.60 ERA, his no-hitter was his only shutout.

The 1984 Tigers won and won and won — their first nine games, 19 of their first 21 — and the fervor for them built and built and built. Non-fans became casual fans; casual fans became fanatics. By the time the Tigers finished the season, 104-time winners and a 15-game lead in their division, they had set a team attendance record — more than 2.7 million — and made the Wave a national pastime.

A CINCH OF A CLINCH

By Mike Downey

Call Yogi. Tell him it's over.

Tell him the Tigers never looked back. Tell him all that "it ain't over till it's over" stuff is for some other team, some other time. Tell Yogi Berra, the Yankees manager, that no one since the 1927 New York Yankees had won their league or division wire-to-wire until the Tigers took care of their last remaining American League East business. But Yogi, baby, this one was over in April.

Maybe sooner. The pizza man, Tom Monaghan, bought the ballclub last October, when the Baltimore Orioles were just beginning their American League pennant series. In Detroit, the new season already had begun. Bill Lajoie had just been promoted as the team's general manager. The Tigers had taken the 1983 season practically to the limit, but the Orioles still had something extra, something the Tigers were missing.

So, Mr. Monaghan pulled out his checkbook and signed a man with a bat, Darrell Evans. That was December. Mr. Lajoie picked up his telephone and traded two warm bodies for a man with an arm, Willie Hernandez, and a man with a glove, Dave Bergman. That was March. Next thing anybody knew, the Tigers had played 40 baseball games and won 35.

For the next few months, the rest of the division waited for the Tigers to go into the tank. But they didn't. They wouldn't.

The team had just been built too solidly, too strategically. Suddenly, the Tigers seemed to have two of everything: Two owners, John Fetzer and Monaghan. Two GMs, Jim Campbell and Lajoie. Two sluggers, Kirk Gibson and Lance Parrish. Two aces, Dan Petry and Jack Morris. Two rally starters, Lou Whitaker and Alan Trammell. Two rally killers, Aurelio Lopez and Hernandez. And most of all two fan clubs, home and away. Tigers caps started appearing all over the country, from Austin to Boston, from Anaheim to Cucamonga.

By the time the Tigers put down the Milwaukee Brewers, 3-0, behind a kid pitcher named Randy O'Neal and the ridiculously successful Hernandez, there wasn't a baseball fan in the country who believed the Tigers weren't going to win the division. For weeks, it had only been a question of when. And when it happened, with Hernandez smoking a third strike past Milwaukee's Jim Sundberg, only a ring of police kept Tiger Stadium from being dismantled piece by piece.

The Tigers themselves finally got to chug the champagne that had been waiting for them for days. The magic number was zero. The fans in the stands, filled with beer and filthy language, had the time of their lives, taunting cops into chasing them into the seats. Several of them pleaded only to be permitted to touch home plate, as if it were a Blarney stone waiting to be smooched. Not since 1972 had the Tigers won a division title, and a dozen years is a long time to go without being able to kiss a real dish.

The end had finally come. The new people in the organization had put the club over the top, but the division title also belonged to the old guard, the guys like Campbell who had convinced Old Man Fetzer to fork over the bucks required to keep fast-improving players like Parrish, Trammell and Whitaker on the premises.

The title also belonged to old standbys such as Milt Wilcox, the pitcher who came through with the season of his life, and Johnny Grubb, who had come off the pines so many times to pitch in, and Tom Brookens, who watched the Tigers do everything but re-activate Eddie Mathews to solve their problems at third base. When Brookens homered home the final run in the division clincher, it felt good to him. "It was the least I could do," this total team player said.

There was shouting and singing. The opera was over and the fat lady had sung. Actually it was Fat Bob Taylor, the Singing Plumber, who did the national anthem on the night Detroit won the division, but he'll do nicely, thank you. Call Yogi, somebody. Tell him to start thinking about 1985. ◆

Willie Hernandez rocketed off the mound and the Tigers out of the dugout after he struck out Jim Sundberg, clinching the American League East title. It was good practice: Hernandez also was on the mound for the final out of the playoffs and the World Series. Rookie Randy O'Neal started the 3-0 title-clincher, despite lobbying by Jack Morris and Dan Petry. O'Neal, 9-10 after a season in the minors, gave up four hits and struck out six in seven innings. Hernandez finished for his 30th save in 30 save opportunities.

In contrast to the Tigers' runaway, the 1984 Kansas City Royals won the American League West by only three games and with 84 victories — fewer than the fifth-place team in the East. The difference showed in the playoffs. The Tigers won at Kansas City, 8-1 and 5-3 in 11 innings, then came home for Detroit's first playoff game in a dozen years.

ONE, TWO, THREE, SWEEP

By Bill McGraw

Tiger Stadium flipped its lid when the Tigers beat the Royals to win a nail-biting game that gave them the American League pennant.

Champs!

Marty Castillo caught Darryl Motley's pop foul to put the finishing touch on a tense, 1-0 game that was the Tigers' 107th victory of the year. The crowd of 52,168, largest of the season, exploded like a firecracker as long phalanxes of leather-jacketed police held back the minority that rushed the field. A joyous throng gathered at Michigan and Trumbull.

The team that startled baseball with a 35-5 start and never relinquished its hold on first place swept the Royals in three straight games, sending the Tigers to the ninth World Series in their 84-year history and their first since 1968.

It was the closest of games, a pitching battle between Charlie Leibrandt and Milt Wilcox. "It was a nail-biter of a game," said Kirk Gibson, the series' most valuable player. "Everybody's having fun. We had fun. All season long, we always came up with the big play in the big game when we needed it."

"Nobody would have dreamed one run would hold up in this park," said manager Sparky Anderson. "When a man shuts you out in this ballpark, you know he's pitched a hell of a game."

Wilcox has a rusty hinge of a shoulder and a weird assortment of pitches that include such breaking-ball hybrids as a "slurve" and a "yackadoo." The Tigers nearly dropped him after last season, but he came back and had the best season of a 14-year career. He allowed just two hits over eight innings, striking out eight and walking two. Tigers pitchers held the Royals to four runs and a .170 batting average over the three games. The best in the American League West never had a lead.

Wilcox, who said he was as "nervous as a rookie," had a 17-8 regular-season record that was the best of a career that began at Cincinnati in 1970, when he won a playoff game for Anderson's Big Red Machine. Wilcox struck out the final two batters in the fourth and the first two in the fifth; he also struck out four in a row during the 1970 playoffs. Willie Hernandez, bouncing back from strep throat, finished off the Royals in the ninth.

"Wilcox did his job through eight innings," Anderson said. "And when you have left-handers coming up in the ninth and Willie in the bullpen, you've got to go to him. And he did his job once again for us."

Leibrandt, who started the season in the minors, was nearly as effective. He gave up only three hits, none after the second. The Tigers had early opportunities but scored only in the second, when Chet Lemon came home on Marty Castillo's fielder's choice. "When I first hit it, I said, 'You better go,'" said Castillo, who played a major role in the series after being a little-used sub all year. "I knew I didn't hit it hard, but I knew it was a run if I made it."

The grounder, hit to shortstop Onix Concepcion, was slowed by the Tiger Stadium grass, something that would not have happened on the artificial turf at Royals Stadium.

The play of the game came in the eighth, when first baseman Darrell Evans dived to snare a Willie Wilson grounder, then beat Wilson to the bag by sliding. As the crowd roared, Evans flung his fist into the air in triumph. He later called it the biggest play of his 16-year career.

"You win ball games like that," he said. "But those kinds of plays sort of go unnoticed until you get in a series like this." ◆

Middle reliever Juan Berenguer never pitched because of outstanding efforts like Milt Wilcox's in Game 3. Dave Bergman also gave his all on the basepaths, pulling a hamstring while beating Frank White's tag in Game 2.

1984

◆

Sixteen years before, Detroit had found solace in sports as it recovered from the wounds of horrible rioting. The 1968 Tigers, the city's last world champions, remained a source of pride, a presence in Detroit's psyche, for years. Now, a city aching from a severe recession rallied again around its baseball team. Once again, Detroit was a winner.

THE NIGHT DETROIT ROARED

By Bill McGraw

The season that began in a rush of high hopes and good omens ended as everyone with an old English "D" on his heart knew it would.

The Tigers won the World Series. They won it with a bang. They won it with drama. They won it before 51,901 hell-bent-for-hangover fans at Tiger Stadium.

They crushed the San Diego Padres, 8-4, taking the Series, four games to one. It was the 84-year-old club's fourth world championship. When it was over, it set off madness in the streets — bottles were thrown, autos were overturned and a police car

was burned — and chaos in the stands.

Kirk Gibson touched off the celebrating well before the game ended. He clobbered two timely homers into the upper deck, knocking in five runs. One started the scoring; the other ended it. The second came off menacing Goose Gossage after the fans had taunted the multimillion-dollar ace reliever with repeated chants of "Goosebusters." It also came after Gibson had made a $10 bet with manager Sparky Anderson from the on-deck circle. Anderson said the Padres would walk Gibson; Gibson bet they wouldn't — and won.

Kirk Gibson, the unruly local kid who became a Tigers star. Kirk Gibson, who last season exchanged insults with the public and press during a summer-long slump. Kirk Gibson, who always bragged how he lived for the magic moment in the important game. "There's a little bit of luck involved," Gibson said. "As Alan Trammell said, I've come a long way."

After the second blast, Gibson thrust his fist into the air, circled the bases slowly and blew kisses to the roaring crowd. It was the ultimate scene of an impossibly delirious, delightful summer, a mind-boggling six months when Tiger Stadium truly became the epicenter of the baseball cosmos.

The Tigers did exactly what Anderson — who became the first manager to win a Series in both leagues — had promised the town in 1979. They gave Detroit a winner. And did they ever win: Their overall record was 111-59, a .653 winning percentage. They tore through the American League in April and May with a 35-5 mark, then spent the rest of the schedule taking on all comers. Over the past six days they made official what nearly three million paying customers recognized all along: The Tigers are world champs.

"Thank you for the thrill of my life," outfielder Ruppert Jones told Anderson. ◆

They were the signs of the time: Detroit's first world championship since 1968 and Willie Hernandez and Lance Parrish intertwined. Hernandez, naturally, got the final out of season — on a breaking ball that Tony Gwynn lifted gently down the leftfield line to Larry Herndon. In three Series appearances, Hernandez had two saves and a 1.69 ERA.

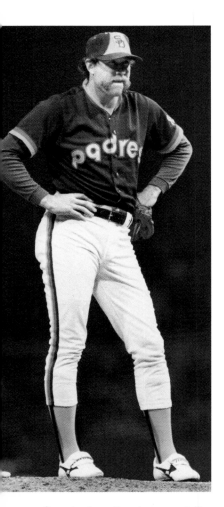

Goosebusters, the slugger and the MVP. Goose Gossage stood tall on the mound until Kirk Gibson blasted an eighth-inning fastball into the upper deck in rightfield for a three-run homer and an 8-4 lead. With runners on first and second, Padres manager Dick Williams wanted Gossage to walk Gibson, who in his first major league at-bat had struck out on three Gossage pitches. Gossage figured he could strike him out again. "I can't second-guess myself now," Gossage said. "But I did apologize to Dick. What can I say? I felt confident I could get him out." Despite Gibson's heroics, the Series MVP went to shortstop Alan Trammell. He belted a pair of two-run homers — scoring Lou Whitaker each time — in the 4-2 Game 4 victory. He hit .450 (9-for-20) with two homers and six RBIs.

"We have a bunch of great players and great people on this club," said Darrell Evans, the Tigers' first major free agent, who joined the club last December. "Chet Lemon said it best coming off the field: 'This is us. *We* won.'"

"There is nothing like this," said Dave Bergman, who came to the Tigers in the Willie Hernandez trade. "Absolutely nothing. The only thing that is close is your first-born child. I'm on a high. There's no weight on my feet. What a way to finish the season!"

Nothing else, of course, would have counted. A Series victory was the only acceptable conclusion to a gilt-edged season in an old ballpark that shimmered each game with human waves and mystic moments. This was simply the *piece de resistance.*

And it came close to being a classic Tigers victory in a Series that will not be remembered as one of baseball's best. The team that led the majors with homers peppered the seats with three. The team that relied on bench strength got a key hit from a pinch hitter. The team whose bullpen saved its soul received yet more key relief.

Rusty Kuntz, one of the nicest guys in spikes, a journeyman who played an important role on a major league team for the first time in his career, broke a tie game with a bases-loaded sacrifice fly in the fifth. He joined Marty Castillo as bench warmers who became heroes during the greatest week of the year.

Said Kuntz: "I'm numb. I'm so happy for Detroit."

Lance Parrish added a solo home run off Gossage in the seventh. That became a key when Hernandez allowed an eighth-inning homer to another sub, Kurt Bevacqua, whose home run in Game 2 gave the Padres their only Series victory. Hernandez topped a wonderful season by retiring the Padres with no other problems. He picked up his second Series save.

Aurelio Lopez turned in one of the best performances of his life and got the victory. He entered in the fifth, with a Padre on second, and struck out Bevacqua to end the threat. He sailed through the sixth and seventh, getting the side in order, firing 21 strikes and only four balls.

"It was one more chance to show myself," said Lopez, 36, who labored in the Mexican League until he was 29. "To show my teammates and myself who the real Lopey is."

With Gibson's first-inning home run and an RBI single from Chet Lemon, the Tigers took a 3-0 lead. But just as they did when they beat the Cubs in the deciding game of the National League playoffs, the Padres came back, driving Dan Petry from the mound after 3⅔ innings. It was his second poor outing in two Series starts. "I felt bad for Dan," Parrish said. "He wanted to be an important part of this."

After Kuntz's sacrifice fly broke the tie and Parrish's homer gave the Tigers a slight cushion, the game came down to the confrontation between Gibson and the Goose.

"Gibson was up to the test; that's how he is," Lemon said.

Gossage debated with manager Dick Williams about what to do with Gibson. Two runners were on base. Gossage, who struck out Gibson in Gibby's first at-bat in the majors, didn't want to load the bases with an intentional walk.

"I guess it's kind of 50-50," Gossage said. "He's a power hitter. . . . He's either going to miss it or hit it. Today, he hit it."

And how. ◆

A diamond of police couldn't hold back the 51,901 fans inside Tiger Stadium. And good judgment couldn't hold back the thousands of fans outside the stadium, where violence and vandalism tainted a night of celebration at Michigan and Trumbull.

AWARD-WINNING WILLIE

By Joe Lapointe

The date was June 23, the baseball season wasn't half over, and Tigers pitching coach Roger Craig was talking about relief pitcher Willie Hernandez. At that point, Hernandez's goals were modest. He hoped to play in the All-Star Game for the first time in his career.

"He is our most valuable player at this point," Craig said. "I don't know if there's a better pitcher going than Willie Hernandez."

Craig's statement might have been the first time the words "Hernandez" and "most valuable player" were used in the same sentence. And his words proved prophetic.

Hernandez made the All-Star team. He was voted Tiger of the year. He won the Cy Young Award as best pitcher in the American League.

And now Hernandez has been voted American League most valuable player by the Baseball Writers Association of America. Next in the voting were Minnesota first baseman Kent Hrbek and Kansas City reliever Dan Quisenberry. Denny McLain, in 1968, was the only other Tiger to win the Cy Young and MVP awards.

"It's unbelievable, winning these two awards in the same year," Hernandez said from his grandfather's home in San Juan, Puerto Rico. "It was like I have another win, like winning the World Series again."

Hernandez, who will turn 30 next week, was 9-3 with a 1.92 ERA. He saved 32 games in 33 opportunities and was on the mound when the Tigers clinched the American League East title, the AL pennant and the World Series.

"He had a once-in-a-lifetime season," said manager Sparky Anderson.

In the spring of 1984, Willie Hernandez, who had pitched in the major leagues for seven years without fame or distinction, joined the Tigers. He was one of several potentially useful spot players manager Sparky Anderson hoped to blend with his few established stars. By season's end, the chant "Wil-lie, Wil-lie" filled Tiger Stadium. Hernandez was a star.

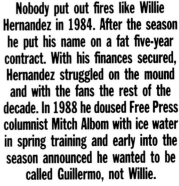

Nobody put out fires like Willie Hernandez in 1984. After the season he put his name on a fat five-year contract. With his finances secured, Hernandez struggled on the mound and with the fans the rest of the decade. In 1988 he doused Free Press columnist Mitch Albom with ice water in spring training and early into the season announced he wanted to be called Guillermo, not Willie.

Hernandez, whose best pitch is a screwball, had 27 saves in seven previous major league seasons. He was acquired by the Tigers in a four-player spring trade that also brought first baseman Dave Bergman to Detroit. The Tigers gave up outfielder Glenn Wilson and catcher John Wockenfuss. At the time, Hernandez was supposed to be the left-handed complement to right-handed reliever Aurelio Lopez. The first time he appeared in a Tigers uniform, he retired three St. Louis Cardinals batters on six pitches. And once he started stringing together save after save without a miss, team officials admitted that Hernandez was much more than they had bargained for.

"I said he'd be a good acquisition," Craig said, "but I never knew he'd be this good." ◆

FOR OLD-TIME'S SAKE

By Mitch Albom

OCT. 2,

1985

◆

When the Tigers left on a 12-game, mid-May road trip, Darrell Evans had one homer, four RBIs and a future on the bench. He turned 38 during the trip but returned with five more homers and 13 more RBIs. And he kept slugging the rest of the season, finishing with 40 homers — most in the majors — and 94 RBIs. Evans became the first Tiger to win the home run title since Hank Greenberg in 1946 and the oldest American League home run champion ever.

And now, three words about Darrell Evans. Home Run King.

OK, so he doesn't have the title clinched yet — there are still four games left — but he'll get it, as sure as God makes little green apples and Piggy loves Kermit and somewhere over the rainbow, way up high, good things come to those who wait. Because Evans has been waiting 38 years. And nobody deserves it more.

This is a professional, a leader, a guy who would keep an even keel in an earthquake, who always faces the cameras, good or bad, who epitomizes the words gentleman, dignity, grace. That might explain why even a few sports writers smiled when Evans cracked his record-setting 40th homer of the year.

It soared toward the seats of Tiger Stadium on a glorious arc. Gone. Out. No questions asked. One for the good guys.

Evans watched it go. He clenched his fists and raised them to his head, then quickly pulled them back and finished running the bases.

That, by the way, was a big display of emotion.

For Darrell Evans. Swat Man.

Sure, it would be nicer if Detroit were celebrating another division title right now. "I'd trade this for that in a second," Evans said.

But it's not. And with all the bad news on baseball's doorstep this season, we shouldn't let Evans' feat get swept aside too easily.

Tell the juries to take five. Put the lawyers on hold. Drugs. Money. Put them aside, just for a moment. Let's remember that a home run is still the biggest play in the biggest sport in the most sports-crazed country in the world.

It is baseball's Stud Meter. One swing. Pow! The most macho you can get while wearing a cap.

And this season, at age 38, in a year when many predicted he would simply crust and fade away, Darrell Evans has more home runs than anybody else. More than Dale Murphy, Pedro Guerrero, Darryl Strawberry — that whole pile of young muscle. It has to be sweet, because Evans came to Detroit under the toughest of circumstances — as the Tigers' first dip into million-dollar free agency.

He was a rich curiosity, like a farmer bringing home a cherry-red Corvette. Everyone expected fireworks. Instead, Evans hit only 16 home runs and batted .232 in 1984. And he started 1985 in a terrible slump. There were whispers. What a waste. He's through. The Tigers had him all but traded.

And how did he handle it? Grace. Manners. Courage. You try being asked "What's the matter?" by a dozen reporters every night. Or being told the team owner has called you a "bad investment." He never balked. Never bit back.

He is a baseball player. He kept swinging.

The reporters were around him again. He had just become the first man to hit 40 home runs in both leagues. How did it feel?

"Oh, it was great, really great running around those bases," he said. "I'll never forget that."

And you're 38 years old.

"Yeah, but maybe you get better as you get older. I hope so, anyhow."

The obvious question. What did it all mean?

"Well," he said, "I love this game. All I want is to keep playing it. I really want to play longer. If this helps me get that chance, it's great."

I love this game. Evans can say that, and you believe him. You really do. In this age of cynicism, that might be the highest compliment you can give a ballplayer.

In years to come, we'll remember it applied to the Home Run King of 1985.

Three words about Darrell Evans.

He deserved it. ◆

Darrell Evans got a hand for belting his 24th homer — a grand slam against Milwaukee in early August. Typical of the Tigers' disappointing '85 season, manager Sparky Anderson had catcher Lance Parrish bunting in the inning with runners at first and second. Evans did not homer the season's final weekend, finishing with 40, three more than Carlton Fisk of the White Sox and Dale Murphy of the Braves. "It's a big thrill," Evans said. "You've got to enjoy everything you are lucky enough to obtain."

THANKS, HANKUS PANKUS

By George Puscas

Hank Greenberg's impact on Detroit struck as solidly as his 331 home runs. He helped keep alive the spirit of fans during the time of a dead economy. His grace and power at the plate were rewarded with unmatched popularity in a city of baseball worshipers.

With Al Kaline's No. 6, the Tigers retired their first number. In 1983 they retired numbers of their aging G-Men — second baseman Charlie Gehringer and first baseman Hank Greenberg. Besides hitting 331 career homers, Greenberg batted .313 and drove in 1,276 runs. In 1956, he became the first Jewish player inducted into the Hall of Fame.

It's strange how descriptions from long ago, nearly a half-century and another baseball age ago, suddenly pop into mind.

"Hankus Pankus," radio announcer Ty Tyson called him.

The name reflected the city's affectionate embrace of one of the greatest of baseball sluggers. Hank Greenberg, 75, has died of cancer. For thousands of aging lovers of the game, the memory of Greenberg, the tall, shuffling first baseman who powered the Tigers to four pennants and two World Series championships, cannot die.

The record books will show others have hit more home runs, but the numbers are misleading. Without a doubt, he was the greatest home-run hitter the Tigers ever had. He was, in fact, one of the great home-run hitters in history, although the record shows him with what seems today only a respectable 331.

The numbers were magic in his time. He ignited the town: "Going . . . going . . . gone!" Tyson would say, and on porch after porch down the city blocks, men and women, relaxing with the afternoon radio broadcast, suddenly leapt off their swings and waved and shouted to their neighbors.

There was not much else to shout about in the 1930s. But Greenberg had a grip that spanned neighborhoods, reached into markets, factories, schools. Few players are so blessed. Greenberg found everybody had a grip on his bat. They all swung with him, and when he connected, Detroit scored.

Babe Ruth was nearing the end of his career in 1933 when Greenberg arrived in Detroit for his first full major league season. Greenberg had hoped to play with his hometown Yankees, but they had no need for him — not then. It was an era when not everyone could reach the outfield seats with a fly ball. Many players were delighted to have a half-dozen home runs a season. Soon, the great bangers of the game were Jimmie Foxx, Lou Gehrig, Hack Wilson and Hank Greenberg.

In Greenberg's second full season, the Tigers won the American League pennant and in his third, 1935, they won the World Series. That season, Greenberg led the American League with 36 home runs. This might have been the best of all Tigers teams — catcher Mickey Cochrane and second baseman Charlie Gehringer are rated among baseball's best-ever at their positions. In 1937, Greenberg's reputation as a slugger began to crest. He hit 40 home runs. The next year, he had the nation following his every swing as the season wound down. He hit 58, a tantalizing two short of the 60 Ruth had set as the major league record 11 years earlier.

In 1940, the Tigers won the pennant again. This time Greenberg was in leftfield, leaving first base so slugger Rudy York could be inserted in the lineup. Greenberg knocked in 150 runs — and that wasn't his high. He had driven in 170 in 1935 and an astounding 183 in 1937.

Soon after the Tigers lost the 1940 World Series to Cincinnati, Greenberg, then 29, was drafted into the U.S. Army. He was out of baseball — except for 19 games in 1941 — until 1945, rejoining the Tigers in time to help them to another pennant. He hit a grand slam that clinched it, then helped lead a World Series triumph over the Chicago Cubs.

The next year, Greenberg was sold after the season to the Pittsburgh Pirates in a deal that brought public condemnation upon team owner Walter O. Briggs Sr. Briggs, a wealthy industrialist known for pinch-penny operations, never really explained what prompted his move. But word soon leaked out that Greenberg dared demand a pay raise. Some fans never forgave the owner.

Nor, apparently, did Greenberg. He seldom returned to Detroit, although he was active in baseball as part-owner of the Cleveland Indians from 1948 to '58 and vice president of the Chicago White Sox from 1959 to '63.

After his retirement from baseball, Greenberg became active in recreational tennis in Los Angeles and achieved national ranking. He was a slugger there, too. ♦

No Tiger was ever more appropriately named than Norm Cash, who gave fans their money's worth with his home run displays and other performances. Whether it was a home run over the rightfield roof or bringing a table leg to the plate during a no-hitter by Nolan Ryan, Cash flourished in the spotlight and made baseball his own stage.

MIGHTY BAT, MIGHTY MAN

By George Puscas

Norm Cash is dead. Another of our great baseball heroes is gone.

Norm Cash, the friendliest, most likable of the old Tigers. Stormin' Norman — the fun-loving jokester, always ready to play. On the field or off.

The year has been unkind. Only a few weeks ago we lost Hank Greenberg, another great Tigers slugger of the past. And now Cash, 51, in an apparent drowning accident in Lake Michigan.

He made the rightfield roof at Tiger Stadium a special attraction. Others before him, and more since, had used that 93-foot-high roof as a target and a symbol of hitting power, and cleared it with magnificent home run blasts. But nobody did it with the flair of the left-handed Cash, the Tigers' first baseman of the 1960s and early 1970s.

It seemed that every time he came to the plate, the roof was his aim. And those four times he did clear it with Ruthian swings, it was as if he had conquered a world of his own.

For years, he was a favorite baseball enigma. Who could understand how a guy could hit .361 to win the American League batting championship, as Cash did in 1961, and then never come anywhere near that average again. Only later, when Cash explained, did it seem to make some sense. After that phenomenal year, when he also hit 41 home runs, Cash began thinking of himself more as a power hitter than a consistent stroker.

"The world is full of guys who can hit singles," he said. "But you always have to make room for somebody who can hit home runs."

Cash clearly established himself as a leader of a home-run banging collection of Tigers — Jim Northrup, Al Kaline, Bill Freehan among them — who powered Detroit to the 1968 World Series championship over the St. Louis Cardinals in seven games. The next Tigers champions, in 1984, lacked the drama of Cash's champions, who rattled late-inning home runs with such frequency that a recording of broadcasts of their game-winning blows became a popular hit itself.

Cash's death was a shock, although he was not in the best of health. Five years ago, he suffered a serious stroke. It was that episode that rekindled the public's affection for Cash, a Texas native who had spent 15 seasons with the Tigers, retiring in 1974.

Cash was a marvelously uncomplicated man who loved his world, and his world loved him back. He was lucky that way. ◆

Norm Cash — older, heavier and slowed by a stroke — still had a good old time at a Tiger Stadium old-timers game six weeks before his death. The Tigers hadn't staged an old-timers game since 1958. Cash led the charge out of the dugout, clowned around at first base to upset pitcher Mickey Lolich and walked in the first inning, the team's only baserunner in the first two innings of a 6-3, three-inning loss.

A CATCHER SCORNED

By Mitch Albom

MARCH 15,
1987
◆

They learned the game together in the farm system. They tasted World Series champagne together. Trammell. Whitaker. Gibson. Brookens. Morris. Petry. And the rock behind the plate, Lance Parrish. After 13 years in the organization, Parrish signed a free-agent contract with the Philadelphia Phillies — for less money than the Tigers offered. The Tigers of the '80s were breaking up.

He pulled the new uniform over his broad shoulders and tugged on the zipper. Up came the pants around his waist, and the red belt went through the loops.

"It fits," he mumbled.

"Pinstripes," said an observer. "Nice. You look like an inmate."

"Yeah?" He smirked at the irony.

And out he went, into the Clearwater, Fla., sunshine, into a strange stadium and a strange team and a strange league. He's somebody else's hero now. After two years of trying to stay with the Tigers, he signed with another team. His story has many implications. But before Detroit writes him off as a traitor, and before fellow players canonize him as a martyr, and before baseball lawyers make him Exhibit A in their collusion file, know this: None of that really mattered to Lance Parrish.

How can a guy who turned down a guaranteed $1.2 million from Detroit — a team he loved — settle for a guaranteed $800,000 from Philadelphia — a team he knows almost nothing about? Listen:

"For the last few years I felt I might have been playing below the pay scale for a catcher like myself. But because I had signed a contract, I was determined to honor it. I figured the Tigers would take care of me when the contract was over. I'd done everything they asked of me. . . . I was naive. I felt like I had such a good relationship with the Tigers that they would do what was fair. And it wasn't even close.

"I understand they were concerned about my back. But I made concessions to that. Originally, I wanted a three-year contract. When I realized it would not have been a good business decision for them to sign me for three years, what with my back, I resigned myself to a one-year contract. I was willing to prove I could play healthy. I would take a chance if they would."

As Parrish talked, he slowly pounded a bat into the bullpen grass. He would say he was happy. It was obvious he was not. Other free agents in this winter of discontent may have been trying to make a statement to the owners about their curiously conservative contracts. But Parrish — who has ended up doing just that — tumbled into the role out of hurt and resentment.

"People aren't going to understand this," he said, "but I thought of the Detroit Tigers as my family. They raised me in baseball. And in the end . . . " He paused.

"What?" someone asked. "You felt betrayed? What?"

He nodded. "That's exactly how I felt. Betrayed." ◆

Out the final two months in 1986 because of a back problem, Lance Parrish always figured he would be back in Lakeland, Fla., in the spring. Instead, he was in Clearwater, and Tigers outfielder Kirk Gibson was his Grapefruit League opponent. Parrish was the first everyday player gone from the '84 team. One spring later, after baseball's owners were found guilty of collusion, Gibson also became a National Leaguer.

◆

He had it all. Then he had nothing — but trouble. Denny McLain, the toast of baseball as a 31-game winner with the Tigers in 1968, tumbled from stardom soon afterward with off-field troubles, eventually landing in an Alabama prison on drug and loan-sharking convictions. Now, all he wanted was to be safe at home.

FREEDOM FIGHTER

By Eric Kinkopf

The first thing Denny McLain did after he was released from prison in Talladega, Ala., was visit Sister Veronica at St. Francis of Assisi Catholic Church to tell her he found an inmate organist to replace him at Sunday prison mass. Then he went to Burger King and wolfed down two bacon double cheeseburgers, two ketchup-laced orders of fries and a Diet Pepsi, talking — giddily, euphorically — about the wonders of freedom and his plans for getting on with his life and being reunited with his wife, Sharon, and their four children.

"There are no words to describe how I feel," said McLain, 43 and graying, as he was driven away from the medium-security federal correctional institution. "I probably won't believe it until I get in bed tonight, and I don't mean a sexual encounter. I'm talking about being home — and arguing with the kids."

McLain, the former Tigers pitching ace, was wearing old tennis shoes, a yellow tennis shirt and blue polyester prison-issued slacks that were about four inches too long. He carried a rumpled gym bag and limped slightly — the result of a year-old tennis injury. McLain joined his wife and daughters Kristi, 21, and Michelle, 15, at the Talladega Airport. They flew to Tampa, Fla., where the McLains live.

"If there's one thing I know, it's that I love Sharon," he said. "I've made a lot of mistakes in my life, but she has always been home. She's been my home."

McLain had spent the last 29 months in prison on drug and loan-sharking charges. He had been sentenced to 23 years. His convictions were overturned by an appeals court Aug. 7. He had been waiting four weeks for his release.

He said some inmates

Denny McLain, who as a young man found his niche on a Detroit mound, seemed to find his niche as a middle-aged man behind a Detroit microphone. He left Ft. Wayne, Ind., in spring 1989 to host a three-hour, afternoon drive-time radio talk show.

threw a going-away party for him his final night.

"This morning I just sat around waiting for something to go wrong," he said. "I've been in a moment of panic for hours. There's no way to describe the loss of freedom. There's no way to appreciate it until you walk out that gate."

At Burger King, he marveled at being able to hold a $10 bill. "I've got to get a job — I have no idea what, where, whom," he said. "No idea. Two things I'd like to do: Get into some full-time position writing — God, I really enjoy writing — or get back into baseball in some way. I don't know if those opportunities will come along."

"Oh, I forgot to pick up my mail. No," he said with a laugh. "I don't want to go back." ◆

A GIANT LEAP

By Mitch Albom

OCT. 4, 1987

◆

This said it all: Frank Tanana darting off the mound, scooping up the ball, turning to first baseman Darrell Evans and — with a lollipop smile already on his face — flipping it underhanded for the final out.

One, two, three, leap!

Happy ending.

"Whenever I think of this game from now on," Evans said, champagne soaking his face, after the Tigers had beaten Toronto, 1-0, to capture the American League East, "that's the moment I'm going to see. Frank coming towards me, the ball in his hand, his eyes as big as saucers. . . . Oh, man. Oh, man. I'll never forget that."

Forget it? Are you kidding? For years in this city, people will be talking about where they were when the Tigers turned that final out, beat the Blue Jays, leapt into each others' arms having done what everybody dreamed and nobody expected — on the final day of the season.

American League East champions.

Happy ending.

They won! They won! In an instant, the field was filled with leaping Tigers, mounted police, fans who had made it over the wall. In the Detroit clubhouse, the staff wheeled out champagne and pulled down rolls of plastic over everything that could be protected.

And in the stands, the sellout crowd was on its feet, giving thunderous applause, basking in a gloriously winning feeling. As their Tigers heroes galloped en masse toward the dugout, Tanana, in the center, looked up, his hair in bangs on his forehead, a wad of pink chewing gum in his mouth, and gave an expression of joy that was captured in 100 camera clicks and a delightful page of history.

"I felt like I was 6 years old again," Tanana said."

Happy ending.

What a moment! What a day! What a finish! Here was the final piece of a jigsaw season, that suddenly, finally, made sense. "If you had told me this would happen back in April, I would have said you're crazy," said pitcher Jack Morris. "We were playing terrible (11-19 in May). That was the truth then. But there's a different truth now."

It was downright chilling to watch these final seven games with the Blue Jays — three this weekend, four last weekend at Toronto — all of them decided by a single run. History will surely remember this as one of the finest title chases in baseball. ➡

The '87 Tigers weren't expected to roar. They were 11 games behind first-place Milwaukee four weeks into the season. They were eight games under .500 five weeks into it. By mid-July they were within striking distance but couldn't pass first-place Toronto. Then on Aug. 12 the Tigers traded a minor league pitcher, John Smoltz, to Atlanta for Doyle Alexander, a 36-year-old veteran of eight teams with a 5-10 record and 4.13 ERA.

Overnight he became Alexander the Great. He made 11 starts; the Tigers won all 11. He went 9-0 with a 1.53 ERA. Still, with one week left in the season, Detroit trailed the Blue Jays by 3½ games.

The Tigers hadn't won a 1-0 game all season until Frank Tanana's six-hitter on the final day, for which Chet Lemon more than thanked him. In four games against Toronto, Tanana went 3-0 and didn't allow a run in three games.

"I've never been involved in seven games like this," said shortstop Alan Trammell, his voice a rasp, lost to screams, shouts, a million interviews. "A week ago, we were really down, trailing Toronto by 3½. But we never gave up. And now . . . this. I'm so emotionally drained right now. But it's the greatest feeling. God, it's great."

It was. Seven head-to-head games in the last 11 days. And it all had come down to this — the last one on the schedule. Tigers win, it's over. Blue Jays win, there's a one-game playoff. Tanana, who two weeks earlier had been slumping so badly he was removed from the rotation, was back and pitching for the Tigers. And Jimmy Key, Toronto's ace, was going against him. A duel in the afternoon shadows. How would this one go?

A better question: What was left? Already there had been games as raucous as a 10-9 Blue Jays victory at Toronto, and as tense as the previous day's 3-2 Tigers victory in 12 heart-stopping innings. What was left? What hadn't we seen? How about a 1-0 game —

the slimmest possible victory in this sport — on a wobbly home run by Larry Herndon in the second inning?

Perfect. How absurdly perfect. A series full of big hitters and big talkers won on a single swing by the quietest man in a Tigers uniform. "Pretty fitting, huh?" said Evans, winking. Indeed. Herndon even gave a brief interview afterward.

"How do you feel?" he was asked.

"Great," he said.

What more need be said?

Great. Grreeaaat. Couldn't have been better. And Tanana wins it? The homegrown Detroit hero? A shutout? A complete game? A six-hitter? "Did you ever think two weeks ago this might happen?" he was asked.

With one out in the second inning, Larry Herndon lofted a Jimmy Key fastball to leftfield. George Bell acted as if he would make the catch on the warning track. Key thought Bell would catch it. The flag, after all, was blowing out toward right. But at the last instant, something — the wind, said Bell; Tigers' momentum, said something else — grabbed the ball and shoved it over the fence. Bell, who edged shortstop Alan Trammell for the American League MVP award, also finished the season luckless at the plate, mired in a 2-for-26 slump.

"No," he said, "I hoped I'd get a chance. But I wasn't even pitching. My job then was to be a cheerleader." That is characteristic of this team. Subs root for starters. Slumpers root for the hot hands. Remember, this is not 1984, a season of power and dominance. Uh-uh. This season has been spit and glue. A leak springs, you take the gum out of your mouth and plug it.

And because of that, this was the year of Sparky Anderson's life — probably the best managing of his storied career, no matter what happens in the playoffs. "That guy," said pitcher Dan Petry of Anderson, "is the key. In May, when we stunk, he came to us and said we could win it. And a lot of us said privately: 'The guy's nuts.' "

In the spritz-a-second Tigers clubhouse, Anderson, 53, talked to microphone after microphone, dressed only in T-shirt and shorts, his white hair soaked with champagne. "I've had it all now," he croaked. "If I die and go to heaven — and I hope I go to heaven — I can say I've had it all."

OK. A moment here for Toronto, a great team, a team that should be playing more baseball this season. The Blue Jays might not realize the ugly pitch fate will toss them now, but they will soon enough. The despair of one lost afternoon will not compare to the disgust at 100 afternoons of questions next spring, next summer, forever: "How could you guys lose your last seven games? What happened?"

Who knows? History will record that the Jays finished only two games behind the Tigers, with the second-best record in baseball. But who really reads history? People will remember that they lost the last game of their series with Detroit at Toronto — some say the turning point of the season — then lost three straight to Milwaukee and three straight to the Tigers. Their last seven games? Yes. People will cast the Blue Jays as losers, chokers, and that is unfair. They deserve better.

"This series had gotten to be so good," Trammell said. "I kind of wanted to keep playing them." No need for that now. The division is won. The Tigers got it. ◆

GOOD-BYE AND GOOD SHOW

By Mitch Albom

OCT. 12,
1987
♦

One by one, they took their last at-bats of summer. Darrell Evans said good-bye with a fly to rightfield, and Alan Trammell signed off with a hard line drive to shortstop. . . .

In a matter of moments, the Detroit baseball season would end the way it had begun six months earlier, on a cool Monday afternoon at Tiger Stadium. A loss then. A loss this day. But oh, what transpired in between! A magical regular season, full of twists and turns and rapid heartbeats; and a post-season that fell horribly flat, lost its sheen and was finally packed away with a bouncer from rookie Matt Nokes to Minnesota pitcher Jeff Reardon, who threw to first for the out, the joyous leap, and the American League championship.

End of story. The Tigers went down badly in their final game, lost 9-5, suffered the indignity of an explosive ninth inning by the Minnesota Twins, a team nobody expected, few respected, but a team that won the American League pennant. "Nothing seemed to bother those guys," Sparky Anderson said, shrugging. And he was right. Twins were everywhere this day, this series, whacking hits, dashing around the bases, playing the infield like God's chessmen.

Did they make any wrong moves? Not that we remember. And when they jumped into that victory pile before a stunned Detroit crowd, no one could deny them their celebration. They had defeated, in four of five games, the team with the best record in baseball. "Outpitched us, outhit us, outfielded us and beat us," Jack Morris said.

That about covers it. End of story.

Here were some last glimpses of this remarkable Tigers team: Manager Sparky Anderson, sitting in the dugout, expressionless, yet shaking inside, chewing sunflower seeds as his team was skinned to its last out; Darrell Evans, 40, the team leader, staring out to the field and beyond, perhaps wondering whether he'll ever see another of these championships; Kirk Gibson, whiskered, intense, desperate to make up for a lousy series, standing on first base, ready to run, ready to explode, but stuck there, stranded in the bottom of the ninth.

Sad faces. Disappointed faces. Yes. That is the signature of defeat. But when this was all over, when the Minnesota players were popping champagne and dumping Gatorade on themselves, the Tigers returned to their clubhouse, sighed and thanked each other for a year that was too good to be ruined by any single series — even a championship one.

Once upon a time, we had a hell of a baseball team. . . . That will be how these '87 Tigers are remembered long after the sting of defeat is forgotten. How far had they come? How unlikely a journey? Oh, my. Here was a group of third-place finishers in 1986 who had lost their catcher and leader, Lance Parrish, and done nothing to improve except age. Even the players didn't predict a high finish. They suffered a dismal April and May. Yet there began — what shall we call it? — a small rumble. A turnaround. Minor at first, a few victories here and there.

Bill Madlock joined the team — cost the Tigers just $40,000 — and his bat went happy-go-lucky. Alan Trammell clicked in his clean-up spot as no one had imagined. Chet Lemon, Larry Herndon, guys criticized for living on past laurels, began to create some new ones. Victories. More victories. Home runs. More home runs. And then Doyle Alexander, a quiet larceny, slipped on a Detroit uniform and won once, twice, three times, four times . . . and — look at this! — first place was within reach. On Aug. 19 (against these same Twins in this same Tiger Stadium), the Tigers tasted that honey for the first time. From then on, it was a race for the hive. ➡

Despite opening the American League playoffs on the road, the Tigers were prohibitive favorites. They had baseball's best record (98-64); the Minnesota Twins won the West at 85-77. But nothing went right at Minneapolis. In Game 1, the Tigers took a one-run lead in the top of the eighth inning, but the Twins scored four times in the bottom, winning 8-5 and handing Doyle Alexander his first loss as a Tiger. In Game 2, Detroit led early, but the Twins ended Jack Morris' eight-game Metrodome winning streak, 6-3. The Tigers returned to Detroit desperate and doomed.

The third-base pickoff of Darrell Evans in Game 4 helped bring the Tigers to their knees. They trailed, 4-3 in the sixth inning and 2-1 in the series, with runners at second and third and one out. The next day, Tiger Stadium fans still gave Evans a standing ovation.

After his series-ending grounder to
pitcher Jeff Reardon, Tigers catcher
Matt Nokes found himself in the wrong
place at the wrong time. Reardon won
Game 1, lost Game 3 (on Pat
Sheridan's eighth-inning, two-run
home run) and saved Games 4 and 5.
But the MVP award went to third
baseman Greg Gaetti, who hit .300 (6-
for-18) with two homers, five RBIs,
five runs scored and a sacrifice fly.

And, oh, how the lungs ached in this one! Remember? The Tigers won a game at Minnesota with a ninth-inning, bases-loaded single by their rookie catcher, and another against Cleveland with one hit. They lost a game to Milwaukee when Willie Hernandez walked in the winning run, and another to Toronto when Lou Whitaker threw wildly to home plate. And then, the finish. The best final baseball chapter ever? Seven games against the Blue Jays? All one-run thrillers?

"It would have been a great story if we'd gone all the way, huh?" asked Trammell after the defeat. Hey. It's a great story anyhow.

And this is how it wound down: A wild pitch by Eric King led to a Twins run. A throw to first baseman Evans grazed off his glove and rolled away, allowing another score. Pat Sheridan, Evans, Trammell, all at the plate with runners in scoring position; all walked back slowly to the dugout, snuffed out, dead.

The Twins, picked by many to go down easily, were like one of those computer quizzes

in an electronic arcade. An answer for everything. Clutch hit. Clutch pitch. Almost spookily successful. This is a young team? The worst record of any division winner? Well, yes. But if April through September is a safari, then October is a vine swing. Pick the right one and you get there first. The Twins got revved by their amazing crowd and didn't stop until the champagne popped.

How different might this have been had the series begun in Detroit? How different if Trammell had swung like the MVP he is, or if Gibson had clicked, or if Morris and Terrell had . . . ahh, why wonder? In the end, it was the Twins who won two on the road, a place where they had won only nine games since the All-Star break. And Detroit will remember names like Greg Gagne, shortstop; Gary Gaetti, the hurricane at third; Tom (Bruno) Brunansky and Dan Gladden and Dan Schatzeder. Not the biggest names.

But, for today, the best.

End of story. During these final five games, it was as if all the magic was gone, turned back to pumpkin. Alexander (who lost Games 1 and 5 of this series) was not the same Alexander as before. Madlock (only five at-bats all series) was gone, out of the lineup. Scott Lusader and Jim Walewander, the young spark plugs of that magical finish, were spectators, ineligible for the playoffs. "We had the best record, but they won the series," Gibson said. "Does that make them the best? Does that make us horsebleep?"

Neither.

Ah, but these Tigers — we grew older with them, lost hair worrying about their bullpen, lost voices screaming at Hernandez, lost composure with the giddiness of their title. Our nerves were rattled like jangled car keys with every late home run, every deadly double play, every weird error, ball through the legs, strikeout, leap for joy, high-five celebration. How good was this season? Think about how many games left you emotionally drained. Wasted. Sweaty and exhausted. That's how good it was. We grew older, and, in a funny way, we grew younger, too. That is what baseball will do for you.

How, in days to come, will this crazy season be summed up? Who knows? Perhaps it will take a book, lots of chapters and pictures and quotes and stories. And perhaps it can be said this simply: Once upon a time, we had a hell of a baseball team. And once upon a baseball team, we had a hell of a time. ♦

Jack Morris went the distance in Game 2 but got tagged with six Minnesota runs. That was a typical performance for a Detroit starter in this series. The starters combined for a 6.70 ERA. "They outpitched us in the series," Morris said. "It's that simple." Doyle Alexander lasted only 31 pitches — 1⅔ innings — in Game 5, surrendering four runs and dropping his career post-season record to 0-5.

1988

◆

Kirk Gibson left for Los Angeles in another contract dispute. Dan Petry, struggling after surgery, was dealt to California. The Tigers of the '80s kept breaking up — but the remainder kept winning. The '88 team, expected by many to finish in the second division, took first place on June 20 and, except for two days in August, held it until Sept. 5. Could the Tigers stage another miracle?

NO SURVIVING THIS DIVE

By John Lowe

The Tigers need binoculars to see the Boston Red Sox, and a parachute to slow their descent.

They fell 5½ games behind first-place Boston and into a third-place tie with Milwaukee as they suffered what has become a typically dismal defeat. The Toronto Blue Jays scored two eighth-inning runs — on two walks, two singles and a run-scoring wild pitch — to win, 3-2, at Toronto's Exhibition Stadium.

Fred Lynn's leadoff homer in the ninth brought the Tigers within a run. Then winner Duane Ward retired the next three hitters.

With 16 games left, the Tigers are further out of first place than they have been all season. It's the first time they have not been in first or second since early June.

"That's hard," manager Sparky Anderson said in a voice not far above a whisper. "That's really hard."

The loss capped a 1-6 trip, which followed a 1-6 home stand, which followed a 2-7 trip. That's a 4-19 dive that began with the Tigers leading second-place Boston by four games.

On Sept. 4, the Tigers and Red Sox were tied for first. Since then, the Tigers are 2-8, the Red Sox 7-2.

As usual in the Tigers' 2-12 September, the circumstances of this defeat were just as bitter as the consequences.

Walt Terrell was in a 1-1 tie and throwing a

two-hitter when he lost his control in the eighth. "I walked batters," he said, "I had no business walking."

He walked No. 9 hitter Manny Lee to start the inning. With Tony Fernandez up, the infield looked for a bunt. First baseman Ray Knight was charging and was no more than 70 feet from the plate when Fernandez swung and shot a single past him. That sent Lee to third. Then Terrell walked pinch hitter Rance Mulliniks on a 3-2 pitch, loading the bases with none out. The previous pitch had bounced away from catcher Matt Nokes. Guillermo Hernandez relieved and struck out left-handed Fred McGriff. Right-hander Mike Henneman took over to face right-handed George Bell in an attempt to get the inning-ending double-play grounder. On an 0-1 pitch, Bell nudged a one-hop single the other way into right, about five feet to the left of second baseman Jim Walewander. One run scored. Henneman struck out Ernie Whitt. But with Jesse Barfield up, Henneman threw a wild pitch, and Fernandez scored with the 3-1 run.

A typical night for the Tigers. You don't see a good team struggle like that so often. You don't see a first-place team take a 4-19 dive very often, either. ◆

Boston officially eliminated the Tigers with three games to play. Still, a final-weekend sweep of the Yankees moved the Tigers into second place. The fans said thanks that final weekend for a winning — yet weird — season. And Darrell Evans, on the final day in what would be his final game as a Tiger, drove home the winning run with an 11th-inning single. Manager Sparky Anderson gave Evans the ball he hit for the winner. "When he handed it to me," Evans said with a laugh, "I almost gave it back."

Sparky Anderson took time out to talk with Bob Taylor, the singing plumber, before his first game back with the Tigers. "Really, the only time Sparky could relax was during batting practice when he went behind the cage," said broadcaster Ernie Harwell. "Someone was always after him for something."

LOWER-VOLTAGE SPARKY

By Gene Guidi

Managers try not to take games home with them. But early in a woeful season for the 1989 Tigers, a sparkless Sparky Anderson had taken so many games home that there was no room for him anymore. Taking doctors' advice, the physically exhausted Anderson went to his Thousand Oaks, Calif., home while coach Dick Tracewski took over the team.

Sparky's back. Or is he?

A soft-spoken, very much out-of-character Sparky Anderson returned to reclaim the team he left May 19. Tigers physicians had sent him to his California home to recover from what was diagnosed as severe physical and mental exhaustion.

Anderson looked tanned and well-rested on his first day back on the job as manager, but his actions and speech were noticeably subdued. He was not at all like the Sparky Anderson to whom Tigers fans had grown accustomed in his nearly 10 seasons in Detroit. Rather, he was more like the George Anderson who all but ignores baseball in the off-season. Anderson said he was going to have to be George, not Sparky, as much as he could from now on.

"My problem has always been losing," Anderson said. "I take it too hard. I don't know that you can change entirely. But at my age (55), I suggest that I had better try."

Before putting on his uniform to lead the Tigers against the Red Sox, Anderson held a press conference at Tiger Stadium. He talked about the condition that forced him to leave the team, but he answered only a few questions before leaving the assembled reporters. Anderson said he was responsible for the exhaustion that forced him to miss 17 games.

"I didn't listen to my own advice," Anderson said. "I have always told players like Alan Trammell, Matt Nokes and Jack Morris that nothing about baseball is so important that it will ruin your life. But no one took losses harder than I did. Inside, I would die a thousand deaths. After 20 years of that, I wasn't just mentally tired, I was mentally exhausted."

Afterward, in his office, Anderson talked more about the condition. He said it started to worsen when the team was in Toledo for a May 11 exhibition game against the Mud Hens. Then the Tigers went to Cleveland, where they lost two of a three-game series. "I hardly slept at all those three nights," Anderson said.

The Tigers returned home for a three-game series with the White Sox and won the first two. They lost the third game, blowing a ninth-inning lead. That was the last game Anderson managed.

After Clarence Livingood, a team doctor, observed Anderson, he urged team president Jim Campbell to send Anderson home, where he could get as much rest as needed before returning. "I was extremely wore out," Anderson said.

Anderson's wife, Carol, intercepted hundreds of phone calls to their Thousand Oaks home, telling callers that her husband wouldn't talk to anyone. Old friends such as Roger Craig, the San Francisco Giants' manager and former Tigers pitching coach; Red Wings coach Jacques Demers and Pistons coach Chuck Daly tried to get through to Anderson — sometimes more than once.

Anderson said doctors who examined him in California found him in good physical shape. He said he never thought about not coming back.

During the season, Anderson has always made himself available to the media and to several charitable causes. Now, he said, he must change his life-style to prevent a relapse.

"Before I left California to come back here, my wife told me to make sure I remembered to eat regularly," Anderson said. "I was in the habit of being on the go so much that all I would do is grab a sandwich on the run.

"You know what I did today before I came to the ballpark? I stopped and had lunch at a restaurant. I don't think I've done that two or three times without my wife since I've been the manager in Detroit. I had Boston scrod, vegetables, corn and carrot cake. That's the kind of thing I've got to do more of."

He returned to an injury-riddled team that was 22-32. How is a manager who takes losing so hard going to cope with that?

"If this club continues to lose, I'm just going to have to learn to live with it," Anderson said. "I'm going to have to try to learn from my mistakes." ◆

The Tigers went 9-8 under longtime coach Dick Tracewski but couldn't claw back into the pennant race.

A spring 1984 portrait — real Tigers up the middle: second baseman Lou Whitaker, shortstop Alan Trammell, centerfielder Chet Lemon and catcher Lance Parrish.

BY THE NUMBERS

Detroit Tigers (American League)

YEAR	W-L	PCT	FINISH	BATTING	HOMERS	RBI	WINS	SAVES
1980	84-78	.519	5th, 19 GB New York	Trammell (.300)	Parrish (24)	Kemp (101)	Morris (16)	Lopez (21)
1981**	31-26	.544	4th, 3½ GB New York	Gibson (.328)	Parrish (10)	Kemp (49)	Morris (14)	Saucier (13)
	29-23	.558	T-2nd, 1½ GB Milwaukee					
1982	83-79	.512	4th, 12 GB Milwaukee	Herndon (.292)	Parrish (32)	Herndon (88)	Morris (17)	Tobik (9)
				Wilson (.292)				
1983	92-70	.568	2nd, 6 GB Baltimore	Whitaker (.320)	Parrish (27)	Parrish (114)	Morris (20)	Lopez (18)
1984	104-58	.642	1st, 15 GA Toronto	Trammell (.314)	Parrish (33)	Parrish (98)	Morris (19)	Hernandez (32)
1985	84-77	.522	3rd, 15 GB Toronto	Gibson (.287)	Evans (40)*	Parrish (98)	Morris (16)	Hernandez (31)
1986	87-75	.537	3rd, 8½ GB Boston	Trammell (.277)	Evans (29)	Coles (86)	Morris (21)	Hernandez (24)
						Gibson (86)		
1987	98-64	.605	1st, 2 GA Toronto	Trammell (.343)	Evans (34)	Trammell (105)	Morris (18)	King (9)
1988	88-74	.543	2nd, 1 GB Boston	Trammell (.311)	Evans (22)***	Trammell (69)	Morris (15)	Henneman (22)

Led American League
*** Season split into halves because of 50-day players' strike.*
**** Fred Lynn hit 25 but spent most of season with Baltimore.*

Manager: Sparky Anderson (1980-88), 780-624 (.556). Total: 780-624 (.556).

Post-season: Beat Kansas City, 3-0, in 1984 American League playoffs; beat San Diego, 4-1, in 1984 World Series; lost to Minnesota, 4-1, in 1987 AL playoffs.

Award winners: Manager Sparky Anderson, Manager of the Year (1984, 1987); rightfielder Kirk Gibson, Playoff MVP (1984); relief pitcher Guillermo Hernandez, Cy Young (1984), MVP (1984); catcher Matt Nokes, Silver Slugger (1987); catcher Lance Parrish, Silver Slugger (1980, 1982, 1983, 1984, 1986), Gold Glove (1983, 1984, 1985); centerfielder Gary Pettis, Gold Glove (1988); shortstop Alan Trammell, Gold Glove (1980, 1981, 1983, 1984), Comeback Player (1983), World Series MVP (1984), Silver Slugger (1987, 1988); second baseman Lou Whitaker, Gold Glove (1983, 1984, 1985), Silver Slugger (1983, 1984, 1985, 1987). (All awards selected by the Baseball Writers Association of America, except for the Silver Slugger and Gold Glove by the Sporting News.)

All-Star Game representatives: 1980 (Lance Parrish, Alan Trammell); 1981 (Jack Morris); 1982 (Parrish); 1983 (Aurelio Lopez, Lou Whitaker, Parrish); 1984 (Guillermo Hernandez, Chet Lemon, Morris, Parrish, Trammell, Whitaker); 1985 (Dan Petry, Hernandez, Morris, Parrish, Trammell, Whitaker); 1986 (Hernandez, Parrish, Whitaker); 1987 (Matt Nokes, Morris, Trammell); 1988 (Doyle Alexander, Trammell); 1989 (Mike Henneman).

Hall of Fame inductees: Al Kaline, rightfielder (1980); Ernie Harwell, broadcaster (1981); George Kell, third baseman (1983); Rick Ferrell, front office (1984). From the Negro leagues: Ray Dandridge, third baseman, Detroit Stars (1987).

Notable deaths: Ray Oyler, shortstop (1981); Fred (Dixie) Walker, outfielder (1982); Vic Wertz, first baseman-outfielder (1983); Jim Hegan, catcher (1984); Waite Hoyt, pitcher (1984); Charlie Lau, catcher (1984); Ed Browalski, official scorer (1985); Syl Johnson, pitcher (1985); Bob Scheffing, manager (1985); Dick Wakefield, outfielder (1985); Harry H. Sisson, front office (1986); James (Skeeter) Webb, infielder (1986); Joe Sparma, pitcher (1986); Hank Greenberg, first baseman-outfielder (1986); Norm Cash, first baseman (1986); Paul Richards, catcher (1986); George Smith, infielder (1987); Ray Coles, scout (1987); Don McMahon, pitcher (1987); Ed Katalinas, scout (1988); Harvey Kuenn, shortstop-outfielder (1988).

RACING

Pied Piper, skipped by Dick Jennings
of Evanston, Ill., crossed the finish line
first in the Port Huron to Mackinac
sailboat race in 1986 and 1989.

The Renaissance Center provided a
photographic backdrop for the first
Grand Prix in downtown Detroit.

THE PRIX PREMIERE

By Charlie Vincent

JUNE 6,
1982
◆

A twist of automotive irony. Here was the Motor City — where many citizens considered driving a foreign car an immoral act — opening its hearts and closing its streets for the world's best foreign cars and drivers. It was the Detroit Grand Prix, a Formula One race through a tight, bumpy downtown course that the drivers despised. When the city got its first taste of the European-style auto racing, more than a little confusion ruled the day.

No one seems quite sure how fast he went, or how far, or how many people watched him do it, and some even question whether he did, indeed, win the first Detroit Grand Prix.

But John Watson, a 36-year-old Irishman driving for Team McLaren, took the checkered flag and easily beat Eddie Cheever, the only American on the Formula One circuit, to the finish of the time-shortened race. Although the first race of its kind in mid-America was scheduled for 70 laps, it was stopped after one hour, 58 minutes, 41.043 seconds of racing time, complying with a Formula One rule that no race go more than two hours. Watson completed 62 laps. Behind Watson and Cheever — who had the best finish of his career — were Didier Pironi, Keke Rosberg and Derek Daly, all on the same lap, and Jacques Laffite, one lap behind.

A number of protests were filed, an action that seems *de rigueur* in Formula One. But by nightfall, Watson's victory was still in the record books.

"The car was bloody awful in practice," Watson said. "I wasn't particularly hopeful, based on that." He started 17th in the 26-car field and, early in the race, showed no signs of improving his position much.

He had moved up only to 14th when the race was stopped after six laps because of an accident involving Riccardo Patrese and Roberto Guerrero in Turn 1. Both walked away from the wreck, but Patrese's car caught fire, halting the race for almost an hour. Formula One rules call for a minimum 30-minute delay once cars are called off the track, but the decision on when that half-hour period begins rests with the clerk of the course. Bob Swenson, serving in that capacity, decided the 30 minutes did not start until the course had been cleared of debris, significantly lengthening the delay.

Also complicating matters was another Formula One rule. When the race was stopped, Prost led Rosberg by 3.299 seconds and Watson by 26.526. Although they would start right behind Prost when the race resumed, Formula One says they must make up that time when the race is restarted.

Prost began having trouble with his electronic fuel injection system, and Rosberg overtook him 18 laps after the restart. Rosberg led for 16 laps, but when he started having gearbox difficulty, Watson was in his rearview mirror.

"I found I could pass people in a few places, and once I found that, it seemed to happen relatively easy," Watson said. "I didn't expect to be able to overtake people. I didn't see places to do that in practice, but today I did."

Once he got past Rosberg, though, he still had to pass him on the clock. Because he trailed Rosberg by more than 23 seconds at the restart, Watson had to pull that far ahead of the Finn before he would take the official lead.

Rosberg's speed slowed dramatically after the race's halfway point. After 42 laps — an hour and 20 minutes into the race — his lead over Watson was 3.728 seconds. And by the time he came to the start-finish line again, Watson led by more than seven seconds. Rosberg continued to slide back into the field, passed by Cheever and Pironi.

Watson's winning speed was announced as 78.2 miles an hour, but that is open to question because various race officials differ on their opinion of the length of the course. Swenson announced the day before the race that the circuit's official length was 2.493 miles. But on race day, Rod Campbell, spokesman for Detroit Renaissance Grand Prix Inc., said his organization still was calling the circuit 2.59 miles.

"John was unbeatable today," Cheever said. "He would have been the winner, under any circumstances."

The crowd for the first Grand Prix was a matter of controversy, too. Though many of the 65,000 seats were empty during the race — some observers thought there were no more than 45,000 spectators — spokesmen for the promoters said Detroit police estimated the crowd at 100,000. ◆

In the early '80s accidents killed unlimited hydroplane racing's two biggest names — Detroit native Bill Muncey and Miss Budweiser driver Dean Chenoweth. An always-dangerous sport, many thought, had finally crossed the line. Then came a fresh face from Seattle, Chip Hanauer. Gar Wood's river and Bill Muncey's river was now Chip Hanauer's river. And it was never more evident than in 1986, the 70th anniversary of powerboat racing on the river and Detroit's 25th Gold Cup race.

UNLIMITED SUCCESS

By Wylie Gerdes

Chip Hanauer seems to have a love affair with Detroit.

"I wish I could take Detroit home with me," Hanauer said after winning the Gold Cup unlimited hydroplane race on the Detroit River. Instead, Hanauer takes a record-tying fifth straight Gold Cup home to Seattle. Gar Wood is the only other to win five straight in more than 80 years of Gold Cups.

After a day of frustrating weather delays, Hanauer's Miller American defeated the Miss Budweiser turbine boat in a thrilling final. Miss Bud's Jim Kropfeld pressed Hanauer all through the six laps, never more than the length of a roostertail or two back. Hanauer's average speed was 123.872 m.p.h.; Kropfeld averaged 121.872. A Griffon-powered Miss Budweiser, driven by Scott Pierce, was third.

Hanauer broke into tears briefly after greeting boat co-owner Fran Muncey and crew chief John Walters at the dock. Hanauer won his first Gold Cup in Detroit in 1982, the season he replaced the late Bill Muncey as driver.

"I said during the week that nothing could top the first one, but this does," Hanauer said. "And most of the reason it does is because of Jim Kropfeld. He's a great driver, and he drove a great race. I have nothing but respect for him."

Hanauer said the race was won before the start, when he grabbed inside position on Kropfeld. The Budweiser turbine had handled so poorly during the week, it appeared in no position to challenge the Miller, which ran flawlessly during qualifying.

In a Free Press pre-race diary, Chip Hanauer wrote: "Winning the Gold Cup is every driver's dream. Winning the Gold Cup in Detroit is the ultimate. . . Detroit is the oldest site on the circuit and the most historic. It has the biggest crowds and most knowledgeable fans. Detroit is also the most difficult to drive." He won his record-tying fifth straight Gold Cup on the Detroit River. He made it six straight the next year at San Diego.

Hanauer said he had written off the Bud turbine until it ran a 127.9 m.p.h. lap in a preliminary heat. "We were going to leave him alone," Hanauer said. "But when he turned in that 127, I knew we just had to attack. . . . We were duking it out pretty good at the start."

Hanauer had to overcome equipment problems. The Miller American developed steering troubles, he said. Team manager Lance Morris said the boat also had problems with the drive train.

"I felt it was my day early," Hanauer said. "Then I couldn't get the boat to steer, and when Jim ran that 127, I thought we were dead. I thought it was curtains."

Not quite. Still, Hanauer was a little bit stunned by the fifth straight Gold Cup.

"I wanted to be a boat racer all my life," he said. "But I just can't believe what's happened. There's a force bigger than me involved in all this." ◆

THE WIND AT HIS BACK

By Drew Sharp

With miles and miles run and races won, Doug Kurtis of Northville became a marathoner known around the world. But for one reason or another, he was winless in three tries in his own backyard — the Detroit Free Press International Marathon. Would the winds of fortune finally shift?

After playing bridesmaid three times in the Detroit Free Press International Marathon, Doug Kurtis finally became best man.

Kurtis, from Northville, easily outdistanced the field and won in two hours, 18 minutes, three seconds, more than three minutes ahead of runner-up Loren Bandt of Livonia, the 1984 champion and Kurtis' training partner. Kurtis was runner-up in 1980, 1981 and 1986, falling prey to misfortune in the late stages each time. But nothing could deny him this year. At 35, Kurtis became the oldest winner in the race's 10-year history.

As he crossed the finish line at Belle Isle with his 13th marathon victory overall, Kurtis pumped his fists into the air. The man who had raced more sub-2:20 marathons than any other American (37), finally won before the home crowd.

"This is the most special of all of my wins," Kurtis said. "I loved it because I had so much support out there with people cheering me. Everyone was rooting, 'This is your year! This is your year!' I never once worried about what could go wrong the last few miles. I was more concerned with my time, wondering if I was going to make 2:20."

The marathon turned into a three-man race at the 9½-mile point, Woodward and Forest, among leader Kurtis, Bandt and 23-year-old Michael Kavulich of Berkley. The trio headed west down Michigan Avenue into a fairly strong wind. At the halfway point, Bandt dropped back several seconds. But Kavulich, a first-time marathoner, stayed on Kurtis' heels. The decision proved his undoing. When the pair turned back on Michigan at 17 miles, Kurtis pushed out front with the wind at his back. Kavulich didn't have the strength to hang on and fell out of contention.

"I was hoping that he would come out with me," Kurtis said with a devilish grin. "While I was running into the wind, I kept in mind that it was going to be at my back eventually, and then Michael appeared to be having some problems."

With six miles left, Kurtis looked over his shoulder to find the competition, but he couldn't see it. He was more than 30 seconds ahead of Kavulich and Bandt.

No one was going to catch Kurtis. His time was a minute slower than the previous year's runner-up effort. But that couldn't wipe the smile off Kurtis' face after the race. He delightedly accepted the hugs and handshakes of fellow runners and spectators, who finally saw Michigan's finest marathoner win its biggest marathon. ◆

After winning his hometown marathon for the first time in 1987, Doug Kurtis became its first repeat male champion in 1988. "It's so nice to get the recognition of being the hometown boy," he said. "It's exciting to be from Detroit and win this race."

◆

Tired of hassling with the Europeans, the Detroit Grand Prix made a big switch to Indy-style racing. The cars were different, but the course was its usual difficult self. And the result was remarkably similar to previous years.

BRASIL '89

By Steve Crowe

The transformation of the Detroit Grand Prix from Formula One to Indy cars was to be an Americanization process, of sorts. Instead, it was largely a process of elimination.

When the 155-mile race over the 2.5-mile, 17-turn downtown street course was over, a Brazilian stood atop the victory stand for the fourth straight year and fifth time in eight races. The more things change, the more they stay Brazilian.

Emerson Fittipaldi, last month's Indianapolis 500 winner, passed Scott Pruett at the beginning of the 59th lap and took the checkered flag 29.544 seconds ahead of Pruett, whose fuel-starved Lola T89-Judd came home on fumes.

It was the eighth Indy-car victory in 76 starts for Fittipaldi, 42, Formula One world champion in 1972 and '74. And it gave Pat Patrick of Jackson, owner of Fittipaldi's Penske PC18-Chevrolet, his 31st career Indy-car triumph.

In finding his way to the victory stand, Fittipaldi literally walked in the footsteps of fellow countryman Ayrton Senna, winner of the last three Formula One races in Detroit. Fittipaldi said beforehand that he would reveal after the race the Detroit-course secrets he learned from Senna during a recent visit at Fittipaldi's home in Miami Beach, Fla. But he reneged on that promise, saying, "Well, next year I'm coming back again."

Finishing third in his Lola T89-Chevrolet was Mario Andretti, who collided with Fittipaldi on Lap 48 in front of Cobo Center when Fittipaldi attempted to pass inside. It took only a few seconds for race marshals to push Andretti back onto the course, but Fittipaldi was stalled for nearly one minute before rejoining the field. "I owe the corner workers a few beers," Andretti said. "They did a great job."

The mishap seemed to give pole winner Michael Andretti — who led for 52 laps in all — a free ride to victory. After 49 laps, he led Pruett by 62.11 seconds. But eight laps from the finish, Andretti felt "something tapping my foot." It turned out to be a loose radio antenna wire that gradually wrapped itself around the throttle. On Lap 55, he slowed considerably. A 26-second pit stop did not eliminate the problem, ending Andretti's day on Lap 56 when the throttle stuck open again and he nudged the wall.

"I was just coasting for a while, looking for a gear," Andretti said. "It's the smallest things that will get you. It just shows you that there's nothing minor in these cars. It was something that could have been prevented. But it's not going to happen to me again, I'll tell you."

The first lap of the race was run under a yellow flag, when Steve Saleen's March 88C-Cosworth stalled in the middle of Turn 3. On the first green lap, Fittipaldi and Mario Andretti's wheels touched, spinning out Andretti's car and puncturing a tire on Fittipaldi's.

The run-in sent Fittipaldi to the pits and then to the rear of the field after starting third. After 29 laps, Fittipaldi had cruised past most of the field into fourth place, behind the Andrettis and Pruett, the Indy 500 co-rookie of the year.

What was expected to be a battle of attrition ended with 12 of the 28 cars running.

"It was a very exciting race for the public, and the drivers, too," said Fittipaldi, whose victory earned him $144,160 of the CART-record $1 million purse. "And I think the Indy-car race proved very dynamic." ◆

Emerson Fittipaldi followed in the skid marks of countryman Ayrton Senna and Nelson Piquet, other Brazilians to win on Detroit's streets.

People power was almost as important to Emerson Fittipaldi as pedal power. On the first lap, Fittipaldi and Mario Andretti's wheels touched, spinning out Andretti's car and puncturing a tire on Fittipaldi's. On Lap 48, Andretti collided with Fittipaldi, who was stalled for nearly one minute before rejoining the field.

BY THE NUMBERS

Detroit Free Press International Marathon

A running event starting in Windsor, Ontario, and ending in Detroit.

YEAR	MEN	WOMEN	MEN WHEELERS	WOMEN WHEELERS
1980	Greg Meyer	Debby Froehlich	Kris Lenzo	
1981	Mike McGuire	Maureen Griffin	Kris Lenzo	
1982	Dave Hinz	Karen Hubbard	Kris Lenzo	
1983	Dave Olds	Cindy Barber	Marty Ball	Jennifer Smith
1984	Loren Bandt	Karen Hubbard	Marty Ball	Jennifer Smith
1985	Tim Fox	Liz Watch	Mike Trujillo	Jennifer Smith
1986	Ahmed Ismail	Patricia Wassik-Hinson	Mike Trujillo	Candace Cable-Brookes
1987	Doug Kurtis	Christine Iwahashi	Philippe Couprie	Candace Cable-Brookes
1988	Doug Kurtis	Ella Willis	Doug Wight	Chantal Petitclerc

Stock cars

NASCAR races at Michigan International Speedway in Brooklyn, Mich.

YEAR	RACE	WINNER	CAR	SPEED
1980	Gabriel 400	Benny Parsons	Chevrolet	131.808
1980	Champion Spark Plug 400	Cale Yarborough	Chevrolet	145.352
1981	Gabriel 400	Bobby Allison	Buick	130.589
1981	Champion Spark Plug 400	Richard Petty	Buick	123.457
1982	Gabriel 400	Cale Yarborough	Buick	118.101
1982	Champion Spark Plug 400	Bobby Allison	Buick	136.454
1983	Gabriel 400	Cale Yarborough	Chevrolet	138.728
1983	Champion Spark Plug 400	Cale Yarborough	Chevrolet	147.511
1984	Miller High Life 400	Bill Elliott	Ford	134.705
1984	Champion Spark Plug 400	Darrell Waltrip	Chevrolet	153.863
1985	Miller 400	Bill Elliott	Ford	144.724
1985	Champion Spark Plug 400	Bill Elliott	Ford	137.430
1986	Miller American 400	Bill Elliott	Ford	138.555
1986	Champion Spark Plug 400	Bill Elliott	Ford	135.465
1987	Miller American 400	Dale Earnhardt	Chevrolet	148.454
1987	Champion Spark Plug 400	Bill Elliott	Ford	138.648
1988	Miller High Life 400	Rusty Wallace	Pontiac	153.553
1988	Champion Spark Plug 400	Davey Allison	Ford	156.863
1989	Miller High Life 400	Bill Elliott	Ford	139.023
1989	Champion Spark Plug 400	Rusty Wallace	Pontiac	157.704

Michigan 500

A CART race at Michigan International Speedway in Brooklyn, Mich.

YEAR	WINNER/SPEED
1981	Pancho Carter (132.890 m.p.h.)*
1982	Gordon Johncock (153.925)
1983	John Paul Jr. (134.862)
1984	Mario Andretti (133.482)
1985	Emerson Fittipaldi (128.220)
1986	Johnny Rutherford (137.139)
1987	Michael Andretti (171.493)
1988	Danny Sullivan (180.654)
1989	Michael Andretti (160.210)

* Norton-Michigan 500, '81-82; Michigan 500, '83-86; Marlboro 500, '87-89.

Detroit Grand Prix

A Formula One race in downtown Detroit from 1982 to 1988; a CART race in downtown Detroit in 1989.

YEAR	WINNER/COUNTRY
1982	John Watson (Great Britain)
1983	Michele Alboreto (Italy)
1984	Nelson Piquet (Brazil)
1985	Keke Rosberg (Finland)
1986	Ayrton Senna (Brazil)
1987	Ayrton Senna (Brazil)
1988	Ayrton Senna (Brazil)
1989	Emerson Fittipaldi (Brazil)

Port Huron to Mackinac

Michigan's premier sailing event, sponsored by Detroit's Bayview Yacht Club. (Because of sailing's handicap systems, the first boat across the finish line may not be the winner. But the first across, usually one of the largest boats, earns that year's bragging rights.)

YEAR	FIRST ACROSS/SKIPPER
1980	Heritage (Don Wildman)
1981	Heritage (Don Wildman)
1982	Heritage (Don Wildman)
1983	Heritage (Don Wildman)
1984	Sassy (Dutch Schmidt)
1985	Sassy (Dutch Schmidt)
1986	Pied Piper (Dick Jennings)
1987	Sassy (Dutch Schmidt))
1988	Sassy (Dutch Schmidt)
1989	Pied Piper (Dick Jennings)

Unlimited hydroplanes

An American Hydroplane Series race on the Detroit River off Belle Isle.

YEAR	WINNER/DRIVER
1980	Miss Budweiser (Dean Chenoweth)
1981	Miss Budweiser (Dean Chenoweth)
1982	Atlas Van Lines (Chip Hanauer)*
1983	Atlas Van Lines (Chip Hanauer)
1984	Miss Budweiser (Jim Kropfeld)
1985	Miller American (Chip Hanauer)
1986	Miller American (Chip Hanauer)*
1987	Mr. Pringles (Scott Pierce)
1988	Miller High Life (Chip Hanauer)
1989	Circus Circus (Chip Hanauer)

* Gold Cup race

Michigan Mile

Michigan's premier thoroughbred horse race, at Detroit Race Course in Livonia, Mich. The race is 1⅛ miles.

YEAR	WINNER/JOCKEY
1980	Glorious Song (John LeBlanc)
1981	Fio Rito (Leslie Hulet)
1982	Vodika Collins (Joe Judice)
1983	Thumbsucker (Tony Russo Jr.)
1984	Timeless Native (Don Brumfield)
1985	Badwagon Harry (Ricardo Lopez)
1986	Ends Well (Randy Romero)
1987	Waquoit (Chris McCarron)
1988	Lost Code (Craig Perret)
1989	Present Value (Frank Olivares)

PREPS

Mary Lillie-Cicerone, a University of
Detroit star in the early '80s, coached
Birmingham Marian to the Class A
girls basketball title in 1988.

Farmington Hills Harrison won the Class B football title in 1981. The following season, because of changing enrollment, Harrison was promoted to Class A, the state's toughest, and the Hawks returned only one starter. Still, Harrison had won 22 straight games and needed only one more victory for a second straight title.

John Miller, only a sophomore, scored 12 points for Harrison in the title game. Despite a slightly separated shoulder and a cut on his chin that needed six stitches at halftime, Miller gained 70 tough yards on the ground and caught five passes for 132 yards. A punishing prep runner, Miller went on to star in Michigan State's defensive backfield. He picked off four passes in a victory over Michigan and two passes in the Rose Bowl.

ONE KICK DESERVES ANOTHER

By Mick McCabe

Farmington Hills Harrison was kicked up to Class A this season, and Dave Blackmer kicked the Hawks to the state championship in a double-overtime thriller. Blackmer's 24-yard field goal gave Harrison a 17-14 victory over Dearborn Fordson at the Silverdome.

The first overtime Class A championship game was easily the most exciting Class A final in the eight-year history of the playoffs. How exciting? Harrison came within two yards of ending the game on the final play of regulation. How exciting? Fordson scored a fourth-down touchdown to force a second overtime. That exciting.

"It's fantastic," said Harrison coach John Herrington. "It speaks so well for the kids coming up. We don't play a lot of juniors, but they still work hard in practice, and when they're seniors they feel it's their turn. We have 13 seniors and they all start." Blackmer was the only starter back from last year's team, which beat Muskegon Catholic Central for the Class B title. Ken Kish, Harrison's senior quarterback, completed only four passes as a junior; against Fordson, he completed 15 of 27 passes for 208 yards.

Fordson (10-2) took a 7-0 lead with 31 seconds left in the first half. After Blackmer missed a 37-yard field goal, the Tractors marched 80 yards in 14 plays. Kevin Harris scored from the 3-yard line.

The score remained 7-0 until the fourth quarter. Harrison launched a scoring drive on the period's first play, and sophomore back John Miller ended it on a dive from one yard out with 8:03 left.

After Fordson missed a 35-yard field goal with 3:33 left, Harrison nearly pulled off a last-second victory. Kish threw to Miller, who raced toward the end zone. But Fordson's Harris caught him at the 2 as time ran out.

In overtime, the teams took turns trying to score in four downs from 10 yards out. Miller ran three straight times for Harrison, scoring from three yards out. Blackmer booted the extra point for a seven-point lead. The Tractors took their turn and scored on a fourth-down, two-yard run by Harris. Richard Brooks' kick was good, forcing a second overtime.

The Tractors, with the ball first, gained only two yards on three plays. On fourth down, Brooks missed a 25-yard field goal. "I thought our kicker was going to make that," said Fordson coach Charlie Jestice. When Harrison got the ball again, Miller carried twice for three yards. Then Blackmer, a first-team All-State kicker last year, lined up to kick on third down. His kick was perfect, and the title belonged to Harrison. ◆

THE QUALITY OF MERCY

By Mick McCabe

DEC. 11,
1982
◆

Farmington Hills Our Lady of Mercy had won the Class A girls basketball championship in 1977. Since then, Flint Northern, coached by Dottie Kukulka, had won four straight titles. Flint Northern led Mercy by 19 points going into the last quarter of the 1982 title game. A fifth consecutive title for the Vikings seemed assured.

Farmington Hills Our Lady of Mercy basketball coach Larry Baker walked around the court at Calihan Hall repeating: "I can't believe it, I can't believe it."

Neither could anyone else.

Mercy had staged a fantastic fourth-quarter rally to end Flint Northern's four-year reign as Class A girls basketball champion with a 61-58 upset of the state's top-ranked team. Entering the fourth quarter, Mercy (22-1, No. 6) trailed Northern by 19 points. With less than seven minutes left, the Marlins still were down by 18.

"Our goal at the quarter was to keep our self-respect," Baker said. "We said we would scratch, kick, claw and bite because we had nothing to lose."

Led by Sarah Basford and Carolyn Burt, the only senior starter, the Marlins reluctantly applied a full-court trapping press against the speedy Vikings and cut the deficit to four points with three minutes left. "We wanted to flash the press on them occasionally," Baker said, "but we absolutely didn't want to go to it — that was our last resort."

After Vickie Prince hit a free throw to give Northern a five-point lead, the Vikings (25-3) turned the ball over four straight possessions. Sophomore Amy DeMattia (13 points, 10 rebounds) scored three straight Mercy baskets, giving the Marlins the lead.

"When Mr. Baker said to get the ball to me," DeMattia said, "I felt I had to do it. I wanted this game so bad I wasn't thinking about the shot at all. It just had to be there. I wanted it really bad."

Northern had

a chance to regain the lead, but Annette Ruggiero, a 5-foot-4 sophomore, intercepted a pass, sabotaging an uncontested lay-up. Ruggiero was fouled and hit a free throw to give Mercy a two-point lead. She finished with a career-high 11 points. Northern then missed two shots and Mercy sophomore center Mary Rosowski grabbed the rebound and was fouled. Her free throw with 11 seconds left iced the game. "I had to make it," Rosowski said. "I tried to block everything out and look at nothing but the rim."

Evette Ott scored 18 points to lead Northern, which committed 31 turnovers. "It was like everything was in a state of chaos," Ott said. "I guess we lost our composure."

Basford, a junior guard, scored 20 points and kept Mercy within striking distance the first three quarters. The Marlins trailed by 10 points, 20-10, after one quarter, by 13, 35-22, at the half.

"I've never experienced anything like this before," Baker said. "We beat the epitome of girls basketball. We pulled the rabbit out of the hat." ◆

Our Lady of Mercy had a difficult path to the title game — a 38-34 victory over Detroit Cass Tech in the quarterfinals and a 43-39 victory over Lansing Everett in the semifinals.

Glen Rice, the scorer, would be taken in the first round — in the 1989 NBA draft. Andre Rison, the playmaker, would be taken in the first round — in the 1989 NFL draft. Anthony Pendleton, the shooter, would tickle the twine for Southern California. They were the backbone of an incredible Flint Northwestern basketball team.

And after winning its semifinal by 37 points, Northwestern was after more than its second straight title.

No Michigan athlete could compete with Andre Rison's versatility his senior year. Rison made all-state in football, second-team all-state in basketball and finished third and fourth in state track sprints. He played quarterback, tailback, slot back, wide receiver and defensive back for the football team and also did the kicking. He was the point guard for the unbeaten basketball team.

THE BEST TEAM EVER

By Mick McCabe

Glen Rice. Andre Rison. Daryl Miller. Anthony Pendleton. Michael Avery.

Those were the Flint Northwestern starters on what many observers think was the best team to play high school basketball in Michigan.

That was the main topic of conversation in the second half as top-ranked Northwestern won its second straight Class A title, beating Detroit Southwestern, 69-55, before a capacity crowd at Crisler Arena. It was the fifth straight Class A title won by a Flint team (Flint Central won the first three) and the fourth straight time Southwestern (24-3) had lost in the finals.

"I'd say that Flint Central team was the quickest team I've ever seen," Michigan State coach Jud Heathcote said. "Northwestern does so many things well. They're so much better defensively. It's hard to score on them."

The Wildcats own four straight Class A basketball titles — two boys, two girls. Both teams were undefeated this season. The boys have won a Class A-record 46 straight games — 28 this season.

How good was Northwestern? Michigan coach Bill Frieder won Class A titles in 1971 and '72 at Flint Northern. His undefeated '72 team included Wayman Britt and Terry Furlow. "Furlow and Britt had great college careers," Frieder said, "but I think Northwestern has more balance. They hurt you from every direction in so many ways. We won all our games, but we didn't destroy teams like Northwestern. We had some close games, but they didn't."

The Wildcats took a 19-10 lead in the first quarter and later ran off 16 straight points for a 39-19 halftime lead. Rice — the state's first Mr. Basketball to win a state championship during his senior season — dominated the first half, scoring 15 of his game-high 25 points.

Northwestern coach Grover Kirkland, who had been hedging on the subject all season, finally agreed that this Northwestern team was better than last season's.

"We worked so hard for the first one that we couldn't enjoy it," he said. "This one, we've been more relaxed, and we've enjoyed it all along."

"This feels good," Rice said, "but it hasn't set in exactly what has happened." ◆

A RICH, RICH LIFE

By George Puscas

MAY 20, 1987

◆

Hal Schram, overcoming a severe sight handicap, covered high school athletics for the Detroit Free Press for more than 40 years. He was the best in the business. What he couldn't see, he illuminated with 20-20 insight. His annual prognostications on the state football and basketball tournaments made him famous statewide as the all-seeing "Swami." He wasn't always right, but he was always entertaining. And he was dear to all who knew him and all who worked with him.

Hal Schram is dead. Good ol' Swami. He was one of ours — longer, better, more beloved and admired than many of us can ever hope to be.

There's a sadness about this day that won't soon fade.

He was our guy, the one with the corny jokes and the giggle, the endless list of friends and news sources, the one who preferred to write about kids trying to play like men, rather than men trying to play like kids. Our Swami. He was something else.

Nothing showed it more clearly than our last conversation, a month or so ago. The end was coming, he knew it, and it never scared him, not for a moment. "I know I'm going to

die someday soon," he said. "But I've had a good life, far better than I ever expected. I was lucky. The Lord blessed me."

He was blind and ailing with lung cancer.

All of it seemed to hit him suddenly after he retired from the Free Press in 1983. But there was no suggestion of bitterness or regret in him. I had tried to call him at his son's home in the morning, and nobody answered. It was too early in the day for Swami to visit the racetrack, that I knew. Several hours later, word came that he had died. He was 68.

He wrote about one generation of athletes and another would come along, and he often found he would be writing about the sons of athletes he had known years before. Nobody knew high school athletics as thoroughly as Schram, and nobody did more to foster its growth and improvement.

It was fun to know him, to work and play with him. In print and around the office, he could be a tease, never mean but always persistent and clever enough to stir a reaction. For instance, he loved to phone his co-workers at home at 2 a.m. "I was just closing this tavern," he would giggle, "and I was thinking of you. What are you doing?"

He was a fun-loving guy nobody could dislike, no matter how much he teased. He had a hobby that never was intended to produce riches, but one time it almost did. He shared a $6 double trifecta bet with Bill Kofender, a photographer, at Detroit Race Course some years ago, and they had a $27,000 jackpot locked 100 yards from the finish line. Then, for reasons never known, their horse collapsed and fell on its face. "It wasn't meant for me to be rich," he said, and he never referred to the incident again.

Ol' Swami was wrong, and he came to know it. He was rich. ◆

The Swami knew how to tease the followers of high school teams. Once, in predicting that Dimondale would lose in the state basketball tournament, he wrote, "I wouldn't give a dime for Dimondale." He suspected what would happen; outstaters always reacted strongly to the least put-down from Hal Schram. Within 48 hours, the office was flooded with letters containing dimes. One large poster board, covered with nearly $20 in dimes, arrived. "Boys," he said, giggling as always, "Ol' Swami's treating you all tonight."

Sam Washington dedicated his life to providing a safe haven for inner-city recreation. St. Cecilia's gym in Detroit became a favorite place for kids to play basketball. Its summer league became legendary. Whenever college recruiters or NBA scouts wanted to watch good players on the basketball floor, they knew all they had to do was call on Sam.

Sam Washington's funeral attracted people from all over — white, black, old, young, basketball players, kids in sneakers, mothers, fathers, coaches. The service was called "Celebrating the Life of Samuel Lee Washington."

ST. SAM OF CECILIA'S

By Scott Walton

Summertime at St. Cecilia gym will never be the same now that Sam Washington is gone. Washington, the driving force behind the famed St. Cecilia's basketball league, died 21 days after suffering a stroke at his office. He was 51.

The summertime youth league, which he founded after the Detroit riots of 1967, attracted some of the state's best players to the sauna-like St. Cecilia gym in northwest Detroit. Magic Johnson played there. So did George Gervin.

"Sam had the ability to mend and heal people," said Father Thomas Finnigan of St. Cecilia's Rectory. "The whole community respected him so much; they respected the

gym and the program, too. It's going to create a tremendous vacuum because he was so well-known and so well-loved by athletes, coaches, parishioners, people on the street."

Washington had been coach and athletic director at St. Cecilia's middle school since 1968, and in the early '80s he was coach and general manager of the Detroit Spirits of the Continental Basketball Association. In March 1987, he suffered a severe stroke, but he came back to direct his 20th season at St. Cecilia. "If something is going to happen to me," Washington said at the time, "I would rather have it happen here at the gym." Then, Nov. 8, he suffered another stroke after a practice with St. Cecilia's seventh- and eighth-graders. A three-sport star at Detroit's Western High, Washington later concentrated on football. He played professionally for the AFL's New York Titans and in the Canadian Football League before returning to Detroit.

"He ran the best basketball program in the state in terms of developing young talent," said Will Robinson, a friend and Pistons assistant to the general manager.

Michigan State football coach George Perles played with Washington in the early 1950s at Western. "I'm just shocked," Perles said. "The real loss is the kids that he's not going to be able to help. He's been kind of a father to a lot of those guys; he got them into colleges and universities. That's a well-known facility because of all the work he's done."

Jim Boyce, Detroit Mumford and former Eastern Michigan coach, was a longtime friend. "How do you replace a man like Sam?" he said. "Hopefully, somebody else will step up to the challenge of giving the kids a good setting in which to play and offer them a good role model, too." ◆

COOLEY'S CROWNING MOMENT

By Mick McCabe

MARCH 18,
1989
◆

Only two teams in Class A history had won three state basketball championships in a row. Detroit Cooley, coached by Ben Kelso and featuring Michael Talley and Daniel Lyton, wanted to be the third. Old nemesis Detroit Southwestern, which had lost six of the last seven title games but had beaten Cooley for the Public School League title, hoped this would be the year it would finally be champion.

Seventeen seconds remained on the Crisler Arena clock when Ben Kelso sent substitutes into the game.

Daniel Lyton, Detroit Cooley's mountain in the middle, made his way to the bench, where Kelso shook his hand and hugged him. Then came Michael Talley, Cooley's all-state point guard, and Kelso nearly crushed him with a bear hug.

Kelso, Talley and Lyton had completed their mission — their third straight Class A championship — by ripping Detroit Southwestern, 85-73, before a packed house. Cooley joins Kalamazoo Central (1949, '50, '51) and Flint Central (1981, '82, '83) as the only

teams in Class A history to win three consecutive titles.

This could be Kelso's most satisfying championship because it was his most difficult. From the season's start, the Cardinals were the team to beat and many great teams never live up to their billing. "For the first time, I looked all around the state and said: 'Damn, I've got the best team,'" Kelso said. "That worried me. Now I had to get the team to perform. Along the way there were certain things I had to do."

There were player suspensions and other discipline problems that may have prevented Cooley from winning the Detroit PSL championship. But Kelso never lost sight of his team's main goal — the state championship.

"I used to read a book that said Lincoln's best generals were the ones who were able to see the big picture," Kelso said. "Along the way you may lose some battles, but you're still closing in all the time. That's why I could tell you this morning we were going to win."

Cooley (25-1 and ranked No. 2) launched a ferocious attack on top-ranked Southwestern (25-2), which lost in the championship for the seventh time in eight years. Cooley hit an amazing 67 percent of its shots (33 of 49). The Cardinals scored on all but five possessions in the first quarter, jumping to a 25-9 lead. Southwestern scored on only four of 14 possessions and got stung when coach Perry Watson was hit with a technical foul with 2:56 left in the quarter. Talley went to the line and made one of two technical free throws. On the ensuing possession, he hit a three-point basket.

That forced Southwestern out of its zone defense, and the Cooley guards took complete control of the game. Talley hit 10 of 13 shots for 27 points and eight assists. Lyton, a 6-foot-7 center, had his way inside, hitting eight of 11 shots for 20 points.

"I'm proud of myself and the whole team," Lyton said. "Now I can relax." ◆

Michael Talley, the first point guard to win the Mr. Basketball Award, finished his career with three state titles. "There was a lot of hard work involved," he said. "I'm glad to be Mr. Basketball, but I'd rather have the three state titles."

Dream teams

◆

Mick McCabe, a.k.a. the Son of Swami to Free Press readers, weighed a decade of outstanding performances to create Michigan's high school Dream Teams of the '80s. When creating the teams, McCabe only considered athletes' prep performances, ignoring subsequent successes or failures in college or the pros.

Center Terry Mills owned 1986 — winning the Class A championship and the Mr. Basketball Award.

THE DECADE'S BEST

Boys basketball dream team

PLAYER	HIGH SCHOOL
Mark Macon	Saginaw Buena Vista
Dan Majerle	Traverse City
Tim McCormick	Clarkston
Terry Mills	Romulus
Glen Rice*	Flint Northwestern
Coach: Ben Kelso, Detroit Cooley	

Boys basketball Class A team

PLAYER	HIGH SCHOOL
Darryl Johnson	Flint Central
Antoine Joubert	Detroit Southwestern
Michael Talley*	Detroit Cooley
Eric Turner	Flint Central
Sam Vincent	Lansing Eastern

Boys basketball Class B team

PLAYER	HIGH SCHOOL
Mark Brown	Hastings
Derrick Coleman	Detroit Northern
Roy Marble*	Flint Beecher
Matt Steigenga	Grand Rapids South Christian
Garde Thompson	East Grand Rapids

Boys basketball Class C team

PLAYER	HIGH SCHOOL
Willie Burton	Detroit St. Martin dePorres
Ron Fillmore	Sanford Meridian
Mark German	Bronson
Negele Knight*	Detroit DePorres
Randy Morrison	Olivet

Boys basketball Class D team

PLAYER	HIGH SCHOOL
Anthony Grier	Detroit East Catholic
Dennis Kann	Mio
Mark Kraatz	Allen Park Inter-City Baptist
Sander Scott*	Northport
Jeff Warren	Litchfield

Captain

Girls basketball dream team

PLAYER	HIGH SCHOOL
Annette Babers	Saginaw
Tonya Edwards	Flint Northwestern
Dena Head*	Plymouth Salem
Nikita Lowry	Detroit Cass Tech
Franthea Price	River Rouge
Coach: Larry Glass, Leland	

Girls basketball Class A team

PLAYER	HIGH SCHOOL
Kim Archer	Livonia Bentley
Marline Ferguson	Detroit King
Regina Pierce	Jackson
Jennifer Shasky*	Birmingham Marian
LaTonya Thomas	Detroit King

Girls basketball Class B team

PLAYER	HIGH SCHOOL
Tracey Bloodworth	St. Joseph
Regina Clark	Saginaw Buena Vista
Kris Emerson	Caledonia
Sue Nissen*	Dearborn Divine Child
Sue Tucker	Okemos

Girls basketball Class C team

PLAYER	HIGH SCHOOL
Daedra Charles	Detroit DePorres
Carrie Lawless	Traverse City St. Francis
Carol Szczechowski*	Wyandotte Mt. Carmel
Keri Thomas	Newaygo
Vonnie Thompson	Carrollton

Girls basketball Class D team

PLAYER	HIGH SCHOOL
Char Durand	Peck
Becky Glass	Leland
Erica Ledy	De Tour
Julie Polakowski*	Leland
Laura Wiesen	Maple City Glen Lake

Captain

Football dream team

OFFENSE	HIGH SCHOOL
E: Todd Lyght	Flint Powers
E: Cedric Gordon	Ann Arbor Pioneer
T: Mark Garalczyk	Fraser
T: Rob Doherty	Sterling Heights Stevenson
G: Bud Gereg	Warren De La Salle
G: Matt Vanderbeek	Holland West Ottawa
C: Jim Kreutzer	Walled Lake Central
QB: Mill Coleman*	Farmington Hills Harrison
RB: Tony Boles	Westland Glenn
RB: Eric Ball	Ypsilanti
RB: John Miller	Farmington Hills Harrison

DEFENSE	HIGH SCHOOL
E: Kevin Brooks	Detroit Mackenzie
E: Tim Ridinger	Hazel Park
T: John Ghindia	Trenton
T: Ron Zielinski	Sterling Heights Stevenson
NG: Mark Messner*	Redford Catholic Central
LB: Pat Shurmur	Dearborn Divine Child
LB: Kevin Egnatuk	East Lansing
LB: Pepper Johnson	Detroit Mackenzie
DB: Greg Washington	Detroit Western
DB: Dean Altobelli	Escanaba
DB: Andre Rison	Flint Northwestern
K: Mike Gillette	St. Joseph

Coach: John Herrington, Farmington Hills Harrison

Class A football team

OFFENSE	HIGH SCHOOL
E: John DeBoer	Grosse Pointe South
E: Keith Karpinski	Warren De La Salle
T: John Keenoy*	St. Johns
T: Jason Ridgeway	Detroit Chadsey
G: Bob Kula	Birmingham Brother Rice
G: Cornelius Simpson	Highland Park
C: Mike Battaglia	East Detroit
QB: Dave Yarema	Birmingham Brother Rice
RB: Aaron Roberts	Redford Catholic Central
RB: Torin Dorn	Southfield
RB: Aaron Bailey	Ann Arbor Pioneer

Captain

Class A football team

DEFENSE	HIGH SCHOOL
E: Jamal Al	Dearborn Fordson
E: Joe Holland	Birmingham Seaholm
T: Bryant Hill	East Lansing
T: Jim Szymanski	Sterling Heights Stevenson
NG: Mark Nichols	Birmingham Brother Rice
LB: Gary Rakan	Traverse City
LB: Marc Spencer	Birmingham Seaholm
LB: Brad Money	Midland
DB: Joel Blankenship	Detroit Murray-Wright
DB: Mike Kenealy	Royal Oak Kimball
DB: Paul Bobbitt*	Southfield-Lathrup
K: Mike Prindle	Grand Rapids Union

Class B football team

OFFENSE	HIGH SCHOOL
E: Ken Higgins	Battle Creek Lakeview
E: Derrick Alexander	Detroit Benedictine
T: Chris Baar	Grand Rapids West Catholic
T: Chris Trainor	Royal Oak Shrine
G: Mike Bruns	Frankenmuth
G: Brent Myers	Gr. Rapids Forest Hills Northern
C: Gary Shreve	Millington
QB: Terry Andrysiak	Allen Park Cabrini
RB: Steve Palmateer	Marysville
RB: Perry Foster	Grand Rapids Catholic Central
RB: Matt Morse*	Grand Rapids South Christian

DEFENSE	HIGH SCHOOL
E: Jim Scarcelli	Warren Woods
E: Joe Sklenar	Muskegon Catholic Central
T: John Wojciechowski	Warren Fitzgerald
T: Tom Spoelhof	Grand Rapids Kenowa Hills
NG: Dave Wolff	Southgate Aquinas
LB: Jim Morrissey	Flint Powers
LB: Scott Lamphere	North Branch
LB: Mike Reinhold	Muskegon Catholic Central
DB: Paul Agema	Wyoming Park
DB: Courtney Hawkins*	Flint Beecher
DB: Bobby Morse	Muskegon CC
K: Pete Stoyanovich	Dearborn Heights Crestwood

Captain

Class C football team

OFFENSE	HIGH SCHOOL
E: Steve Hatch	Saginaw St. Peter & Paul
E: Brian Oosterhouse	Middleville
T: Brian Williams	Haslett
T: Skip Confer	New Lothrop
G: Scott Kowalkowski	Orchard Lake St. Mary's
G: Hiram Jackson	Birmingham Detroit Country Day
C: Kevin Haverdink	Hamilton
QB: Ron Fillmore*	Sanford-Meridian
RB: Rodney Culver	Detroit DePorres
RB: Tony Jackson	Saginaw Nouvel
RB: Brian Stephens	Country Day

DEFENSE	HIGH SCHOOL
E: Tom O'Sullivan	Ann Arbor Richard
E: John Harry	Iron Mountain
T: DeMond Winston	Lansing Catholic Central
T: Mike Boyle	Redford St. Agatha
NG: Pat Lee	St. Ignace
LB: Joe Gray	Detroit Benedictine
LB: Joe Connolly	Traverse City St. Francis
LB: Bob Fata*	Lansing CC
DB: Tony McNichols	Parchment
DB: Gordie Sekerak	Allen Park Cabrini
DB: Derek Bowman	Erie Mason
K: Todd Winters	Muskegon CC

Class D football team

OFFENSE	HIGH SCHOOL
E: Triando Markray	Detroit DePorres
E: Jeff Crosby	Martin
T: Chuck Pellegrini	Norway
T: Bryan Cook	North Adams
G: Jason Derby	Sand Creek
G: Bill Ross	Crystal Falls
C: Todd Maki	Baraga
QB: Larry Hoskins	Schoolcraft
RB: Shawn Ampey	Gobles
RB: Tony Ceccacci*	Rudyard
RB: Eric George	Mendon

DEFENSE	HIGH SCHOOL
E: Scott Parsons	Frankfort
E: Steve Mills	Rudyard
T: Dick Wheeler	Crystal Falls
T: Rob Dahlin	Bessemer
NG: Todd Baker	Allendale
LB: Gary Guidos*	Flint Holy Rosary
LB: David Slade	Detroit Servite
LB: Todd Marlatt	Atlanta
DB: Rich Ledy	De Tour
DB: Trevor Martin	Frankfort
DB: Brian Johnson	Schoolcraft
K: Jeff Martin	Martin

Captain

BY THE NUMBERS

Football champions

YEAR	CLASS A	CLASS B	CLASS C	CLASS D
1980	Birmingham Brother Rice	Muskegon Catholic Central	Munising	Norway
1981	Escanaba	Farmington Hills Harrison	Elkton-Pigeon-Bay Port	Detroit St. Martin dePorres
1982	Farmington Hills Harrison	Muskegon Catholic Central	Detroit St. Martin dePorres	Mendon
1983	Birmingham Brother Rice	East Grand Rapids	Detroit St. Martin dePorres	St. Ignace LaSalle
1984	Ann Arbor Pioneer	Wyoming Park	Detroit St. Martin dePorres	Gobles
1985	Traverse City	Dearborn Divine Child	Lansing Catholic Central	Battle Creek St. Philip
1986	Muskegon	Marysville	Birmingham Detroit Country Day	Saginaw Michigan Lutheran
1987	Ann Arbor Pioneer	Gr. Rapids Catholic Central	Erie Mason	Martin
1988	Traverse City	Farmington Hills Harrison	Detroit St. Martin dePorres	Schoolcraft

Boys basketball champions

YEAR	CLASS A	CLASS B	CLASS C	CLASS D
1980	Lansing Eastern	Ypsilanti Willow Run	Reed City	Detroit East Catholic
1981	Flint Central	Okemos	Stephenson	Detroit East Catholic
1982	Flint Central	Okemos	Orchard Lake St. Mary's	Covert
1983	Flint Central	Corunna	Kalamazoo Christian	Detroit East Catholic
1984	Flint Northwestern	Oak Park	Hamilton	Powers-North Central
1985	Flint Northwestern	Flint Beecher	Detroit St. Martin dePorres	Allen Park Inter-City Baptist
1986	Romulus	Saginaw Buena Vista	Detroit St. Martin dePorres	Detroit East Catholic
1987	Detroit Cooley	Flint Beecher	Saginaw Nouvel	McBain Northern Mich. Christian
1988	Detroit Cooley	Grand Rapids South Christian	Saginaw Nouvel	Northport
1989	Detroit Cooley	Saginaw Buena Vista	Birmingham Detroit Country Day	Mio

Hal Schram Mr. Basketball Award winners: Sam Vincent, Lansing Eastern (1981); Robert Henderson, Lansing Eastern (1982); Antoine Joubert, Detroit Southwestern (1983); Demetreus Gore, Detroit Chadsey (1984); Glen Rice, Flint Northwestern (1985); Terry Mills, Romulus (1986); Mark Macon, Saginaw Buena Vista (1987); Matt Steigenga, Grand Rapids South Christian (1988); Michael Talley, Detroit Cooley (1989).

Worth noting: Chris Coles made the shot of the decade — a 54-footer at the buzzer in Saginaw Buena Vista's 33-32 victory over Flint Beecher for the 1986 Class B title. The two-handed push from just shy of midcourt was Coles' only shot of the half and only points of the game.

Girls basketball champions

YEAR	CLASS A	CLASS B	CLASS C	CLASS D
1980	Flint Northern	Flint Beecher	Battle Creek Pennfield	Leland
1981	Flint Northern	Okemos	Carrollton	Leland
1982	Farmington Hills Mercy	Manistee	Carrollton	Leland
1983	Flint Northwestern	Livonia Ladywood	Flint Hamady	De Tour
1984	Flint Northwestern	River Rouge	Newaygo	McBain
1985	Detroit King	Livonia Ladywood	Newaygo	Potterville
1986	Saginaw	Dearborn Divine Child	Wyandotte Mt. Carmel	Peck
1987	Detroit Cass Tech	Flint Beecher	Detroit St. Martin dePorres	Walkerville
1988	Birmingham Marian	Grand Rapids South Christian	St. Joseph Lake Michigan Catholic	Walkerville

Miss Basketball Award winners: Julie Polakowski, Leland (1982); Sue Tucker, Okemos (1983); Michele Kruty, Manistee (1984); Emily Wagner, Livonia Ladywood (1985); Franthea Price, River Rouge (1986); Daedra Charles, Detroit St. Martin dePorres (1987); Dena Head, Plymouth Salem (1988); Jennifer Shasky, Birmingham Marian (1989).

COLLEGE HOCKEY

Michigan State puts the finishing
touches in 1989 on its sixth CCHA
playoff title, all won at Joe Louis
Arena, "Munn East" to Spartans fans.

Despite a bumpy 11-7-1 start,
Michigan State finished No. 1 after
beating the Harvard Crimson.

Spartans' Heaven on Ice

By Joe Lapointe

MARCH 29,
1986
◆

W hat a long, strange trip this had been. Michigan State's hockey team, with seven freshmen, was in a rebuilding year. But after Christmas, the Spartans had lost only two games, and there they were in the NCAA tournament final against Harvard.

Coach Ron Mason admitted his team had been inconsistent and unpredictable all year but it also had been tenacious. And all three were true throughout the final game in Providence, R.I. The Spartans fell behind, 2-0, trailed two other times by two goals, but came back to tie the score in the third period.

And with 2:51 left, Mike Donnelly of Livonia, Mich., scored his second goal of the night and his 59th of the season, most in college hockey. It was 6-5, Spartans.

But even then there was stress. After Harvard pulled its goalie for an extra attacker in the last minute, it looked as if the Spartans had scored in the empty net to seal a 7-5 victory. But . . . no. The whistle had blown — unheard in the din of the MSU fans. The Spartans had been penalized for having too many men on the ice.

Harvard, for the last 18 seconds, would have a power play. And by pulling the goalie again, the Crimson would have two extra men in the MSU zone to storm the net after the face-off.

"I thought, 'Is it going to happen all over again?' " Doug Weaver, the MSU athletic director, would say. He was referring to the football season, disappointing at the end when the Spartans lost, 17-14, to Georgia Tech in the All American Bowl after thinking they had it clinched. He was referring to the basketball season, disappointing in the end when MSU lost to Kansas, 96-86 in overtime, in the NCAA tournament in part because of a malfunctioning scoreboard clock in Kansas City's Kemper Arena.

But this one would end with no such disappointment. Harvard got the puck and moved it near the crease. But MSU held tight and eventually cleared it away. As the seconds ticked down, the Spartans (34-9-2) threw their sticks into the crowd, their gloves in the air and hugged one another, rolling in twos and threes on the ice, laughing and shouting, celebrating the school's first major national title since the basketball crown in 1979 and the first hockey championship since 1966 (a 6-1 victory over Clarkston).

"It's like heaven," Mason said. "There were times in the game when Harvard had shut us down and I wasn't sure we could get back. . . . I thought after a while I'd be a Ray Meyer and I wouldn't be able to catch one of those championships."

Harvard led, 2-0, midway through the first period. The Crimson (25-8-1) also had two-goal leads at 3-1 and 4-2. But Donnelly cut the lead to 4-3 with a power-play goal off a rebound with 1:30 left in the second period. MSU tied the game when freshman Brad Hamilton scored on a slap shot at 1:06 of the third period. The Spartans took their first lead, 5-4, at 2:15 when Brian McReynolds put a wrist shot past the Crimson goalie. But Harvard's Andy Janfaza tied it, 5-5, with a wrist shot at 6:46.

A crisis developed during the first intermission when the Zamboni — the machine used to resurface the ice — broke down halfway through its work. It was replaced by a machine from nearby Providence College. The other Zamboni arrived after a 20-minute drive with a police escort.

As the machine came onto the ice, the fans cheered and the MSU band serenaded the driver with "I Get Around." But, as he left, the fans booed him for missing a narrow slice of the ice in front of one of the nets.

The game-winner came on a hard slap shot; Donnelly said a Harvard player touched the puck.

"I just banged at it," Donnelly said. "It was a lucky goal, but those things happen. I'll take it."

He also will take his award as the tournament's most valuable player.

"It's the best moment of my life," Donnelly said. "I still can't believe it. It hasn't sunk in yet. It's a great moment. We're No. 1 — finally." ◆

Ron Mason won the 1972 NAIA hockey championship with Lake Superior State. He moved on and kept winning — first at Bowling Green, then at Michigan State. He kept winning tournaments, regular-season titles, playoff titles — but never an NCAA title. His '82 and '83 MSU teams lost in the NCAA first round. His '84 team reached the Final Four as the No. 1 seed but lost in the semifinals to Bowling Green. His best team, the '85 squad that won an NCAA-record 38 games, lost in the first round when Providence goalie Chris Terreri made 50 saves. Would Mason ever get his title?

Lake Superior State, a two-time NAIA champion, struggled in NCAA hockey. But on Jan. 1, 1983, Frank Anzalone took over the team. Within two years he had a winner. Within six years he had the Lakers on the verge of a national title.

A SUPERIOR EFFORT

By Steve Crowe

When they gather in Sault Ste. Marie this summer to commemorate 20 years of hockey at Lake Superior State, the focus is likely to be more immediate, rather than the distant past.

The Lakers — who defeated St. Lawrence, 4-3, in overtime at Olympic Arena in Lake Placid, N.Y., in their first NCAA final — return home as the undisputed kings of college hockey, the little school that not only could, but did.

Even if it was at the expense of an even smaller school.

Lakers junior right wing Mark Vermette, a runner-up to Minnesota goalie Robb Stauber for the Hobey Baker Award, scored 4:46 into overtime, sliding the puck past Saints goalie Paul Cohen during a wild scramble in front of the net.

"I took the final whack at it," said Vermette, from Cochenour, Ontario. "I consider that pretty lucky. I just closed my eyes and it went in."

The title game, before a mostly hostile, standing-room-only crowd of 8,600, seemed almost as formidable as the semifinal, when the Lakers turned back top-ranked Maine, 6-3. In the title game, the Lakers (33-7-6) won despite being outnumbered in fan support by at least 30-to-1.

By the thousands, St. Lawrence fans made the winding, 1½-hour drive from Canton, N.Y., to cheer their Saints (29-9), informally known as the Larries in these parts.

The victory capped a six-year road to excellence paved by Lakers coach Frank Anzalone, 33, an intense Brooklyn, N.Y., native who may have finally halted comparisons with former Lakers coach Ron Mason, now at Michigan State. Mason led the Lakers to an NAIA championship in 1971-72, Lake Superior's first of two NAIA titles.

Freshman goalie Bruce Hoffort was superb in the first period, stopping 20 St. Lawrence shots as the Lakers took a 2-0 lead. Cohen made only six saves in the period and allowed goals by Lake Superior freshman right wing Tim Harris and sophomore defenseman Kord Cernich. Both came on slap shots: Harris scored at 5:46 after cutting in on Cohen and beating him cleanly to the stick side with a 20-footer. Cernich gave the Lakers a two-goal advantage at 16:48 on a shot just inside the blue line that Cohen got a pad on but could not keep from trickling into the net.

But the Saints started to march in the second period, outscoring Lake Superior, 3-1. Doug Murray tipped a shot past Hoffort at 1:57, and Russ Mann scored an unassisted wrap-around goal at 7:49. Cernich's second goal, at 12:19 on a power play, regained the lead, 3-2, for the Lakers in the second period. A Brian McColgan slap shot from the blue line with 2:36 left in the second found its way through a crowd, beating Hoffort to his glove side for a 3-3 tie.

With 6:30 left in the third period, Hoffort robbed Saints right wing Pete Buckeridge with a glove save from point-blank range on a shot that appeared headed for the upper corner, probably the best scoring chance of the period. With 1:23 left and the Saints swarming around Hoffort, Lakers sophomore left wing Pete Stauber — Robb's brother — pushed the net off its magnets with nobody within 10 feet of him, clearly intending to stop play. No penalty was called.

Hoffort, who made 49 saves, was named tournament MVP and, along with right wing Mike de Carle and defenseman Cernich, made the all-tournament team.

It was an amazing journey for Hoffort, who began the season hoping to make the team as a backup. "I wasn't impressing anybody in camp," he said. "Not even myself. And now to win a national championship. . . . It's amazing."

After the victory, about 200 Lakers fans attended a reception for the champions. In Sault Ste. Marie, Mich., citizens were honking horns and generally making merry until the wee hours. The entire experience, de Carle said, was draining.

"But once I get that ring on my finger, it'll probably finally hit me," de Carle said. "I'm going to just keep looking at it, and it's going to keep ringing bells." ♦

Once the small-school champion of college hockey, Lake Superior State suddenly ruled over the NCAA's big boys. The Lakers did the same in the CCHA, winning the regular-season championship by 10 points, widest margin in league history.

Ronald Reagan gave the presidential seal of approval to Lake Superior State after the Lakers beat Harvard for the 1988 NCAA championship.

BY THE NUMBERS

College hockey

YEAR	CCHA SEASON	CCHA PLAYOFFS	CCHA PLAYER OF YEAR	WCHA SEASON	WCHA PLAYOFFS
1980	Northern Michigan	Northern Michigan	Steve Weeks, Northern Michigan	North Dakota	Minn., North Dakota
1981	Northern Michigan	Northern Michigan	Jeff Pyle, Northern Michigan	Minnesota	Michigan Tech, Minn.
1982	Bowling Green	Michigan State	George McPhee, Bowling Green	North Dakota	Wisconsin
1983	Bowling Green	Michigan State	Brian Hills, Bowling Green	Minnesota	Wisconsin
1984	Bowling Green	Michigan State	Paul Pooley, Ohio State	Minnesota-Duluth	Minnesota-Duluth
1985	Michigan State	Michigan State	Ray Staszak, Illinois-Chicago	Minnesota-Duluth	Minnesota-Duluth
1986	Michigan State	Western Michigan	Dan Dorion, Western Michigan	Denver	Denver
1987	Bowling Green	Michigan State	Wayne Gagne, Western Michigan	North Dakota	North Dakota
1988	Lake Superior State	Bowling Green	Mark Vermette, Lake Superior State	Minnesota	Wisconsin
1989	Michigan State	Michigan State	Bruce Hoffort, Lake Superior State	Minnesota	Northern Michigan

CCHA denotes Central Collegiate Hockey Association
WCHA denotes Western Collegiate Hockey Association

NCAA tournament appearances

Lake Superior State: 1985: Lost to Rensselaer Polytechnic Institute, 10-6, in total goals. 1988: Beat Merrimack, 8-4, in total goals; beat Maine, 6-3; beat St. Lawrence, 4-3 (OT) (NCAA championship game). 1989: Beat St. Cloud State, 2 games to 0; lost to Harvard, 2 games to 0.

Michigan State: 1982: Lost to New Hampshire, 9-4, in total goals. 1983: Lost to Harvard, 9-8, in total goals. 1984: Beat Boston College, 13-8, in total goals; lost to Bowling Green, 2-1; lost to North Dakota, 6-5 (OT) (consolation). 1985: Lost to Providence, 6-5, in total goals. 1986: Beat Boston College, 10-6, in total goals; beat Minnesota, 6-4; beat Harvard, 6-5 (NCAA championship game). 1987: Beat Maine, 11-5, in total goals; beat Minnesota, 5-3; lost to North Dakota, 5-3 (NCAA championship game). 1988: Beat Harvard, 11-8, in total goals; lost to Minnesota, 8-5, in total goals. 1989: Beat Boston College, 2 games to 1; lost to Harvard, 6-3; beat Maine, 7-4 (consolation).

Michigan Tech: 1981: Beat Providence, 13-8, in total goals; lost to Minnesota, 7-2; beat Northern Michigan, 5-2 (consolation).

Northern Michigan: 1980: Beat Minnesota, 4-3; beat Cornell, 5-4; lost to North Dakota, 5-2 (NCAA championship game). 1981: Beat Cornell, 10-7, in total goals; lost to Wisconsin, 5-1; lost to Michigan Tech, 5-2 (consolation). 1989: Lost to Providence, 2 games to 1.

Western Michigan: 1986: Lost to Harvard, 11-4, in total goals.

Worth noting: Michigan Tech's Damian Rhodes, according to the best available research, became the first collegiate goaltender to score, Jan. 22, 1989, at Colorado College. A shot tipped Rhodes' glove, bounced off the glass behind the net and to a Colorado player, who fired the puck the length of the ice into an empty net. Being the last Huskie to touch the puck, Rhodes was credited with the goal, at 19:51.

PRO HOCKEY

The Red Wings' ninth coach of the '80s, Jacques Demers finally turned the team around. He was voted NHL coach of the year in 1987 and 1988.

GORDIE'S CURTAIN CALL

By Joe Lapointe

FEB. 5,
1980

◆

Gordie Howe, it seemed, would go on forever. He played 25 years with the Red Wings before retiring. Then he joined the World Hockey Association, playing with sons Mark and Marty. When the leagues merged for the 1979-80 season, Howe was back in the NHL. And possibly the most memorable night of Howe's 26th — and final — NHL campaign came in the All-Star Game in his old hometown.

For two minutes and 35 seconds, his old fans cheered and chanted the name of the best 51-year-old hockey player in the world for all the memories he brought back with him to a town he had called home for 25 years.

If not the best, Gordie Howe was certainly the guest of honor for the NHL All-Star Game at Joe Louis Arena. Somebody asked him whether there were tears in his eyes when he was introduced to a standing ovation.

He answered without missing a blink.

"What ovation?" he asked, before telling it like it was. "Yeah, they were getting close. It was getting to me pretty good. It was beautiful, but awkward."

So he skated over to the bench, where Red Wings trainer Lefty Wilson was helping with the Prince of Wales team. "I said, 'Lefty, help me,'" Howe said. "And Lefty said something you can't print."

And then Gordie Howe laughed, and everyone laughed with him.

Howe didn't score as his team beat the Campbell Conference team, 6-3, but had an assist, and he put three shots on net and a couple of others just wide. And, as happens whenever the former Red Wing returns home, the 21,002 fans chanted "Gordie, Gordie." The crowd in the Wings' new home (two months after leaving Olympia) set an All-Star

Game record.

Howe's first shot was his best, a slap from between the face-off circles, right in front of goalie Tony Esposito. It hit Esposito on his sore left hand, forcing him to leave the game.

"I wish I'd had less time to think about it," Howe said. "You might not believe this, but that shot was meant for the lower right-hand corner."

Later, he took a quick wrist shot that was kicked away by Philadelphia rookie goalie Pete Peeters. Another wrist shot went wide, and late in the game he was set up in the clear but stopped by Peeters. Moments later, Howe's pass set up a goal by Real Cloutier, and Howe was on the All-Star score sheet — perhaps for the final time in his career.

The game was tied, 2-2, after two periods. The Campbell Conference took a 3-2 lead on a goal by Brian Propp, another Flyers rookie, 4:14 into the third. That's when the Wales Conference went to work, scoring four straight goals by Ron Stackhouse, Craig Hartsburg, Wings defenseman Reed Larson and Cloutier.

Howe's return to the NHL for a 32nd major league season hasn't gone as well as he had hoped. He has 11 goals with the Hartford Whalers, but he hasn't scored for two months. Lately, he has spent considerable time on the bench.

"It could very possibly be my last one," he said. "I know damn well I can't go forever. But I'll be sly about it. I'll tell my family first." ◆

Gordie Howe stole the show at the All-Star Game. Howe, after a 15-goal, 26-assist effort, finally retired after the 1979-80 season. Even at 51, he played in all 80 games. He also took time out to play in an old-timers game at Olympia Feb. 22, scoring the final goal in the building's history. Howe finished his 26-year NHL career with 801 goals, 1,049 assists and 1,850 points. He had 174 goals, 334 assists and 508 points in six WHA seasons.

Two Michiganders — Ken Morrow of Davison and Mark Wells of St. Clair Shores — shared a golden moment at the 1980 Winter Olympics, part of the U.S. hockey team's Miracle on Ice. For Morrow, it was a stepping-stone to an illustrious NHL career, which he began less than a week after the Olympics. And, playing for the Islanders, he finished his Olympic year with his name on the Stanley Cup.

GOLDEN OPPORTUNITY

By Bill McGraw

A s rookie debuts go, this one was different. But then, this one was solid gold.

Ken Morrow, a shy 23-year-old defenseman from Davison, Mich., skated for the New York Islanders in his first NHL game to rounds of applause and tons of publicity in Uniondale, N.Y. He was even interviewed on regional television.

And the fact that the Red Wings were the opponents meant something to Morrow, who once played at Olympia for the Junior Wings. "It was," he said, "a little special." But Morrow took a penalty that led to the Wings' first goal. And Detroit ended up beating the Islanders, 4-3.

"It distracts you a lot, all this stuff that goes on," Morrow said. "It's been nuts, it really has. My wife and I tried to sneak away at her parents' house. But it ended up we were getting calls all through the day. I'm really happy but I haven't had time to relax."

A week ago Sunday, the 6-foot-4 Morrow and his USA teammates became the toast of the nation after they won the gold medal in the Winter Olympics at Lake Placid, N.Y. There was the White House on Monday, Lansing on Thursday, New York on Friday and a multi-year contract in between.

Before he even touched the puck, 14,995 fans in the Nassau Coliseum applauded Morrow. After play finally started, "I really can't even tell you what happened because I was in a daze out there," Morrow said. "But it was great to just step on the ice. Great feeling." Then he was whistled off for tripping Wings center Paul Woods. Nine seconds later, Detroit had its first goal. "I didn't think it was a penalty," Morrow said, clutching a photo showing his stick in front of Woods' legs.

He arrived at the rink more than three hours before game time. He had called his wife, Barb, and his mother, Loretta, the night before because he had trouble sleeping in his Long Island hotel. "It just settled me down, hearing her voice," Morrow said of his mother.

Morrow said the main difference between the NHL and Olympic play was that "guys up here have more poise . . . the little things are perfected here."

Morrow gets the key to New York City next week along with his Olympic pals. More solid gold memories. ◆

Ken Morrow, in his first game after the Miracle on Ice, went to the penalty box for tripping Red Wings center Paul Woods. Morrow disputed the call.

BON VOYAGE, BRUCE

By George Puscas

The Norris family owned the Red Wings for 50 years, through good times and bad. But they were mostly bad after Bruce Norris took over the Stanley Cup champions in 1955. He put the team, badly in disrepair, up for sale in March 1982. It would be purchased in June by Detroit native Mike Ilitch, the Little Caesars pizza magnate and a former Tigers farmhand. Ilitch, a long-time Wings fan, promised that the proud franchise would see better days soon.

Well, we won't have Bruce Norris to kick around anymore, either. Doggone it. He was such an inviting target, and he deserved every last boot anybody could lay on him.

His announced intention to sell the Red Wings should be greeted as a sign of hope for the future, if only because there appeared no hope so long as he remained in control, stumbling from one ill-conceived move to another.

It is not the easiest thing to take one of the finest franchises in sports history and run it so deeply into the ground nobody can find a way out. But Norris managed.

He once opened a travel bureau, and cynics said he needed it for all the people he was

shipping out of town — the good with the bad. You cannot say Bruce didn't try, but whatever he tried backfired so badly the Red Wings disintegrated almost beyond repair.

Ultimately, in professional sports, a team reflects its owner and management. When Bruce Norris took over the Wings from his sister, Marguerite, in 1955, the Stanley Cup was resting in their showcase for the fourth time in six seasons. They have not been near it since, nor have they been farther away than they are now as they fall away from the playoffs for the 10th time in 11 years.

When the Red Wings moved into Joe Louis Arena a few years ago, Lincoln Cavalieri, Norris' business smoothie, put the club up for sale for the boss. The price was $20 million. But it was a slicker's deal, investors soon recognized.

Norris, as operator of the arena, would continue to take 15 percent out of every Red Wings ticket as stadium rental. The new owner would be saddled with rent and the expense of restoring the team, while Norris would thrive as landlord. He couldn't find such a sucker. Nor will he this time, unless he prices the team realistically.

This once was a proud and profitable hockey port, made so by Bruce's late father, James Norris. The Wings play in a division named after the founder. But now the game is booming in cities that never saw it played when the Red Wings were the ultimate — and the Wings are now considered a joke.

The Norris family recently celebrated its 50th anniversary of Red Wings ownership. Bruce was on hand, and when he was announced to the crowd, he was booed vehemently. Maybe that convinced him to give it all up and let somebody else try. It's a wonderful idea; it is probably the best move he ever made for the team. ◆

Mike Ilitch and his clan became Detroit's first family of hockey. "I've always had the ambition of owning a major league franchise," Ilitch said at the June 3 press conference announcing the sale. "It's a dream I had as a young boy." Bruce Norris did not attend the press conference to offer final thoughts. He died in 1985.

In 1983, the Red Wings drafted one of the world's best junior players — but not until the fifth round. His name was Petr Klima, and he played behind the Iron Curtain. The next year he scored 23 goals and 22 assists in 35 games with the Czechoslovak army team. He wanted to score his next goal in the NHL.

COMING TO AMERICA

By Joe Lapointe

At 2:30 p.m., a sporting goods shop employee arrived at the Red Wings' camp in Port Huron, Mich., with a special order: a white hockey jersey with red letters and numerals that read, "KLIMA 85."

Less than three hours later, Petr Klima arrived at Metro Airport on a flight from New York. More than a month after defecting from Czechoslovakia, Klima, 20, had become a member of the Red Wings. "I'm very happy to be in Detroit and in the United States," Klima said through an interpreter. "I want to play for the NHL because it is one of the best leagues in the world."

Klima chose No. 85 because it represented the year he gained his freedom. He had been in West Germany since defecting while his national team was training in Rosenheim, Bavaria. "The hearts were beating," said Nick Polano, the Wings assistant general manager, dispatched to Europe to court and deliver Klima. Polano and Klima moved to five West German cities — changing hotels, keeping a low profile. "Petr thought that as soon as he got out he would be in the U.S. right away, and it didn't turn out that way,"

Petr Klima, who could skate with the best of them, learned to shop with the best of them, too. He scored 32 goals as a rookie, including one in his debut against Minnesota. At times brilliant on the ice (he never scored fewer than 25 goals his first four seasons), Klima often struggled mightily off the ice. He canceled a midseason wedding at the last minute. He frequently visited the coach Jacques Demers' doghouse. And he served jail time for drunken driving and probation transgressions.

Polano said. "We both had to keep each others' spirits up."

Once, there was a scare. Klima rented a Mercedes 500 and crashed it on the autobahn, the German expressway. "The car was totaled," Polano said. "Petr thought it was funny." Finally, after they got permission to leave, Klima played a practical joke on his guardian. As they walked to the plane in Frankfurt, Klima stopped dead in his tracks, looked Polano in the eye, shook his head from side to side and waved his hands back and forth as if to say, "No go." Then he started to walk away. "He was just joking," Polano said. "I grabbed him by the arm and said, 'Come on, Petr.'"

Klima arrived in Detroit with only a small bag of clothes and three tennis rackets. His girlfriend, who also defected, is expected to join him later this season. Klima smiled frequently when greeted by Wings owner Mike Ilitch, who operates the Little Caesars pizza chain. Klima said he had never eaten American pizza nor does he know much about Gordie Howe, the former Wing many consider the greatest player of all time.

He'll learn. ◆

LATER, BIG RED BARN

By Neal Shine

JULY 9,
1986
◆

Elvis Presley sang there. So did the Beatles. There were other sports played in the Olympia, but most of all hockey. Gordie Howe and Co. made the Red Barn the Stanley Cup's second home during the Red Wings' glory years in the '50s. But in December 1979 the Wings moved to new Joe Louis Arena in downtown Detroit, and the Olympia stood empty — save for its memories — until a fateful summer day.

In the middle of the morning, right after the rain stopped, Ray Messer moved the machine they call the LS 3400 in close to the building and knocked a hole in the wall. Standing on what used to be Hooker Street, you could now look inside and see the Red Wings' dressing room, jersey numbers inked on squares of adhesive tape still stuck to the inside wall. Richard Peake, the project manager for Cuyahoga Wrecking, went off to talk to the guy from the city who was worried about how much of Grand River would have to be barricaded and for how long.

It was the final indignity. Whatever the old place had been in its nearly 60 years, Olympia Stadium was going to spend its last days as a traffic problem. With the detachment of a gravedigger, Peake explained how it was going to be done.

"No explosives," he said, "and no ball. We'll clear the area around the beams and then reach in and pull it down. This won't be a complicated job. Eighty feet high on one end, about 95 on the other. About five million cubic feet. But it's mostly walls, not much inside. If anything complicates it, it's that it's close to the street. We've got 90 days to take it to grade. Shouldn't be a problem."

It was, after all, just bricks. Somebody put them up, and it was inevitable that some day, somebody was going to have to pull them down.

Jim Martin of Westland, Mich., looking as formidable as he did when he played for the Lions in the 1950s, is the site supervisor on the job. He is less clinical than his colleagues about presiding over the dismantling of a half-century of Detroit history. "This place is as close to me as it is to most people in this town," he said. "I played some hockey here, a benefit game with Gordie Howe and some other athletes. There was a lot of life here, a lot of excitement. Now all that's left are the memories. It's all pretty depressing."

All morning, people showed up at

the lot next to the building. Some wore Wings caps and T-shirts. Some took pictures. Most left carrying bricks or chunks of masonry.

A few yards away, Messer's machine pulled at the red brick wall near the spot somebody had chalked a farewell to Olympia Stadium. It read: "Later, Big Red Barn." ◆

Olympia opened Oct. 17, 1927, with a rodeo; hockey debuted Nov. 22, 1927, when Ottawa beat the Cougars, 2-1.

1987

♦

The Red Wings made the playoffs the second and third years of the Mike Ilitch era. But after they couldn't get past the first round, coach Nick Polano was bumped upstairs. Disaster followed. The Wings fired two coaches — Harry Neale and Brad Park — and finished with a club-worst 40 points in 1985-86. Then they swiped St. Louis' coach, who produced one of the most incredible turnarounds in hockey history.

BACK FROM THE DEAD

By Mitch Albom

The fans were going insane, the players were slapping each other in celebration and even coach Jacques Demers, dressed in his lucky wedding suit, walked out across the ice, raised a fist, and suddenly leapt toward the heavens. Why not? That's where these magic words seemed to be coming from:

The Red Wings are going to the semifinals.

Amazing. The Red Wings? Hockey's little engine that could? The semifinals? This was the worst team in the league last season? This was the joke, the embarrassment, the reason fans around Detroit considered putting bags over their heads, or moving?

This is the team. And this is not the team. These players carry the logo, they carry the uniforms — they do not carry the memories, or the fate, or the weight of failure.

"How far are you now from your lowest point last year?" someone asked center Steve Yzerman, drenched in champagne after the Wings' 3-0 seventh-game victory over Toronto. "It seems like centuries apart," he said, beaming. "I've never won a Stanley Cup, but if the feeling is any better than this, I can't wait!"

Stanley Cup? Dare they talk about that? Well, why not? They have a fresh taste now, these Detroit players, a clean plate. They have an intensity that will not be crushed by odds. They've been pushed now to a Game 7 and they've come out winners.

This morning they have eight playoff victories. And eight'll get you a shot at 16.

"Have you ever heard a cheer that loud?" someone asked right wing Joe Kocur about the final-buzzer explosion from the Joe Louis crowd. "Never," he said, his young eyes bulging. "It was heaven out there." Heaven? Well, hockey-wise, perhaps. What happened at this arena was not merely a victory, it was a refusal to lose. This was a whale of a series, a series the Wings had trailed, 3-1, a long time ago. But they threw the thing on their backs and lugged it back and forth across the Canadian border, and, in the biggest of the big games, Game 7, they simply refused to put it down. Not for a moment.

Here was Adam Oates, circling behind the net and spinning and shooting and getting his rebound and, score! 1-0. Here was Steve Yzerman, goalless in this series, breaking away and . . . score! 2-0. Here was Darren Veitch taking a pass from Oates and slapping that puck as if all the frustrations of hockey in this city were unloosed in one mighty swipe and . . . score! 3-0. And here was goalie Glen Hanlon, called upon as a mid-series replacement, whacking and smacking and flicking away everything, finishing a masterful series in which he would not allow a goal in this country. Not a single goal? Two shutouts?

"I am so proud of these players," Demers said, his eyes watering from a cold and the emotion. "They had plenty of chances to quit. People would have said, 'Hey, you swept Chicago. That was good enough.' But they wouldn't accept that."

All right. Some perspective. True, this was not like beating the Oilers, Detroit's foe in the next best-of-seven series. No doubt outsiders will look at Detroit this morning and say, "Boy, are those people desperate for a party." But remember the failure that has been hockey around here in recent years, the red faces, the "Dead Wings" jokes, the revolving door of coaches and players. It was as if a filmy residue had dried on this franchise. Forget that now. With the final buzzer, these players have brought a cleansing rinse that leaves them fresh and new and ready to establish their own tradition in this town.

"Tell us about that leap!" someone yelled at Demers. "I was . . . I . . . I'm so happy," he said, choking up. "I was . . . you know . . ." Ah, forget the words, Jacques. Go ahead and leap, leap all the way to the sky. Stay up there for a moment with the echoes of words not heard for too, too long. . . .

The Red Wings are going to the semifinals. Amazing. ♦

Jacques Demers pointed the way back from a 3-1 deficit — a deficit only three other teams had overcome. Sweeter still was that the comeback stunned the Maple Leafs, whose coach carried on a season-long feud with Demers. The coach, John Brophy, had flashed a choke sign at Demers after Toronto shut out the Wings.

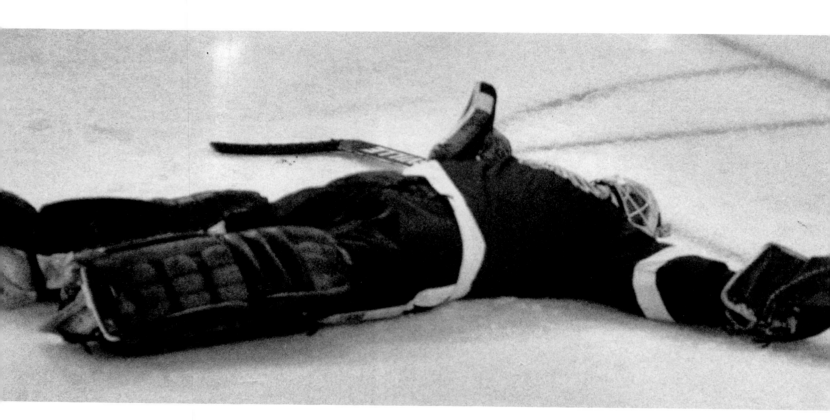

In the biggest game of the season, the Red Wings played two of their worst periods of hockey. They trailed, 6-2, entering the third. But they scored two quick goals. The Oilers were in chaos – until Mike Krushelnyski left goalie Greg Stefan and the Wings for dead with Edmonton's seventh goal.

THE BITTER END

By Mitch Albom

MAY 11,
1988

◆

The challenge was tough enough already. The Red Wings had to beat Wayne Gretzky's Oilers or lose to Edmonton in the Campbell Conference finals for the second straight season. But on the eve of Game 5, the challenge became all but impossible. Six Wings — including Bob Probert and Petr Klima — had been caught drinking after curfew at an Edmonton nightclub, Goose Loonies. A seventh player — Steve Chiasson — later would admit he was out, too.

Long before the puck was dropped, before the Detroit hockey season saw its sad and bitter conclusion with that final 8-4 loss to Edmonton, there was a crack in the heart of this Red Wings team. It may take a long, long time to mend.

We are talking about an incident that left half the team angry and its coach almost numb with disbelief. It is not a story you want to read, not this morning, when we should be paying tribute to the Wings' fine effort all year.

On the night before the biggest game of their season, seven Red Wings players went out drinking. They stayed out well past curfew — a curfew that wasn't being checked because, as coach Jacques Demers would say: "We never ever thought we'd need to enforce curfew when our team reached the final four of hockey."

And one of the culprits was Bob Probert.

This will break your heart. It already has broken Demers.' Probert has been battling alcoholism for years. It has tackled him, trashed him, landed him in jail. Yet recently, with the help of medication, he seemed to have it under control. He was playing his best hockey of the year and was Detroit's top performer against Edmonton.

Yet there he was, less than 24 hours before Game 5 of the Campbell Conference finals, at an Edmonton nightclub called Goose Loonies. He came with Petr Klima (who was out of the lineup because of a broken thumb). By all accounts, Klima encouraged Probert to go out.

"My God, Petr Klima could be ready to play if we reach the finals," Demers said, his face red with anger and disappointment. "If he keeps the big guy eating ice cream, he might get a chance at it. Instead they do this . . ."

He sighed. He looked like he was going to weep. He talked about how Probert and Darren Veitch returned to the hotel drunk, after an assistant coach found them at the bar. John Chabot, Joe Kocur and Darren Eliot also were caught.

"Klima and Bobby could have spent the most wonderful summer of their lives this summer," Demers said. "People thought so much of them. The way they played this year. All the adulation. Now, they'll hear about this instead. For one night. One night. It's not worth it. . . . It's just not worth it."

In Game 5, Probert looked awful on the ice. He was sluggish. The fire from the earlier games was gone. What happened? Was it the night before? Was it the knowledge that he had let his coach down? "It definitely had an effect on our whole team," said a weary Demers. "We came out flat in the first period. There was a loss of respect going on."

No doubt some teams make a practice of drinking the night before games. Fine. But the Wings had rules, an agreement among themselves that they would do whatever it took to be at their very best against Edmonton. "It put a black cloud over what we accomplished," said Steve Yzerman, the captain.

This Detroit team played gallantly all year, and it should be coming home knowing that everyone gave his best to the end. Instead, the Wings lost the game, they lost the playoff series — and a handful of them lost something more important. They lost trust. They lost spirit. They broke their coach's heart, and there's no excusing that. ◆

STEVIE WONDER

By Keith Gave

OCT. 6,
1988
◆

He wasn't the hometown boy the Red Wings really coveted. They didn't have a high enough draft choice in 1983 to take Pat LaFontaine of Waterford Township, Mich. But Steve Yzerman, who grew up in Nepean, Ontario, became the team's heart, soul and captain.

He is the winged wheel personified, an all-Canadian kid Detroiters have adopted as their own. He is the most famous hockey player in Detroit since Gordie Howe. If he does everything expected of him, his No. 19 will be raised to the rafters at Joe Louis Arena next to Howe's No. 9.

Red Wings captain Steve Yzerman is growing up before our very eyes. "I'm getting there, I guess," he said, stifling a laugh, "slowly but surely."

Surely, if not so slowly, Yzerman has reached a stature few athletes achieve. He is the one player immediately identified with the Wings, just as Isiah Thomas is with the Pistons. General manager Jimmy Devellano calls him "a pure Red Wing" because he was drafted, developed and reached stardom in the organization. And he likely will remain with the Wings as long as he can play.

"Nothing would thrill me more than to have Steve Yzerman finish a 15-year career in Detroit," Devellano said. "It's pure. It signifies something special in sports. I know it's the way Jack Adams used to feel about Gordie Howe. He's like a son. I feel a little sad when I think of Gordie Howe in Houston and Hartford."

Yzerman feels the same way.

"I'd like to stay in Detroit my entire career," he said. "I don't know what's going to happen, whether they want me or not, but I know I don't want to go anywhere else. It's very rare, I know, but when you look at a lot of the greats in sports, they all played in one city . . . like Beliveau and Richard in Montreal. I think you lose a little something when you move. You can always move for more money, but I don't believe in that. You see it a lot in baseball, which is why I admire Alan Trammell. He could go a lot of other places and take the money, but he doesn't."

Before the 1986-87 season, at 21, Yzerman became the club's youngest captain, which coach Jacques Demers still considers the best decision he has made since coming to Detroit. At the time, Yzerman was coming off his most disappointing season. He scored only 14 goals and 42 points in 51 games before a broken collarbone ended his year. "I remember a very confused and angry young man," Demers said. "I told him, 'You have another season like that, I'm going to box your ears.' "

The son of a high-ranking official with the Canadian social services department, Yzerman is the third of five children in a family of scholars. Yet he jokes about his own lack of education and dreads thinking of what his life would be were it not for hockey.

"I'd probably be finishing high school," he said, laughing. "I'm not sure, really. I'd probably still be in university, or just graduated. I know it's not good advice to kids, but all I ever thought about was playing hockey. I did what I had to do, nothing else."

And he succeeded. So how has fame and fortune affected him? "Well, fortune hasn't affected me a whole lot, because I don't have one yet," he said. "But I'm working on that."

As for the fame: "It was nice just being a hockey player before, with people knowing who you are. Now, I still enjoy it, but I'm a little more reserved. I like to stay to myself. I'm a little more private. When I was a kid, I used to think that hockey players were like God or something. I thought it would be great to be a hero like that. Then, I got there and it's no big deal. It's really no different than playing midget or pee wee. It's still just playing the game. It's not for the bonuses. It's just winning." ◆

Steve Yzerman was always ahead of his time. As an 18-year-old, he became the youngest player in All-Star Game history. As a 21-year-old, he got a "C" for his jersey, making him the youngest captain in team history. As a 23-year-old, he broke the club record for goals (65), assists (90) and points (155) in a season. After six seasons, only Los Angeles' Wayne Gretzky and Pittsburgh's Mario Lemieux were considered his equals in the NHL.

It wasn't supposed to be like this. The Red Wings and their fans had great expectations for 1988-89. But the Wings' Stanley Cup quest never really got off the ground. Bob Probert was arrested at the border with cocaine. Petr Klima spent time in jail. Joe Kocur ran into trouble with the law. The Wings did win their second straight Norris Division title — but with a .500 record. And then came a first-round playoff series best forgotten . . .

Wayne Presley's Game 6 hat trick polished off his hometown team.

THE SEASON AFTER

By Mitch Albom

The Red Wings died slowly, inevitably, to the delight of the howling crowd. The fog horn that is the signature of rickety Chicago Stadium blew strong and loud after every Blackhawks goal and finally, at 11:29 p.m., it sounded the good-bye moan, almost mercifully, for this most difficult season.

"What day is it, April 15 or something?" captain Steve Yzerman would sigh after the Wings lost, 7-1, surrendering this first-round playoff series in six games. "Last year we were still playing on May 15. I don't think we're going to realize what happened here for a few days."

When they do, they will not forget it. It was sad, and perhaps an unavoidable end to a season that was star-crossed from Day 1. Sure, the Bob Probert and Petr Klima problems had been wrapped up by the playoffs; Probert was gone because of cocaine charges and Klima was back after serving his jail time on drunken-driving charges. But the unhappiness of the regular season — "There were times when you really didn't feel like coming down to the arena," admitted goalie Greg Stefan — had slowed the Wings like a sore hamstring, and they were trying to run anyway.

And the snapshots of defeat were all over the place. Here was Steve Chiasson flat on the ice, injured, after a vicious check to the boards. Here was Yzerman giving his stick to Gilbert Delorme, who had broken his, and trying to play naked, slapping the puck away with his hand, only to see Chicago come back moments later and score anyhow. Here was Steve Larmer flipping a goal between Stefan's legs — 2-1 Chicago — and then, 26 seconds later, Wayne Presley, who grew up in the Detroit suburbs, for Pete's sake, backhanding the puck past Stefan, 3-1. Before the night was over, Presley would score a hat trick, and the Wings would be buried in black hats, flying onto the ice like bullets. "It's going to be a long summer," Stefan said, "and not very much fun."

In a way, this is a stunning upset — the full effect may not be realized for days, maybe weeks. Yet in other ways, you could almost feel it coming. Wasn't this a dark-side season from the start for the Wings? Didn't you hear whispers and mumbles all winter? "I don't know about them. . . . They're not the same. . . . All that off-ice controversy. . . . "

"Are you surprised with this defeat?" coach Jacques Demers was asked.

"No," he said. "Disappointed, yes. Surprised, no. We never had the right chemistry, not from the very start. This was a team that was never at peace with itself."

What will come of all this? Changes, for sure. "Certain players will be traded," Demers admitted. "Certain guys have gotten complacent here in Detroit. It's a great place to work. We need to open training camp on a different note with some different people."

That about says it all for this season of our discontent, a tumble off the rainbow for this team that began, really, with a drinking incident last May in Edmonton and ended with that deathly horn in Chicago. In between have been disillusion, disfavor, discord and disgust. Good players were ignored, bad players were overplayed, and it seemed the lights were always glaring on this team. The Wings could never escape their shadows. And in the end, that was all they had left to look at as the time ran out on the Chicago Stadium scoreboard. Three. Two. One. And here came that sound, no doubts, no questions. We go home now. That fog horn means someone else's ship has just come in. ♦

Coach Jacques Demers had been worried about this team long before the playoffs. He tried to give the appropriate pep talks. He rallied the team before the final period of Game 5: "You don't want to go home and play golf now. Nobody in Detroit will want to talk to you anyhow." It worked. Nothing worked in Game 6.

Nothing says Detroit hockey quite like the octopus. Fans threw the slimy mollusk onto the ice frequently during the late '80s. The octopus made its debut in the '52 playoffs, when its eight tentacles symbolized the victories needed to win a Stanley Cup.

By THE NUMBERS

Detroit Red Wings (NHL)

YEAR	W-L-T	PTS	FINISH	GOALS	ASSISTS	POINTS	PENALTY	GOALIE
1980	26-43-11	63	5th, 44 PB Montreal	Foligno (36)	McCourt (51)	McCourt (81)	Huber (164)	Vachon (3.61)
1981	19-43-18	56	5th, 47 PB Montreal	Ogrodnick (35)	McCourt (56)	McCourt (86)	Korn (246)	Gilbert (4.01)
1982	21-47-12	54	6th, 40 PB Minnesota	Ogrodnick (28)	Osborne (41)	Osborne (67)	Larson (112)	Sauve (4.19)
1983	21-44-15	57	5th, 47 PB Chicago	Ogrodnick (41)	Larson (52)	Ogrodnick (85)	Gare (107)	Micalef (3.62)
1984	31-42-7	69	3rd, 19 PB Minnesota	Ogrodnick (42)	Park (53)	Yzerman (87)	Paterson (148)	Stefan (3.51)
1985	27-41-12	66	3rd, 20 PB St. Louis	Ogrodnick (55)	Yzerman (59)	Ogrodnick (105)	Gare (163)	Stefan (4.33)
1986	17-57-6	40	5th, 46 PB Chicago	Ogrodnick (38)	Kisio (48)	Ogrodnick (70)**	Kocur (377)*	Stefan (4.50)
1987	34-36-10	78	2nd, 1 PB St. Louis	Gallant (38)***	Yzerman (59)	Yzerman (90)	Kocur (276)	Hanlon (3.18)
1988	41-28-11	93	1st, 17 PA St. Louis	Yzerman (50)	Yzerman (52)	Yzerman (102)	Probert (398)*	Stefan (3.11)
1989	34-34-12	80	1st, 2 PA St. Louis	Yzerman (65)	Yzerman (90)	Yzerman (155)	Gallant (230)	Hanlon (3.56)

PB denotes points behind; PA denotes points ahead.
* Led the NHL
** Doug Shedden had 71 points but split the season with Pittsburgh and Detroit.
*** Brent Ashton had 40 goals but split the season with Quebec and Detroit.

Coaches: Bobby Kromm (1979-80), 24-36-11; Marcel Pronovost (1980), 2-7-0; Ted Lindsay (1981), 3-14-3; Wayne Maxner (1981-82), 34-68-27; Billy Dea (1982), 3-8-0; Nick Polano (1983-85), 79-127-34; Harry Neale (1986), 8-23-4; Brad Park (1986), 9-34-2; Jacques Demers (1987-89), 109-98-33. Total: 271-415-114 (.410).

Post-season: Lost to St. Louis, 3-1, in 1984 Norris Division semifinals; lost to Chicago, 3-0, in 1985 Norris semifinals; beat Chicago, 4-0, in 1987 Norris semifinals; beat Toronto, 4-3, in 1987 Norris finals; lost to Edmonton, 4-1, in 1987 Campbell Conference finals; beat Toronto, 4-2, in 1988 Norris semfinals; beat St. Louis, 4-1, in 1988 Norris finals; lost to Edmonton, 4-1, in 1988 Campbell finals; lost to Chicago, 4-2, in 1989 Norris semifinals.

Award winners: Jacques Demers (coach), Jack Adams (coach of the year) (1987, 1988); John Ogrodnick (left wing), post-season All-Star team (1985); Brad Park (defenseman), Bill Masterton (dedication to hockey) (1984). (The Adams winner is selected by the NHL Broadcasters' Association; the Masterton winner and post-season All-Stars are selected by the Professional Hockey Writers' Association.)

All-Star Game representatives: 1980 (Reed Larson); 1981 (John Ogrodnick, Larson); 1982 (Ogrodnick); 1983 (Willie Huber); 1984 (Steve Yzerman, Ogrodnick); 1985 (Ogrodnick); 1986 (Ogrodnick); 1988 (Bob Probert, Yzerman); 1989 (Yzerman).

Hall of Fame inductees: Harry Lumley, goalie (1980); John Bucyk, left wing (1981); Frank Mahovlich, left wing (1981); Norm Ullman, center (1982); Budd Lynch, broadcaster (1985); Leo Boivin, defenseman (1986); Ed Giacomin, goalie (1987); John Ziegler, attorney (1987); Brad Park, defenseman (1988).

Notable deaths: Cecil (Tiny) Thompson, goalie (1981); Jack Stewart, defenseman (1983); Bruce Norris, owner (1985); Carl Mattson, trainer (1985); Ebbie Goodfellow, center-defenseman (1985); Cooney Weiland, center (1985); Joe Carveth, right wing (1987); Normie Smith, goalie (1988); Johnny Mitchell, assistant general manager/scout (1988); John Bell, publicity (1989).

Worth noting: Four Michigan franchises won the International Hockey League's Turner Cup in the '80s: Kalamazoo Wings (1980), Saginaw Gears (1981), Muskegon Lumberjacks (1982, 1989), Flint Generals (1984).

COLLEGE BASKETBALL

The Fishers became the University of Michigan's First Family when Steve coached the Wolverines to the 1989 NCAA basketball championship.

Michigan wasn't invited to the NCAA's party. So the Wolverines showed the NCAA its mistake and bulled their way through the National Invitation Tournament. Michigan edged Virginia Tech, 78-75, in the semifinals, setting up a New York date with one of its favorite opponents — on the gridiron.

With senior forward Tim McCormick and sophomore center Roy Tarpley, Michigan (23-10) pounded Notre Dame (21-12) on the boards. McCormick, the tournament MVP, had 28 points and 14 rebounds. "No question," McCormick said, "this is the thrill of my life. No one can take this away." Tarpley added 18 points and eight rebounds.

BEST OF THE REST

By George Puscas

S top the NCAA! Don't let those pretenders continue.

How dare they play for the national basketball championship without giving Michigan a shot? The Wolverines showed 'em the injustice of it all in Madison Square Garden. They weren't allowed into the 53-team field of the NCAA tournament, and it broke their hearts. But they turned right around and won the next best thing.

They smashed Notre Dame, 83-63, in the rollicking final of the National Invitation Tournament. It wasn't the Super Bowl of college basketball, but you can't tell that to the Wolverines.

Bo Schembechler would have been proud of 'em. He might even be wondering how several of them escaped his eye and landed in Bill Frieder's roundball game.

"People think this is gonna be a heavyweight title bout," said Notre Dame coach Digger Phelps before the game, "and they might be right." Alas, poor Digger. The prediction was too right. It was physical, very much so, but it was the Wolverines who put old-fashioned muscle to Notre Dame.

Michigan jumped on the Irish, jumped over them, stepped on them, and then finally, they simply ran right away from them. The crowd loved it.

Early in the second half, the Wolverines outgunned the lumbering Irish 20-2 over a six-minute spell, breaking away from a 28-28 tie. The Wolverines were zipping around and through the Irish so consistently that over much of the second half, they were clicking on a phenomenal 92 percent of their shots. A thousand and more U-M followers noticed, and they raised a maize and blue racket worthy of the Rose Bowl. At the end, the Irish were thoroughly beaten and the Wolverines were celebrating a victory they suspected from the beginning would not be difficult to achieve.

"We were disappointed we didn't jump to a big lead early," said Tim McCormick, the 6-foot-11 giant from Clarkston, Mich., "but we felt going in that if we played well, we would win easily." McCormick was one reason they did. He grabbed 14 rebounds and scored 28 points to claim most valuable player honors for the tournament.

Frieder, who has had some rough moments in his tenure in Ann Arbor (the Wolverines were 7-20 two years ago), said the day the Wolverines were selected as one of the 32 teams in the NIT field he believed they could win the tournament.

"Remember, we were rated 20 or 21 for much of the season in the power rating," he said. "After the NCAA decided not to invite us to their tournament, our team met and determined to win the NIT. We knew we had the potential."

And now that he had that title in hand, Frieder wasn't ready to let anyone demean it. "This is a prestigious tournament," he said, "the oldest one in basketball. A lot of great teams have won it in the past."

Like a good coach should, Frieder took special care to commend Notre Dame, although, truth be told, the Irish gave one of their saddest performances in yielding to Michigan without a threat.

"They deserve credit," Frieder said. "It was a physical game and they made us do a variety of things to combat them. But our guys play smart. I'm really happy for them. They worked their hearts out."

The Wolverines had built a nine-point lead over the Irish in the first half, but let it slip away with what Frieder called "three minutes of careless play."

"Then, in the second half, we did a great job of getting inside on their big players," he said. "McCormick and Roy Tarpley both had great games because of that. They controlled the defensive boards, and we started getting some easy baskets."

He paused then. He couldn't resist a parting shot.

"I think this team of ours would have done very well in the NCAA," he said. Why deny it? ◆

♦

Michigan's NIT championship in 1984 was the beginning of an exhilarating — yet frustrating — turn of events. In 1985, the Wolverines won the Big Ten by four games. In 1986, only Bobby Knight and his Indiana Hoosiers stood between Michigan and its second straight title.

Gary Grant, who in 1988 would finish as Michigan's second all-time leading scorer, had only six points against Indiana but hounded Steve Alford. The victory was sweet for Butch Wade and Antoine Joubert.

ONCE IS NEVER ENOUGH

By Jack Saylor

The winner ... and still champion ... Michigan.

The Wolverines capped the finest basketball season in their history by clubbing Indiana, 80-52, and running their conference record to 14-4. Michigan becomes the first Big Ten champion to repeat in five years and the first in 10 years to win back-to-back undisputed titles. The victory was achieved in shockingly easy style over a good Indiana team (21-7), Big Ten runner-up at 13-5 and also NCAA tournament-bound.

"They dominated us from the start," said a docile Bobby Knight, the Indiana coach who has been feuding with Michigan coach Bill Frieder. "We didn't really play that poorly. They took it away from us."

Michigan concluded the regular season 27-4, and not even two decades ago in the halcyon days of Cazzie Russell had the Wolverines posted such a glossy record. After the U-M scrubs had mopped up the rout, exuberant fans flooded onto the Crisler Arena floor to celebrate with Frieder and his players, who held the Big Ten championship trophy aloft for the fans and national television audience.

"A great victory," said Frieder, who will take the Wolverines into this week's NCAA tournament on a high note of seven victories in their last eight games. "If this wasn't our best game of the year, it's close — and we've had some good ones. I hope we're peaking because this is the time to peak."

Butch Wade, one of five U-M seniors playing their last home game, bubbled: "It just goes to show you that when Michigan comes to play, there's nobody that can beat us."

"It's harder to repeat than sneak up on somebody and win the championship," Frieder said. "And these kids have risen to the occasion."

Guard Antoine Joubert seconded that. "This title meant more than last year," he said. "We surprised a lot of people last year. This year was a challenge because everyone was trying to knock us off."

Indiana, a Michigan nemesis in years past, was never a threat this time. The Wolverines, led by Roy Tarpley's work under the basket and Gary Grant's steadfast hounding of Steve Alford, hit Indiana with nose-to-nose defense from the start — and never let up. That and a 47-29 hammering on the backboards pressured the Hoosiers into an uncharacteristic 20 turnovers, 13 of them in the first half as U-M ran up a 44-25 lead.

At the opposite end, whatever defensive game plan Knight had planned had to be torn up early as center Daryl Thomas and forward Andre Harris got into quick foul trouble. And Alford, a 6-foot-2 junior guard and the Big Ten's second-leading scorer, was held to 15 points as the Hoosiers shot only 43 percent. Grant limited Alford to two baskets in the first 14 minutes. By then, the Wolverines were on their way to a 20-point lead.

"Grant was superb," Frieder said. "He forced Alford to the side, then our big people helped. It all started with defense."

Tarpley and Joubert fueled an 18-4 U-M run that produced a 36-16 lead over the astonished Hoosiers. And this time the Wolverines didn't rest on their oars. "We've gotten leads before, then gotten lackadaisical and let teams catch up," said Richard Rellford. "Today we played with intensity the whole gamme."

U-M came out winging in the second half as Rellford and Tarpley sparked another scoring surge, of 10-4, as the lead reached 55-29. Tarpley showed the way in his Crisler Arena farewell with 21 points, 11 rebounds, three assists, three blocked shots and three steals, before he left the game with less than three minutes left to a thundering ovation.

Joubert scored 16 points and Rellford 13 as all the Wolverines played and nine of them scored.

The victory ended the U-M home season with an 18-1 record. At Crisler, Michigan has a remarkable 50-4 record over the last three years.

"When they get it together and play hard," Knight said, "they have a helluva chance to go a long way in the NCAA." ♦

After its 1985 Big Ten championship, Michigan struggled in its first-round NCAA game and lost to Villanova, the eventual champion, in the second round. With a second straight Big Ten title in hand, the senior-laden Wolverines expected to go a long way in the 1986 NCAAs.

On the eve of their second-round meeting, Iowa State coach Johnny Orr and his former assistant at Michigan, Bill Frieder, talked about old times. "This is my biggest victory ever," Orr later said. "Our team was ready to play, but I feel sorry for Bill. I'd rather not have played them." Center Roy Tarpley scored 25 points, grabbed 14 rebounds and made three steals but couldn't rally the Wolverines. In the '86 NBA draft, he went in the first round to the Dallas Mavericks.

CAUGHT IN A CYCLONE

By Tommy George

Michigan kept chipping and clawing its way back into the fight against Iowa State. Four times in the final seven minutes — after trailing by as many as 11 points — Michigan cut the lead to one point. The last time was at 64-63, with 1:18 remaining.
The Wolverines' dream was still alive.
And then Cyclone Elmer Robinson, a reserve forward, broke free on an inbounds play for a slam dunk. The Wolverines, stunned, played the remaining seconds in a trance. They still don't know how they let Robinson score so easily. But they knew their season was over, their high hopes in this NCAA tournament dashed.

Iowa State 72, Michigan 69.

For the second straight season, Michigan — 28-5, repeat champ in the Big Ten, the nation's fifth-ranked team — had been ousted from the tournament in the second round.

"At this level you have to play exceptional basketball for a full 40 minutes — we didn't," said Michigan coach Bill Frieder, his tie loosened, his eyes weary. "It's disappointing when you don't go further. Everything hurts."

Guard Gary Grant especially hurt. He shot 1 of 9 from the field and fouled out. "Me and the NCAAs just don't get along. . . . Next year I might have 'em sit me out," Grant said. "I feel bad for the seniors. A lot of things out there were my fault."

Several things hurt the Wolverines before 25,543 in Minneapolis' Metrodome. They were bruised by 15 turnovers. Spotty shooting — 45 percent from the floor and six missed free throws — salted their wounds.

But Robinson's jam broke their backs. The Wolverines had scrapped from a 40-31 halftime deficit and believed the game was turning their way. But Robinson, free off a screen on forward Glen Rice, put the game away.

"He got caught," Frieder said, "and he didn't get help. We didn't do the job." Again.

"This is worse than last year against Villanova," said forward Richard Rellford. "We feel we could have gone so far. But there is no one to blame but ourselves. Yeah, we had our chances before and after Robinson's play. Yeah, we had a real chance to win it all." ◆

TICK-TOCK, BAD CLOCK

By Mitch Albom

I t was too early for heartbreak. The sun was just creeping through the huge glass windows. The plane wasn't ready yet, and the Kansas City, Mo., airport was filled with the lonely echo that comes in those ungodly hours before the coffee shop opens.

It was the first morning of the rest of Scott Skiles' life, the first morning he was no longer a college athlete but a young man with memories behind him and a prison sentence in front of him. It was a hell of a morning, really, and Skiles was coming in on no sleep. "Not one minute," he said, shaking his head slowly. You don't sleep when your insides are on fire.

He was dead now, but seven hours earlier he was still alive, because he was still playing basketball, and anyone who has seen this clenched fist of a man knows if ever a human being needed a ball in his hands for survival, it was Scott Skiles. And, damn, the ball was there, right where he wanted it, in his hands, as the final seconds of the big game against Kansas ticked away, and the score was tied and the crowd was screaming and he was racing up the court with defenders chasing him and his eyes were locked on that basket.

"I had eight seconds," he said softly, narrating it all over again. "I should've dribbled that baby up, 25 feet from the hole. Then I should've pulled up and shot a normal jumper and hit it for the game-winner. . . . I had it in my hands. And I failed."

The shot he fired instead was an off-balance jumper from around 17 feet. It careened off the rim. The clock ran out and the game went into overtime and his team, Michigan State, had nothing left. The Spartans lost a few minutes later, 96-86. They were out of the NCAA tournament.

It wasn't his fault. No way. There was a malfunctioning clock and bad officiating and ➡

Fifteen seconds still are lost in Michigan State basketball history. Fifteen seconds that failed to come off the clock with MSU ahead, 76-72, and 2:21 left in an NCAA regional semifinal against No. 2 Kansas. After the fifth foul on Kansas' Danny Manning, Larry Bates switched on the Kemper Arena clock as the Jayhawks came up the floor and scored. MSU coach Jud Heathcote charged the scorer's table, pointing out that the clock hadn't started. Bates flipped the switch again and the clock worked. Kansas coach Larry Brown, demanding a technical foul on Heathcote, got one when his program hit the referee's whistle. MSU made two technical free throws and a basket on the possession for a six-point lead with 1:07 left. Yet, Kansas tied the game at 80 and won in overtime, 96-86.

Coach Jud Heathcote stood behind his troubled player during the toughest of times. He was even there when Scott Skiles was released in May 1986 after 15 days in the Marshall County Jail in Plymouth, Ind., the town Skiles led to the 1982 state championship.

two missed free throws by teammates and a dozen other good reasons the blame should fall anywhere but on the pale white shoulders of Skiles, whose gritted-teeth style of play had literally carried the Spartans this far, the regional semifinal, way past anyone's wildest expectations. Besides, the game was such a thriller, people left saying, "There was no loser tonight." But Skiles didn't buy it. He blamed himself. And in the showers afterward, as the water ran over his head but the loss would not wash away, he turned to teammate Larry Polec and quietly said, "It's over, isn't it?" and Polec could only nod yes.

To understand Scott Skiles, you must be able to mix the golds of glory with the deep blues of tragedy, for here was a young man splashing through both. It is doubtful we soon will see his likes again, a 22-year-old twister playing an entire college basketball season with the threat of prison hanging over his head. He was forever on the front pages of newspapers this season for his 27.7 scoring average, his dazzling passing game, his fiery leadership. And because he was going to jail. A 30-day sentence for violating the terms of his probation with a drunken-driving arrest last November. Skiles had been arrested before: in August 1984, charged with marijuana and cocaine possession, and in September 1984, charged with driving while intoxicated.

"It's been more difficult than anyone will imagine," he said, leaning forward in the airport chair as he waited with his teammates for the flight back home. "There are a lot of things about the arrests that I'm sure will die with me. I just know I'm damn lucky to have gone to Michigan State. When I got into trouble people didn't say, 'Let's find a way we can phase this kid out.' They stuck by me."

All season, Skiles was greeted in foreign gyms with chants of "GO TO JAIL!" or "D.U.I.!" Some fans waved plastic bags of sugar to suggest cocaine. He had bigger problems. Like the jail sentence this summer. "Sure, I'm scared of jail," he said. "It'd be inhuman not to be scared of it. But isn't that what jail is supposed to be about?"

"The thing is," he added, his voice lowered now, almost pleading, "I don't want to drive drunk. I mean, I don't want to go out and kill someone on the road. God, that's the last thing I'd want to do. I just made a . . . mistake."

He leaned back, quiet. In that last word was the unmistakable plea of conscience, and anyone who had ever messed up in life would have had a hard time not feeling something for the guy. But Skiles is not usually that fortunate. His manner doesn't evoke sympathy. He lacks the sweetie-pie countenance of a Magic Johnson or an Isiah Thomas. What can you do? Some guys buy with their looks and some guys pay for them. Skiles just happens to have the flaring eyes of a marine sergeant in a barroom brawl. And that's during lay-up drills. But it's this same ferocity that is responsible for all the victory in the MSU program this year. And there's the dilemma. You can't have one without the other. Skiles is a fist-wielding, bad-mouthing, rile-'em-up kind of player on the court. Skiles bled from the knee all game in MSU's tournament victory over Washington. Yet he scored 31 points. He led the upset charge against Georgetown even though he had a piercing sciatic nerve injury. He scored 24. "You can count on Scott to spill his guts on the floor," Polec said. And that's what the Spartans needed.

"It all happened so quick," Skiles said. "I thought when Mark Brown was at the line, and we were up, 80-78, if he could have made one foul shot we'd have won it. He didn't. But I missed a foul shot before him and Larry missed one before him, and if we'd have made them, Mark wouldn't have had to be there. Then there was the thing with the clock malfunctioning. It's a shame that had to happen in such a big game. Even worse than that was the officiating. . . . I don't think it's any secret that I thought that I could win the whole thing for Michigan State. That's the way I feel. That's the kind of confidence I had. I had 100 percent confidence we'd be advancing to the Final Four. It's my responsibility. I'm taking the blame. It's something I have to deal with the rest of my life."

Then came an odd question, a question that could only be asked of Skiles, and in whose answer you catch a glimpse of something: If he could do one thing over and make it come out right — the trouble that is sending him to jail or that final, off-balance jumper — which would he choose?

He thought about it for a few seconds. He decided on an answer. "I guess I'd choose both," he said finally.

But he couldn't help it. It showed. His heart was on the side with the net. ◆

Although only 6-feet-1 and slow of foot, Scott Skiles feared no one on the basketball court. He challenged and angered — and then beat — his opponents. Before upsetting Michigan, he told guard Antoine Joubert: "You better lose 20 pounds before you try to guard me, fat boy." In an NCAA second-round game, Skiles destroyed 13th-ranked Georgetown with 24 points and five assists. After 1 of 7 shooting in the first half, he went 6 of 7 in the second. The Hoyas had reached the title game three of the four previous seasons.

It was the year the NCAA Midwest Regional came to the Silverdome, smack in the heart of Big Ten country. Fans hoped Michigan would play there, but the Wolverines were sent to Seattle. Big Ten champion Purdue was a heavy favorite to advance from the Silverdome, but in the end, two schools from the Great Plains — Kansas and Kansas State — battled for a trip to the Final Four.

GOIN' TO KANSAS CITY

By Charlie Vincent

This was the day Danny Manning didn't lead the Kansas Jayhawks into the NCAA Final Four. This was the day people stopped — maybe for just a single day — saying the Jayhawks were a one-man team. This was a day for Milt Newton, who missed two games at the beginning of this season because of an NCAA violation, and for Keith Harris, who was suspended five games for disciplinary reasons, and for Scooter Barry, who grew up feeling just a bit inferior because his dad, Rick, was one of the greatest shooters in basketball history.

Kansas will be in the Final Four in Kansas City, Mo., this weekend because the Jayhawks' bit players became the stars for a day in a 71-58 victory over Kansas State in the Midwest Regional final at the Silverdome. Do not be deceived, though. Of the four teams left from these four months of college basketball, the Jayhawks will be the longest shot. But they were better than Kansas State and that was as good as they had to be.

By the time coach Larry Brown pieced together a workable lineup, the Jayhawks' record had plummeted to 12-8 with a four-game losing streak. Then something happened. Not a miracle. Nothing mystic. Just a human response, just the decision to do better. "We had some kids step forward," Brown said.

Newton is a free spirit, an independent sort who was given the nickname Alfreaka "because I always try to freak someone. I put a move on 'em and try to make 'em look stupid. Freak 'em out."

In 29 minutes, Newton scored 18 points, helped hold Kansas State's leading scorer, Mitch Richmond, to 11 points, and had seven assists.

In the box score, Harris — who scored just 77 points in Kansas' first 35 games — looks like a minor player — four points, one rebound, two steals. But one of those

Chris Piper and Danny Manning were off to Kansas City, where Kansas would stun Duke and Oklahoma to win the NCAA title. In the Silverdome, Manning had 38 points against Vanderbilt and 20 against K-State.

steals may have been the game's most important play. Kansas was behind, 43-42, when he took the ball away from Richmond and headed toward the other basket for a jam.

Then there was Barry, like Harris, a reserve. Only 19 men had scored more points than his dad did in the NBA. But Scooter Barry has a career average of 1.9. "The comparison used to bother me," he said. "But it doesn't any more because I've never scored more than 10 points." It was a fact until this day, when the son of Rick Barry scored 15 points. And helped lead the Kansas Jayhawks into the Final Four. ◆

FIELD HOUSE OF MEMORIES

By Jack Saylor

MARCH 11,
1989
◆

Oh, the secrets Michigan State's Jenison Field House could tell. The stadium, a showpiece in its day, served the Spartans — and prep athletics — well for 50 years. But by the '80s time had passed Jenison by. A new and better facility was needed. So MSU bid its old barn adieu.

Requiem for a heavyweight. That's the tone of Michigan State's season-ending basketball game against Wisconsin — the final college game to be played at Jenison Field House, the Spartans' home for 50 seasons.

Jenison is old and nonfunctional. It is drafty, has hard, bleacher-style seats, and less-than-adequate facilities. Most of all, it is too small.

But it was, indeed, a heavyweight among college arenas in its heyday, a showplace in the '40s and '50s. Consider: Michigan was playing in already rickety Yost Field House, which the Wolverines shared with the bats. Other schools had not yet built slick, modern

coliseums.

"I came from the West Coast, and we didn't have big basketball buildings then," said Pete Newell, who coached the Spartans from 1950 to 1954. "Jenison ranked in beauty with the best of the time. It was a tremendously attractive building — the entranceway with its pictures and trophies."

Jenison Field House, which hosted its first game Jan. 6, 1940 (MSU beat Tennessee, 29-20), is named for Frederick Cowles Jenison, a former engineering student who became a highly successful businessman. It was built for $1,707,750.

Next season, the Spartans move into the Jack Breslin Student Events Center, across Kalamazoo Street from Jenison. It cost upward of $40 million.

Crowds from 13,000 to the record 15,384 (for a 1948 loss to Kentucky) regularly packed Jenison for big games, including high school finals, until the fire marshal set a limit of 10,004 some years ago.

The old barn rocked through the years with the heroics of Julius McCoy, Johnny Green, Terry Furlow, Sam and Jay Vincent, Scott Skiles and the Greg Kelser-Magic Johnson NCAA title season of 1978-79.

Perhaps never did the roof reverberate as it did on the February night in '79 when the Spartans, on the ragged edge of elimination from Big Ten title contention, fell behind unbeaten Ohio State with Magic Johnson in the locker room with an ankle injury. Then the Magic Man limped back onto the court to a tumultuous reception. He sparked a rally that won the game, 84-79, in overtime and started the Spartans on their way to a title and a place in NCAA championship history. ◆

MICHIGAN STATE UNIVERSITY NCAA BASKETBALL CHAMPIONS 1979

The Spartans had a banner year in 1979 when they beat Indiana State for the NCAA title. Michigan State beat Wisconsin, 70-61, in the final regular-season game at Jenison Field House on March 11, 1989. MSU beat Wichita State, 79-76, in an NIT game at Jenison on March 20. And Magic Johnson's '79 Champions beat the MSU All-Stars, 95-93, in an alumni game at Jenison on Aug. 12.

1989

♦

It all happened within 24 hours. Bill Frieder, Michigan's coach for nine years, took the job as Arizona State's coach two days before the Wolverines' opening game in the NCAA tournament. The same day Arizona State introduced Frieder, athletic director Bo Schembechler announced he would go with a Michigan man, little-known assistant Steve Fisher, as interim coach.

Bill Frieder stayed in the same hotel as his former team in Atlanta. He watched Michigan's 92-87 first-round victory over Xavier (Ohio). "It's a big stadium," Bo Schembechler said. "It's a free country." Steve Fisher, holding his son, Mark, couldn't believe his new assignment. "It still seems like a dream," he said. "But I won't change the way I operate, except that I will shout in the assistants' ears."

THE MICHIGAN MAN

By Steve Kornacki

There was a new look to the Michigan basketball program. Everything from the coach to team dress style changed.

Assistant Steve Fisher, 43, was selected interim head coach by athletic director Bo Schembechler. The announcement at the indoor football building came at 12:30 p.m., 2½ hours after Bill Frieder was introduced as Arizona State's new coach. Fisher began his first press conference by saying, "For the benefit of most of you, I'm Steve Fisher." He later added: "I've gone from the guy most of the media used to shove away to get to the stars, to this."

Schembechler, the day after spring football practice started, began his first significant transition period as athletic director with a pep talk and a gift. The Wolverines (24-7), who have no strict dress code, traveled to Atlanta for the NCAA tournament's Southeast Regional wearing beige sweaters with a basketball logo over the heart and this message:

*Michigan on the road
to the Final Four*

"These were given to us earlier, but we probably never would have worn them," center Loy Vaught said. "Bo Schembechler gave us this great speech at about 12 o'clock and asked us to wear them."

And they wore them. It was no big deal on the surface, but said a lot about the discipline Schembechler believed was lacking under Frieder. Schembechler has never publicly criticized Frieder, but it was known by those close to the program that the two disagreed on many matters.

"If there is a problem between Bo and Bill Frieder, it's that I have to replace him," Schembechler said. "I wouldn't have done it the way he did. But that was up to him. I appreciate everything he did here."

Frieder left U-M with a 191-87 record and two Big Ten championships. He also left in a hurry, saying Arizona State wanted an immediate decision. Only 24 hours elapsed between a job offer by Arizona State athletic director Charles Harris — the last of several to Frieder in the last three years — and the announcement that Fisher would coach the Wolverines in the NCAA tournament. Frieder, 47, flew to Phoenix last night after practice. He told Fisher of his plans to take the Sun Devils job at 6 p.m., and departed.

"I know people are going to be negative," Frieder said, "but I didn't have any choice. . . . Bo said he could not understand why we couldn't hold off until the end of the tournament to announce it, but what if I'd have taken the job and not announced it? There would have been tremendous pressures on the kids. There would have been questions all the time."

Schembechler was concerned about how the upheaval would affect the team. "I told them, 'Go on and win this NCAA tournament. Get these things out of your mind and play basketball,' " he said. "They're too good a team not to go into this thinking they can win."

Associate athletic director Jack Weidenbach was the first to receive word from Frieder in Arizona, at 7 a.m. Frieder said he had attempted to reach Schembechler, but could not because of his unlisted phone number. He called Lynn Koch, Schembechler's secretary, at 3:45 a.m. Frieder was instructed to call Schembechler after a 10 a.m. press conference in Tempe, Ariz. He did so at 11.

"I told him I preferred Steve Fisher coach the team," Schembechler said. "Things always turn out for the best. I'm disappointed by the timing. I'm sure he will say he wanted to coach the team, but I did not want an Arizona State coach coaching Michigan. I wanted a Michigan man." ♦

1989

♦

One thing was certain, a Big Ten team would play for the national championship in Seattle's Kingdome. It was just a matter of determining which one would get there — Cinderella Michigan with interim coach Steve Fisher and hot-scoring Glen Rice or powerhouse Illinois, which had defeated the Wolverines twice during the regular season. The Illini had the talent; the Wolverines had destiny.

LIVING A DREAM

By Steve Kornacki

It ended in a most unlikely manner. But then, isn't this an unconventional Michigan team that is headed for the NCAA championship game?

The Wolverines beat Illinois, 83-81, at the Kingdome in Seattle, after losing twice to the Fighting Illini during the regular season. And they did it with their top scorer setting a screen on the final play. They did it with a guy known for rainbows popping in a follow shot.

With the game on the line, 81-81, Glen Rice set a pick for Terry Mills. His shot from the right baseline missed, but Sean Higgins had the angle from the left for the rebound. He grabbed it and wasted no time depositing the winning six-footer with two seconds left.

"It didn't happen picture-perfect," Loy Vaught said. "But it worked."

The play was designed for Rice to shoot behind a double-screen set by Mills and Mark Hughes. "We were in the final seconds and they were keying on me too much," Rice said. "I had to screen to get someone open."

Rumeal Robinson was dribbling in the middle of the lane and noticed that the play had been cut off by a landslide of Illini defenders. "I came about this close from trying to go to the basket," Robinson said, holding his thumb and fingers a half-inch apart. "But I didn't want to force it. I saw Terry open."

Mills didn't hesitate to put up the 18-footer. "Time was running out," he said, "and I would rather have missed the shot than held it and had OT."

"They tell us all year that shots from the right side usually rebound to the left," Higgins said. "I got position (on Nick Anderson) and went after the ball. Then I went straight in for the shot, no glass. I've dreamed of hitting the last shot to win a game my whole life. Then to do it on national TV, in a game like this."

But one second remained and Illinois (31-5) knew something about last-second heroics. With two seconds left at Indiana, Stephen Bardo found Anderson with a three-quarter-court pass. Anderson then fired a shot that beat the Hoosiers. But it wouldn't happen this time.

Rice, who finished with 28 points, caught Bardo's desperation, court-length pass and the buzzer sounded.

Michigan was going to the championship game against Seton Hall (31-6). The Wolverines (29-7) set a school record for victories in one season and broke an Illinois

After so many disappointing trips in the NCAA tournament, Michigan fans found plenty to cheer about in the Pacific Northwest. By beating Illinois, Michigan qualified for its first NCAA final since losing to Indiana, 86-68, in 1976. The Wolverines also lost in the 1965 final to UCLA, 91-80.

streak of 10 straight victories.

When it was over, there was a mob scene on the court before 39,187 fans. Higgins, who scored 14 points, lifted both hands and shouted, "Yeah, man, we're going!" Rice placed a traditional postgame hug on Higgins and said, "I love you and you played a great game." The senior captain has more or less taken the one-time enigma, Higgins, under his wing. "I have another hug left," Rice said. "Oh, I want to have a lot of hugs left. . . . It's sweet because I think the Illinois players thought they were going to come in and beat us a third time."

As the Wolverines mugged for CBS cameras and interviews, Robinson was in the stands, hugging his mother. Hughes was shouting, "Coach of the year" for Steve Fisher, the interim coach living a dream. "Don't wake me up," he said, "until Tuesday morning."

The Illini were gracious in defeat. "I felt they played much harder than they usually play," said Anderson, a junior forward who tried to get a body on Higgins before his rebound-basket. "They were a lot more together than I remember during the season. They played a heck of a game." ♦

Michigan center Loy Vaught took this ball away from an Illinois forward, 6-foot-7 Ervin Small. Vaught, at 6-9, grabbed 12 first-half rebounds and finished with a career-high 16. "How do we expect to get a rebound when we've got four guards out there and they're all 6-8, 6-9?" asked Illinois coach Lou Henson. "Size is important. And that's what beat us." Vaught said: "See, I told you rebounding would be the difference. It was just a lot of extra effort. They live and die on second shots and couldn't get them."

It's the stuff dreams are made of. Three weeks earlier, Michigan had lost its coach and seemingly had no direction. But under the leadership of interim coach Steve Fisher, the team started a sweep through the NCAA Tournament that won't soon be forgotten. Star forward Glen Rice had sent this team on a mission. Seton Hall, a small college in New Jersey, was the final obstacle.

A-MAIZING BLUE

By Mitch Albom

He stood at the free throw line, the loneliest man in the world. All around him was the enemy, hooting and hollering, the demons in Seton Hall uniforms talking trash, the crowd suddenly an army of "MISS IT! MISS IT!" The referee bounced the ball twice, slowly, like an executioner, and tossed it to him. Life came to a standstill. A school and a nation and a glorious destiny held its breath.

Dribble. Shoot. Swish.

Tie game.

"All right, baby!" yelled Glen Rice to Rumeal Robinson. "One more. One more."

Robinson licked his lips. What was riding on this shot? Only an entire season. Only a fairy tale ending. Only the championship of the world in college basketball. Pressure?

Dribble. Shoot. Swish.

Champions.

"WOOOOH! WOOOH! WOOH!" screamed Glen Rice, hugging Robinson three seconds later, crying in his arms, after Michigan had hung on to win the national championship in overtime, 80-79, in the most fantastic finish to a basketball season you could ever imagine. "WOOH! WOOH!"

Were there any other words? How else could you describe it? A game that had everything, classic theater, wonderful drama — the first overtime game in a tournament final since 1963. It had heroes and villains and magnificent plays and bonehead plays and moments when you could cut the pressure with a buzz saw, and moments when all the players, good and bad, succumbed to it.

It had Glen Rice, the tournament's MVP, keeping his team alive all game long with miracle shots, scoring from every angle, yet missing a jumper at the buzzer that could have sealed it. It had Sean Higgins, the young, free-spirited guard, who three weeks ago you wouldn't trust with his own sneakers, sinking two clutch free throws in the final moments of regulation. It had Steve Fisher, the interim coach, calming his players when it seemed like the world was coming down around them, when the Seton Hall Pirates were stealing everything they touched.

And finally it had Rumeal, a kid who has overcome everything you can imagine, a lost childhood, academic woes, a natural shyness, to become a sterling example of what college basketball should be — and there he was, where he belonged, at the free throw line, proving once again that you can't write off any team that believes in itself.

"What were you thinking when you were standing there with the championship on the line?" he was asked in the locker room afterward. "I was thinking, 'Man, I wish the referee would stop stalling and give me the ball,'" he said.

Dribble. Shoot. Swish.

Champions.

Who would believe it?

"Nobody believed us," said Higgins, clutching his little brown box with the championship ring inside. "The people were all saying 'Seton Hall, Seton Hall.' Just like at the beginning they were saying 'Xavier, Xavier.' They didn't know how many nights we sat up talking about a national championship. I think it was all that doubting by everyone else that enabled us to win tonight."

Well, there was certainly enough of that. What a story! Who would ever believe this? A team that three weeks ago had no coach and seemingly no chance? National champions? Not only national champions, but the first Michigan team to ever win that title. Not only national champions, but come-from-behind national champions.

"There were moments when it got a little scary," said Rice, who had 31 points. "Their defense was really good, and they kept getting me out of my type of offense."

The final minutes of this affair were enough to make you lose your hair, misplace your heartbeat. Michigan (30-7) had squandered a 12-point lead in the second half and ➡

Rumeal Robinson, academically ineligible as a freshman, nailed the NCAA-winning free throws as a junior.

Next page: Glen Rice earned his place on the championship ladder by scoring 184 points, breaking Bill Bradley's record of 177, set in the 1965 NCAA tournament with Princeton. Rice's performances: 23 points against Xavier, 36 against South Alabama, 34 against North Carolina, 32 against Virginia, 28 against Illinois and 31 against Seton Hall. Rice, later drafted by Miami in the first round, averaged 30.7 points. He passed Michigan's Mike McGee as the Big Ten's all-time leading scorer with 2,442 points.

missed a chance to win at the regulation buzzer, when Rice's 20-footer thumped the rim once, twice, and out. Overtime? Overtime. The Wolverines fell behind, 79-76. The Seton Hall fans seemed to own the Kingdome. Each Michigan miss brought a roar and fans leaping from their seats, smelling the kill. Wasn't this supposed to be a neutral court? Where did all this blue and white come from?

But Michigan fought back. Robinson brought the ball up court against a chorus of jeers — "Terry, it's your shot," he yelled at Terry Mills — and Mills made that shot, a leaping banker, to cut it to 79-78. The Pirates (31-7) came back down court, dripping the time off the clock, 20 seconds left, 10 seconds left, finally they took a shot, it missed badly, and Rice caught the ball and dished to Robinson.

"From that point, I wanted the shot," said Robinson, who raced up court, drove the lane, and was fouled by Gerald Greene. "I didn't want to put the burden on anyone else's shoulders." Can you believe that? Why not? Didn't you see him at that free throw line?

Rumeal Robinson gave new meaning to executive privilege during Michigan's visit to the White House. He allowed President George Bush to shoot his second free throw in a re-enactment of the NCAA title game. Both sank their shots on a portable, regulation basket in the Rose Garden, combining the spirit of "Hail to the Victors" with "Hail to the Chief." Two days before the trip, Steve Fisher lost his interim title, receiving Michigan's standard, one-year contract.

Wasn't he the picture of calm — even as your heart pounded in your throat?

"I told him, 'I made mine, now you make yours,'" said Higgins.

"I told him God helps those who help themselves," said Mike Griffin.

Everyone had a word of encouragement. Everyone had a piece of heavenly advice. But the ball was in Robinson's hands, his alone. Pressure?

"I looked at John Morton and he was grinning at me, trying to unnerve me," Robinson said. "But I just grinned back at him. Because I had the ball and he didn't."

Dribble. Shoot. Swish.

Champions.

Wow. What a story! Michigan basketball: Rice, shooting from the heavens, breaking the NCAA tournament record for points. God, what a tournament. There are rims in Atlanta and Lexington, Ky., that are still too hot to touch. And Robinson, always with the ball, dictating the creative flow, holding in mid-air, then flicking in those two-footers. And Higgins, the baby of the group, with that goofy expression and that flexible-flyer body all over the court. And Mills, with a wing span like a Pterodactyl, rising toward the hoop for a rebound or a jumper. And Loy Vaught, sucking in the rebounds, and Griffin, the unappreciated guy — there's always one, right? — making the steals or the invisible defensive maneuver. Or Mark Hughes. Or Demetrius Calip. Look at them out there now, cutting down the nets.

Champions.

And Steve Fisher, the interim coach. Here is the story to end all stories. The hero of second-fiddles everywhere. He took over for the departed Bill Frieder two days before the tournament and never looked back; six victories later, he is the coach of the national champions. There still may be debate as to whether Fisher earned a five-year contract with this miracle run. There is no doubt he proved himself tournament tough. Tough? He took a wild tornado of talent and harnessed it into a thinking, synchronized unit. In three weeks! "I am the happiest man in the world right now," he said. "I couldn't be prouder of this team and what they did."

For now, however, let's not worry about jobs and futures. Savor these scenes: Michigan clamping on Seton Hall star Andrew Gaze, holding him to five points. Higgins stepping away from the free throw line at the end of regulation, having made the biggest shot of his life, then stepping up and making another. Robinson, standing at the line, waiting for that ball — "C'mon, ref, I'm ready." And finally, when the buzzer sounded, Robinson and Rice locked in that eternal embrace, a hug that would never end, crying, laughing, screaming, doing everything we all would do at a moment like that, all at once.

"WOOH! WOOH! WOOH!" ◆

BY THE NUMBERS

College basketball

1979-80 SEASON	RECORDS	FINISH	TOURNAMENT*	SCORING	REBOUNDS
Central Michigan (MAC)	12-13 (6-10)	9th, 8 GB Toledo	Failed to qualify	Robinson (14.4)	Robinson (9.6)
Detroit (Independent)	14-13			Cureton (20.0)	Cureton (9.1)
Eastern Michigan (MAC)	13-14 (7-9)	T-4th, 7 GB Toledo	Lost in quarterfinals	Blakely (17.3)	Zatkoff (6.7)
Michigan (Big Ten)	17-13 (8-10)	T-6th, 5 GB Indiana		McGee (22.2)	Garner (6.7)
Michigan State (Big Ten)	12-15 (6-12)	9th, 7 GB Indiana		J. Vincent (21.6)	Charles (8.9)
Western Michigan (MAC)	12-14 (7-9)	T-4th, 7 GB Toledo	Failed to qualify	Cunningham (24.2)	Seberger (6.1)

1980-81 SEASON	RECORDS	FINISH	TOURNAMENT*	SCORING	REBOUNDS
Central Michigan (MAC)	12-14 (5-11)	9th, 5 GB five teams**	Failed to qualify	McLaughlin (20.8)	Robinson (11.2)
Detroit (MCC)	9-18 (1-5)	6th, 4½ GB Xavier (Ohio)	Lost in quarterfinals	Kopicki (19.9)	Kopicki (8.7)
Eastern Michigan (MAC)	13-14 (8-8)	6th, 2 GB five teams**	Lost in quarterfinals	Zatkoff (17.5)	Zatkoff (6.7)
Michigan (Big Ten)	19-11 (8-10)	7th, 6 GB Indiana		McGee (24.4)	Garner (5.6)
Michigan State (Big Ten)	13-14 (7-11)	8th, 7 GB Indiana		J. Vincent (22.6)	J. Vincent (8.5)
Western Michigan (MAC)	15-13 (10-6)	T-1st with four teams**	Lost in semifinals	McElroy (16.9)	Seberger (7.1)

1981-82 SEASON	RECORDS	FINISH	TOURNAMENT*	SCORING	REBOUNDS
Central Michigan (MAC)	10-16 (4-12)	10th, 8 GB Ball State	Failed to qualify	McLaughlin (23.2)	Wandzel (6.0)
Detroit (MCC)	10-17 (6-6)	T-4th, 4 GB Evansville	Lost in quarterfinals	Kopicki (18.6)	Kopicki (10.5)
Eastern Michigan (MAC)	15-12 (8-8)	T-4th, 4 GB Ball State	Lost in quarterfinals	Zatkoff (16.6)	Zatkoff (7.9)
Michigan (Big Ten)	8-19 (7-11)	T-7th, 7 GB Minnesota		Turner (14.7)	Garner (6.7)
Michigan State (Big Ten)	12-16 (7-11)	T-7th, 7 GB Minnesota		Smith (15.6)	Perry (5.4)
Western Michigan (MAC)	15-14 (8-8)	T-4th, 4 GB Ball State	Lost in semifinals	Russell (19.9)	Seberger (8.3)

1982-83 SEASON	RECORDS	FINISH	TOURNAMENT*	SCORING	REBOUNDS
Central Michigan (MAC)	10-17 (5-13)	9th, 10 GB Bowling Green	Failed to qualify	McLaughlin (24.1)	Thompson (5.6)
Detroit (MCC)	12-17 (6-8)	T-5th, 6 GB Loyola (Ill.)	Lost in semifinals	D. Chappell (17.6)	D. Chappell (8.1)
Eastern Michigan (MAC)	12-16 (8-10)	T-7th, 7 GB Bowling Green	Lost in quarterfinals	McClain (16.2)	Blevins (5.9)
Michigan (Big Ten)	16-12 (7-11)	9th, 6 GB Indiana		Turner (19.2)	McCormick (6.4)
Michigan State (Big Ten)	17-13 (9-9)	T-6th, 4 GB Indiana		S. Vincent (16.6)	Willis (9.6)
Western Michigan (MAC)	5-23 (3-15)	10th, 12 GB Bowling Green	Failed to qualify	Eley (18.1)	Jones (6.0)

1983-84 SEASON	RECORDS	FINISH	TOURNAMENT*	SCORING	REBOUNDS
Central Michigan (MAC)	11-16 (6-12)	8th, 10 GB Miami (Ohio)	Failed to qualify	Boldon (14.2)	Boldon (6.0)
Detroit (MCC)	8-20 (4-10)	7th, 7 GB Oral Roberts	Lost in quarterfinals	Gray (17.0)	D. Chappell (7.2)
Eastern Michigan (MAC)	12-17 (8-10)	T-6th, 8 GB Miami (Ohio)	Lost in semifinals	Cofield (15.6)	Giles (8.9)
Michigan (Big Ten)	24-9 (11-7)	4th, 4 GB Illinois, Purdue		Tarpley (12.5)	Tarpley (8.1)
Michigan State (Big Ten)	16-12 (9-9)	5th, 6 GB Illinois, Purdue		Skiles (14.5)	Willis (7.7)
Western Michigan (MAC)	4-22 (2-16)	10th, 14 GB Miami (Ohio)	Failed to qualify	James (14.3)	James (6.9)

1984-85 SEASON	RECORDS	FINISH	TOURNAMENT*	SCORING	REBOUNDS
Central Michigan (MAC)	9-18 (4-14)	10th, 10 GB Ohio	Failed to qualify	Boldon (15.7)	Boldon (6.1)
Detroit (MCC)	16-12 (8-6)	T-3rd, 5 GB Loyola (Ill.)	Lost in quarterfinals	Gray (17.5)	Wendt (7.4)
Eastern Michigan (MAC)	15-13 (9-9)	5th, 5 GB Ohio	Lost in quarterfinals	Cofield (20.6)	Giles (9.5)
Michigan (Big Ten)	26-4 (16-2)	1st, 4 GA Illinois		Tarpley (19.0)	Tarpley (10.4)
Michigan State (Big Ten)	19-10 (10-8)	T-5th, 6 GB Michigan		S.Vincent (23.0)	Johnson (10.2)
Western Michigan (MAC)	12-16 (7-11)	T-7th, 7 GB Ohio	Lost in quarterfinals	Petties (19.5)	James (7.4)

1985-86 SEASON	RECORDS	FINISH	TOURNAMENT*	SCORING	REBOUNDS
Central Michigan (MAC)	11-17 (7-11)	T-6th, 9 GB Miami (Ohio)	Lost in quarterfinals	D. Majerle (21.4)	D. Majerle (7.9)
Detroit (MCC)	14-15 (7-5)	T-3rd, 3 GB Xavier (Ohio)	Lost in semifinals	Humes (14.1)	Wendt (7.3)
Eastern Michigan (MAC)	9-18 (5-13)	T-9th, 11 GB Miami (Ohio)	Failed to qualify	Cooper (13.9)	Long (6.6)
Michigan (Big Ten)	28-5 (14-4)	1st, 1 GA Indiana		Tarpley (15.9)	Tarpley (8.8)
Michigan State (Big Ten)	23-8 (12-6)	3rd, 2 GB Michigan		Skiles (27.4)	Polec (5.7)
Western Michigan (MAC)	12-16 (7-11)	T-6th, 9 GB Miami (Ohio)	Lost in quarterfinals	Petties (15.7)	James (7.9)

Conference post-season tournament
** *Tied for first were Western Michigan, Ball State, Bowling Green, Northern Illinois and Toledo. Ball State won the post-season tournament.*

BY THE NUMBERS

College basketball

1986-87 SEASON	RECORDS	FINISH	TOURNAMENT*	SCORING	REBOUNDS
Central Michigan (MAC)	22-8 (14-2)	1st, 3 GA Kent State	Beat Kent State in final	D. Majerle (21.1)	D. Majerle (8.5)
Detroit (MCC)	7-21 (2-10)	7th, 6 GB Evansville	Lost in quarterfinals	Tullos (19.7)	Humes (6.4)
Eastern Michigan (MAC)	14-15 (8-8)	4th, 6 GB Central Michigan	Lost in semifinals	Long (14.9)	Long (9.0)
Michigan (Big Ten)	20-12 (10-8)	5th, 5 GB Indiana, Purdue		Grant (22.4)	Rice (9.2)
Michigan State (Big Ten)	11-17 (6-12)	7th, 9 GB Indiana, Purdue		Johnson (22.1)	Valentine (5.6)
Western Michigan (MAC)	12-16 (7-9)	T-5th, 7 GB Central Michigan	Lost in quarterfinals	James (22.1)	James (10.1)

1987-88 SEASON	RECORDS	FINISH	TOURNAMENT*	SCORING	REBOUNDS
Central Michigan (MAC)	19-13 (10-6)	2nd, 4 GB Eastern Michigan	Lost in semifinals	D. Majerle (23.7)	D. Majerle (10.8)
Detroit (MCC)	7-23 (2-8)	6th, 7 GB Xavier	Lost in final	Tullos (25.1)	McKinney (7.1)
Eastern Michigan (MAC)	22-8 (14-2)	1st, 4 GA Central Michigan	Beat Ohio in final	Long (23.0)	Long (10.4)
Michigan (Big Ten)	26-8 (13-5)	2nd, 3 GB Purdue		Rice (22.1)	Rice (7.2)
Michigan State (Big Ten)	10-18 (5-13)	8th, 11 GB Purdue		Valentine (13.3)	Papadakos (5.7)
Western Michigan (MAC)	12-17 (7-9)	T-5th, 7 GB Eastern Michigan	Lost in semifinals	Brown (19.6)	Riikonen (6.6)

1988-89 SEASON	RECORDS	FINISH	TOURNAMENT*	SCORING	REBOUNDS
Central Michigan (MAC)	12-16 (6-10)	T-6th, 8 GB Ball State	Lost in quarterfinals	Briggs (13.8)	Briggs (5.6)
Detroit (MCC)	7-21 (4-8)	T-5th, 6 GB Evansville	Lost in quarterfinals	McKinney (16.1)	McKinney (6.7)
Eastern Michigan (MAC)	16-13 (7-9)	5th, 7 GB Ball State	Lost in semifinals	Neely (13.1)	Henderson (6.3)
Michigan (Big Ten)	30-7 (12-6)	3rd, 3 GB Indiana		Rice (25.6)	Vaught (8.0)
Michigan State (Big Ten)	18-15 (6-12)	T-8th, 9 GB Indiana		Smith (17.7)	Smith (6.9)
Western Michigan (MAC)	12-16 (6-10)	T-6th, 8 GB Ball State	Lost in first round	Baumgardt (13.9)	Baumgardt (5.7)

Conference post-season tournament

Coaches

Central Michigan: Dick Parfitt (1979-85), 64-94 (.405); Charles Coles (1985-89), 64-54 (.542). Total: 128-148 (.464).

Detroit: Willie McCarter (1979-82), 33-48 (.407); Don Sicko (1982-87), 57-88 (.393); John Mulroy (1987-88), 7-20 (.259); Ricky Birdsong (1988-89), 7-21 (.250). Total: 104-177 (.370).

Eastern Michigan: Jim Boyce (1979-86), 86-98 (.467); Ben Braun (1986-89), 57-46 (.553). Total: 143-144 (.498).

Michigan: Johnny Orr (1979-80), 17-13 (.567); Bill Frieder (1980-89), 191-87 (.687); Steve Fisher (1989), 6-0 (1.000). Total: 214-100 (.682).

Michigan State: Jud Heathcote (1979-89), 151-138 (.522). Total: 151-138 (.522).

Western Michigan: Les Wothke (1979-82), 42-41 (.506); Vernon Payne (1983-89), 69-126 (.354). Total: 111-167 (.399).

NCAA tournament appearances

Central Michigan: 1987: Lost to UCLA, 92-73.

Eastern Michigan: 1988: Lost to Pittsburgh, 108-90.

Michigan: 1985: Beat Fairleigh Dickinson, 59-55; lost to Villanova, 59-55. 1986: Beat Akron, 70-64; lost to Iowa State, 72-69. 1987: Beat Navy, 97-82; lost to North Carolina, 109-97. 1988: Beat Boise State, 63-58; beat Florida, 108-85; lost to North Carolina, 78-69. 1989: Beat Xavier (Ohio), 92-87; beat South Alabama, 91-82; beat North Carolina, 92-87; beat Virginia, 102-65; beat Illinois, 83-81; beat Seton Hall, 80-79 (OT) (NCAA championship game).

Michigan State: 1985: Lost to Ala.-Birmingham, 70-68. 1986: Beat Washington, 72-70; beat Georgetown, 80-68; lost to Kansas, 96-86 (OT).

NIT appearances

Michigan: 1980: Beat Nebraska, 76-69; beat Texas-El Paso, 74-65; lost to Virginia, 79-68. 1981: Beat Duquesne, 74-58; beat Toledo, 80-68; lost to Syracuse, 91-76. 1984: Beat Wichita State, 94-70; beat Marquette, 83-70; beat Xavier (Ohio), 63-62; beat Virginia Tech, 78-75; beat Notre Dame, 83-63 (NIT championship game).

Michigan State: 1983: Beat Bowling Green, 72-71; lost to Fresno State, 72-58. 1989: Beat Kent State, 83-69; beat Wichita State, 79-67; beat Villanova, 70-63; lost to St. Louis, 74-64; lost to Alabama-Birmingham, 78-76 (NIT consolation).

Michigan state colleges

Great Lakes Conference champions: 1980: Saginaw Valley State (11-3). 1981: Hillsdale (13-3). 1982: Ferris State (14-2). 1983: Ferris State, Saginaw Valley State (13-3). 1984: Wayne State (13-3). 1985: Saginaw Valley State (15-1). 1986: Wayne State (14-2). 1987: Ferris State, Wayne State (13-3). 1988: Ferris State (14-2). 1989: Ferris State (16-0).

Michigan Intercollegiate Athletic Association champions: 1980: Calvin (11-1). 1981: Albion, Calvin, Hope (9-3). 1982: Hope (10-2). 1983: Hope (11-1). 1984: Hope (12-0). 1985: Hope (11-1). 1986: Calvin (10-2). 1987: Hope (11-1). 1988: Hope (10-2). 1989: Calvin (10-2).

PRO BASKETBALL

Isiah Thomas held the hardware and
Mark Aguirre the champagne as the
boyhood buddies celebrated the
Pistons' 1989 NBA championship.

THE SAVIOR IS DRAFTED

By Charlie Vincent

JUNE 9,
1981
◆

As the only team to average under 100 points, the 1980-81 Pistons lost 61 games. Then they lost the coin toss to determine the NBA's first draft pick. Dallas used it to take Mark Aguirre, a DePaul forward. The Pistons drafted Isiah Thomas, a sophomore point guard who had led Indiana to the NCAA championship.

A wide, bright grin split the little man's face as he slipped behind the big man who was talking to a circle of furiously scribbling reporters.

"Partner!" 6-foot-1 Isiah Thomas said, slapping 6-6 Kelly Tripucka on the back and extending his hand. The newest Pistons slapped hands and smiled at each other, proving again that adversity sometimes creates the strongest bonds.

If they had been able to select their teams, rather than the other way around, neither Thomas nor Tripucka would have chosen Detroit in the NBA draft. But fate has thrown them together and made them the centerpiece of the Pistons' hoped-for resurgence — after winning just 37 games in the last two seasons.

The Pistons, with two first-round draft choices, made Thomas, a point guard from Indiana, the second overall pick, then selected Tripucka, a forward from Notre Dame, as the 12th overall.

Thomas had made no secret of his desire to return to his hometown of Chicago and play for the Bulls; Tripucka is so impressed with the Pistons that he says Thomas is the only man he knows on his new team.

"I don't think I know one player for them," Tripucka said in the crowded Grand Ballroom of New York's Grand Hyatt Hotel, where the draft was held. "But I know Isiah, and that's all I need to know right now. He's the man with the ball."

Indeed, that will be Thomas' primary role with the Pistons: Getting the ball inside to Tripucka, Kent Benson, Phil Hubbard, Terry Tyler and Greg Kelser.

Five weeks ago, when he announced he was giving up his final two years of eligibility at Indiana, Thomas expressed some doubt about fitting into the scheme of things in Detroit. Now he said he had changed his mind.

"I think I have to," he said, smiling. "I've heard things about their management and they're good people. They're not sit-back-and-wait people. They want to win, and I'll do anything possible to win, too. Within the rules."

Tripucka, who can play small forward and big guard, finished his career at Notre Dame as its fourth-leading scorer, behind Austin Carr, Adrian Dantley and Tom Hawkins. The son of 1949 Lions quarterback Frank Tripucka averaged 15.3 points and almost five rebounds during his four seasons in South Bend.

Until last weekend it was believed that the Dallas Mavericks would make Thomas the first player picked in the draft. But after he met with team officials, stories began to circulate that the Mavericks had soured on him. On draft day, Dallas selected DePaul forward Mark Aguirre.

"I've read where I was called a jerk and things of that nature," Thomas said. "But I can't believe it because I was there and they didn't call me a jerk when I was there." ◆

Before the draft, Isiah Thomas took a shot at the Pistons' forwards. "My job," he said, "is to get the ball to somebody who can score. In Detroit, who would I pass to?" He visited town for the first time a week after the draft and, in trying to apologize, took a shot at the Pistons' guards. "I want to clear up something that I said before. Don (Chaney) has informed me that maybe the players we have here just didn't have anybody to get them the ball. Hopefully I'll be able to get them the ball." In his NBA debut, the 20-year-old rookie played with the poise of a five-year veteran. He had 31 points, 11 assists and three rebounds in a 118-113 victory over Milwaukee before 9,182 in the Silverdome.

The Pistons of the middle '80s could score at will. But so could their opponents. On a December night in Denver, the Pistons and run-and-gun Nuggets scored 370 points, by far an NBA record. The key play, believe it or not, was a free throw missed intentionally.

Kelly Tripucka scored 35 points against the Nuggets, but two teammates scored more. Tripucka averaged 21.6 points in his five seasons with the Pistons. He was dealt with Kent Benson to Utah for Adrian Dantley before the 1986-87 season.

ROCKY MOUNTAIN HIGH

By Mike Downey

By now you may have heard about the Denver Nuggets scoring 184 points and getting beat. You can put it in Ripley's Believe It or Not, right between the woman with three heads and the man who grew a 2,000-pound tomato.

In a prodigious and preposterous professional basketball game, the Nuggets lost to the Pistons in triple overtime, 186-184. The game set NBA standards for points scored and wretched excess.

No, this game did not mark the advent of the league's new experimental 2.4-second clock. It was just an old-fashioned shoot-'em-up out West. No representative of Denver or Detroit did anything special on defense — putting up his hands, for instance. D was something you found only in the teams' names.

At least the Nuggets were trying this time. Earlier this year, coach Doug (Don't Stand So Close to Me) Moe told his players to pose as statues in Portland so that the home team could break the stadium scoring record. The NBA thought Moe behaved like a stooge and made him pay a stiff fine.

But it wasn't as if no one had any idea this many points would be scored.

"Before the game," said Pistons coach Chuck Daly, "I told Doug Moe that we should make it the first team to 140 would win the game. Little did I know how prophetic that would be."

And none of it would have happened had Bill Laimbeer not intentionally missed a free throw with four seconds left in regulation. Isiah Thomas grabbed the rebound and scored on a driving shot, tying the score at 145.

Among the highlights and records:

■ The game took 3 hours and 11 minutes.

■ The 370 points beat the NBA record by 33. The previous record was set March 6, 1982, when San Antonio beat Milwaukee, 171-166, also in triple overtime.

■ Thomas and Nuggets Kiki Vandeweghe and Alex English set career scoring highs. Thomas (18-for-34 from the field, 10-for-19 from the line) scored 47 points, Vandeweghe 51 and English 47. For the Pistons, John Long scored 41 points and Kelly Tripucka 35, including all 12 of the team's points in the second overtime. ◆

INSTANT OFFENSE

By Charlie Vincent

APRIL 27,
1984
◆

After finishing 49-33 — their first winning season since 1976-77 — and only one game behind Milwaukee, the Pistons played a stirring first-round playoff series with the Knicks. The final game was played on a neutral court of sorts — Joe Louis Arena — because a motocross had booked the Silverdome. Isiah Thomas, however, had no trouble revving up in his new surroundings.

The season ended with the shouts of 21,208 reverberating off the walls of Joe Louis Arena. It ended with Isiah Thomas and Bill Laimbeer, the two players perhaps most instrumental in the season's success, sitting on the bench, fouled out of the most important game of their careers.

It ended because the New York Knicks had one more big play, one more stroke of luck, one more dash of whatever it takes to separate the winners from those who must go to the sidelines. "It was," said Pistons coach Chuck Daly, "like a 15-round championship fight and the guy on his feet at the end wins. I guess that's them."

It took the Knicks five full games and one overtime period to do it. But they eliminated the Pistons from the NBA playoffs, 127-123.

Both superstars got in foul trouble in the third period, New York's Bernard King going to the bench with his fourth foul with 8:55 left in the quarter, Thomas leaving with his fourth two minutes later. But in the final 94 seconds of regulation Thomas put on a one-man show that rivaled King's 23 straight points in the second game of the series. He scored 16 points — including a three-point field goal. He was so baffling during that minute and a half that he enticed Rory Sparrow into three fouls in only 30 seconds. He scored on lay-ups, long jumpers and at the free throw line.

He had the crowd dancing and clapping in the aisles when his picture-perfect three-pointer cut cleanly through the nets to tie it 114-all with 23 seconds left. And when John Long harassed Darrell Walker into botching an inbounds pass, the Pistons got the ball back, still with 23 seconds left. The scene was set for the Cinderella ending. Thomas stood at the top of the key, his teammates fanned out on the sides. Walker watched and waited for the move he knew was sure to come, Thomas driving for the hoop.

And when he did, Walker, who had not made a steal all night, slapped the ball away, sending the game into an overtime that would be dominated by New York.

Thomas finished the night with 35 points; King had 41, giving him a record total of 213 for a five-game playoff series.

"With all sincerity," said Knicks coach Hubie Brown, "it's too bad someone had to lose. Isiah Thomas' effort in the fourth quarter was a staggering punch to us. I've been around a long time and I've never been in a game like that." ◆

Isiah Thomas, with 16 points in the final 94 seconds of regulation, finished with 35 points (13-for-25 from the field, 7-for-9 from the line), 12 assists and three rebounds. "Isiah had an unbelievable last quarter," Pistons coach Chuck Daly said. "Only he can play like that."

It was unanimous. After Isiah Thomas scored 30 points and contributed 10 assists to lead the East to a 139-132 victory in the All-Star Game at Dallas, all 15 voters named the Pistons' guard as the best player on the floor. But Thomas, who also was MVP in 1984, was quick to deflect the credit.

By driving around and through the giants of the West — Rolando Blackman, Ralph Sampson and Kareem Abdul-Jabbar — little Isiah Thomas made it big in the '86 All-Star Game. Playing 36 minutes, Thomas had 30 points, 10 assists and five steals. In the '84 Denver game, Thomas won his first MVP award, edging Julius Erving by four votes. In 39 minutes, Thomas had 15 assists, four steals, five rebounds and 21 points, all scored in the second half.

MOST VALUABLE MOM

By Charlie Vincent

siah Thomas stopped smiling. He stopped just long enough to drop his head onto his mother's right shoulder and sob his eyes out.

They stood in the middle of the floor at Reunion Arena in Dallas and embraced and cried together. They cried for joy. They hugged and closed their eyes and tears ran down their cheeks. And what memories must have tumbled through their minds.

The flashbulbs popped, the pens scribbled cryptic notes. But neither the pen nor the camera could record what was in the hearts of Isiah and Mary Thomas.

Only they knew how far he came to get here, to become just the fifth man to be named most valuable player twice in the NBA's All-Star Game.

Bob Cousy did it. And Bob Pettit. And Oscar Robertson and Julius Erving and now Isiah Thomas. No one else. Not Larry Bird. Not Kareem Abdul-Jabbar. Not Wilt Chamberlain.

Think about that. Then think about the odds of Isiah Lord Thomas III, from a crime-ridden, drug-infested neighborhood of Chicago, ever doing it.

Do you know how bad that neighborhood is? When the Pistons first signed him, the Free Press sent me to Chicago to do a story on his childhood. I took a cab to his neighborhood and the driver refused to stop. He wouldn't let me out.

"I don't live far from here," he said. "I know this neighborhood. And I ain't letting you out of this cab here."

That's the kind of neighborhood it is.

Think about the odds of somebody from that neighborhood ever playing pro basketball. Think about the odds of somebody from that neighborhood just surviving to adulthood.

Isiah Thomas has thought about it.

"There are a lot of good people in my neighborhood," he has said. "But a lot of them just didn't have the opportunities I had."

A lot of them died. From drugs. And from guns. A lot of them are locked up.

It's an old story that some of Isiah's family got caught in those traps. Got busted. Got in trouble. Got on the hustle and tried to shortcut their way through life.

Mary Thomas didn't allow that to happen to her youngest son. She got him out of the neighborhood, sent him to a private suburban high school, woke him up in the pre-dawn darkness every day so he could make his bus and get to class on time.

Mary Thomas has never told her baby boy how old she is; he can only guess. He knows she has used up more than half her lifetime raising him and the children that came before.

"That's what I was thinking when we were hugging," he said later, after the tears had dried and the smile had returned. "I was thinking of the hard times she had and the struggles she had gone through and how great it is for her to be able to come here to Dallas and stay in the Sheraton Hotel and be with the best people and see these things. And then I think about what a relatively short time she has, I mean, she's not going to live another 60 years. It was very, very emotional."

Isiah Thomas's first MVP Award is in the living room of his mother's house in Chicago. The second one will probably go there, too.

Nothing he can give her, he feels, will repay what she gave him. Anything he gets, she feels, will be only what he earned.

When Mary Thomas dried her tears she had only one explanation for the emotion that spilled out when they embraced.

"He just works so hard. He deserves it. . . . I'm so proud of him."

That, more than his smile and the quicksilver things he does on the court, is the essence of Isiah Thomas. ♦

They battled fiercely and evenly for six games in the Eastern Conference finals. The Celtics took the first two, the Pistons the next two. In Game 5, with the Pistons five seconds from ending a 16-game Boston Garden losing streak, Larry Bird stole Isiah Thomas' inbounds pass and fed Dennis Johnson for the game-winner. Detroit tied the series again, but Game 7 would be played in hot and ghostly Boston Garden.

Vinnie Johnson kept playing after colliding with Adrian Dantley. But with 7:21 left, VJ took a seat, grabbed an ice pack and never returned. For the Celtics, it was their 13th victory in 15 seventh games in Boston Garden.

A HAUNTING DEFEAT

By Johnette Howard

It was incredible and stirring and even frightening at times. It was a basketball classic unfolding before your eyes, and you knew it before it was even half over.

And for the Pistons it was a sweat-soaked dream that ended sadly on a jump shot by Danny Ainge with 25 seconds left, a shot that propelled the Boston Celtics into the NBA Finals for the fourth straight year with a 117-114 victory in Game 7 of the Eastern Conference finals at sweltering Boston Garden. Boston moves on to meet the Los Angeles Lakers. And the Pistons flew home on a chartered jet, still clinging stubbornly to Isiah Thomas' belief that "we have the better basketball team."

"That's his opinion," retorted Celtics forward Kevin McHale. "That's just sour grapes."

Until the Pistons' last frantic gasp — courtesy of a foul that Dennis Johnson didn't want to commit with seven seconds remaining and the score 112-108 — possession of the grueling game swayed back and forth.

The Pistons hung close despite a late third-quarter collision between Adrian Dantley and Vinnie Johnson that put Dantley in the hospital overnight with a concussion and Johnson out for the final 7:21 because of an injured neck. Both players were hurt after banging heads in a dive for a loose ball.

"I'm not going to say an injury decided that game, because we had a lot of injured people out there," said McHale, one of the walking wounded. "It's not like I'm gonna say I feel so sorry for him I'm gonna cry."

The Celtics put the game away in the fourth quarter by dominating the boards and sinking the second- and third-chance shots, which the Pistons just couldn't seem to convert after entering the quarter trailing, 81-80. By then it had come down to this: 12 more minutes and the kind of attitude McHale talked about two days earlier, when asked how it felt to play despite a broken right foot bone, the flu, teammates with mangled fingers and wrenched ankles.

Add the suffocating afternoon heat and the sight of Dantley being carried off on a stretcher, and McHale could have been speaking for both teams when he explained what it took to press on despite a body that seems tapped out and a mind ready to crack: "You fight that voice every day — that voice that says, 'P— on it. Give up.'" There wasn't an ounce of give-up on either team. Not now.

"They played harder than any team I've ever played," Pistons guard Joe Dumars said softly, wiping the season's last sweat from his brow and staring at the locker-room floor. For most of the game Dumars (35 points) was the unlikely axis the Pistons' offense revolved around. For most of the game it was Dumars' 15-for-21 shooting that helped Detroit weather Thomas' foul troubles, quiet offensive days by Rick Mahorn and Bill Laimbeer, and the Celtics' ability to force Dantley to pass again and again rather than shoot them down to defeat again.

Until that back-breaking shot of Ainge's, the Celtics' main player in the drama was, of course, Larry Bird. He finished with 37 points. Ainge had hit a big shot earlier — a three-pointer that gave the Celtics a 102-99 lead with 3:06 left after they had missed five shots on that possession and had the ball for 1:12.

"I don't know what else we could have done," said Pistons rookie Dennis Rodman. "The ball just kept bouncing over our heads, and he finally hit it. That's more than a kick in the stomach. That's like trying to have a baby."

After that, the Celtics were never tied or behind again, and the Pistons' best last-ditch shot at a tie faded when Thomas (25 points) missed a three-pointer with 20 seconds left that could have tied the game at 108.

"I just shot it a little too hard," said Thomas, who refused to admit he was disappointed by the ending. "You can't cry, because you know you gave your all. Had you not given your all, then you could go home and cry." ◆

Adrian Dantley and Vinnie Johnson, pursuing a loose ball, knocked heads with eight seconds left in the third quarter. The Pistons were leading by a point. Dantley, who had 18 points, insisted the outcome would have been different if he hadn't been hurt. "I didn't dive for no loose ball," he said. "I had to get pushed from behind. . . . We would have had some champagne, that's for sure." Instead, Dantley had fluid served intravenously at Massachusetts General Hospital.

JUNE 21,
1988
◆

The first six games had been spectacular: A stunning Detroit upset in Game 1 at the Forum, Magic Johnson rising from his sick bed to even the series in Game 2, more Magic in Game 3 at the Silverdome as the Lakers pulled ahead, decisive Pistons victories in Games 4 and 5, Isiah Thomas almost winning Game 6 singlehandedly, playing the last 1½ quarters on one good leg. The 1988 NBA Finals were tied at three games apiece when Thomas, still hobbled by his sprained right ankle, led his teammates to the floor for Game 7 at the Forum.

Before each game's opening tip, Lakers guard Magic Johnson and Pistons guard Isiah Thomas threw out an opening kiss. In Game 4, Johnson twice decked Thomas driving the lane and a fight nearly erupted. "Sure, we're friends," Thomas said, "but we're playing for the title now."

TIME RUNS OUT
By Mitch Albom

They lost? They lost. Those are all the words needed. There was only one team in the world for Detroit, and all night long — in this breathtaking Game 7 of the NBA Finals — that team, the Detroit Pistons, fought off defeat like some Atlas in basketball sneakers, the weight of the world on their shoulders. Until finally, with just moments left in the longest season in the history of the game, their shoulders buckled and the world caved in.

They lost. It's over. The most magical of all Detroit basketball seasons ended one victory short of glory, final score 108-105, Los Angeles, a heart-breaking, heart-stopping

final show that wasn't over until A.C. Green beat the Detroit defense for a lay-up with two seconds left that gave LA the win by inches at the Forum.

"We came within a hair's breadth," said Pistons coach Chuck Daly when it was all over. "A hair's breadth. . . . "

"Does that give you any consolation?" someone asked.

"No." he said.

They lost.

Oh, but what a war! Weeks from now, when the bitterness has subsided, these pictures will remain: Here was LA rocking and rolling in its home arena — and here was Detroit, miles from home, refusing to die. Here was LA, playing champion, saying, "Had enough? Ready to quit?" And here was Detroit saying, "Never! Never quit!"

Here was LA's James Worthy — the eventual series MVP — spinning and hooking and seemingly toying with the Pistons, 36 points, 16 rebounds.

And here were the Detroit kids — Dennis Rodman and John Salley — growing up before our eyes, refusing to let anybody intimidate them, playing the games of their lives.

It was all the Pistons had, all the courage, all the desire, all the strength oozing from their pores. Their captain, Isiah Thomas, was hobbled with an ankle injury; he was on the bench down the stretch. Their toughest scoring threat, Adrian Dantley, was on the bench as well. Youthful enthusiasm was carrying them, but youthful enthusiasm would do them in. With 39 seconds left and the Pistons trailing, 103-100, Rodman came downcourt on a fast break, he had a lane to the hoop, and suddenly, dear God, he pulled up for a jumper.

"I don't know what I was thinking," he would say in the locker room afterward, ➡

Only the Pistons stood in the Lakers' way of becoming the first team since the 1969 Celtics to repeat as NBA champion. In a 99-86 Game 3 loss, the Pistons' three centers — Chuck Nevitt, Bill Laimbeer and James Edwards — were sitting ducks.

shaking his head. "I don't know why I did that. I can't explain it."

His shot was long. It bounded off the back of the rim. Daly buried his head in his hands, and moments later the Lakers buried the Pistons, although not before Bill Laimbeer had cut the lead to 106-105 with a three-point bomb with six seconds left. What a final act!

"I left everything I had out on that floor," said a weary Joe Dumars, who scored a team-high 25 points. That close. That scary.

But when that buzzer sounded, the Detroit players walked off the court with that empty feeling, like the last day of school. Out of gas. Out of games. Out of time.

The 1988 Detroit Pistons might be the best team that never won it all. They stayed with this Los Angeles juggernaut, on guts, on effort, on desire. And on courage. And that begins with Thomas. How quickly did your heart go straight to your throat when you saw him hobble out to start this game? Two days earlier, after twisting his right ankle and spraining it in three places, he was in such pain he seemed to be crying as he answered questions. And yet there he was, in the first half, diving into the stands and chasing passes and making steals — until his body gave out.

"What was it like for you, the captain, to have to watch from the bench during that final period?" someone asked.

"I was very proud," he said. "The guys out there played well, they played great defense. It was a joy and a pleasure to be a part of that."

But it was not enough. How sad for these Pistons: for Thomas, who braved more pain than any man should; for Dantley, who thought, after 12 years, he was finally going to see his reward; for Laimbeer, who had his bad games at the worst times; for coach Daly, a second banana his whole life, and a second banana once again this morning.

Theirs will be a postseason of what-ifs. They will haunt the Detroit psyche like empty foundations of buildings never built.

What if Rickey Mahorn had been healthy, a dominating force, as he had been all season?

What if Dumars had hit that running bank shot in the closing pandemonium of Game 6?

What if Thomas had never turned that ankle? What if Rodman hadn't taken that ill-advised jumper? What if Laimbeer had been able to save that ball from going out of bounds in the final minute?

What if? What does it matter? Life goes on. The Pistons stop here. You can remember the heartbreak — Lord knows there was plenty — or you can remember the near-glory, and everything that brought them to this oh-so-close finish.

This was more than a season for these guys, it was a sweet moment in time, a clean and well-lighted place in the history books. They won more games than any Pistons team before them. They went further than any Pistons team before them. They came onto the stage as brutes and left with an entire nation's respect — for their courage, their determination, for their talent. They played

and they fought and they laughed and they shook the world. They took on all comers – the Bullets, the Bulls, the Celtics, the Lakers. They could beat any team in the league.

They just couldn't beat them all. ◆

Isiah Thomas scored 25 points in the third quarter of Game 6 — setting an NBA Finals record. He hit 11 of 13 shots. Thomas twisted his right ankle with 4:21 left in the quarter, yet he returned with 3:46 left and scored 11 more points. "Nobody," Thomas said, "ever said winning the NBA championship would be easy." Teammate Dennis Rodman found the going easy around the basket, especially against Kurt Rambis. But Rodman took an out-of-character, ill-advised jumper that all but doomed the Pistons in Game 7. The shot would haunt him throughout the next year.

A MIDSEASON DIVORCE

By Mitch Albom

FEB. 15,
1989
◆

When the Pistons traded Adrian Dantley to Dallas for Mark Aguirre, players whispered, fans screamed, even Dantley's mother offered an opinion, referring to Isiah Thomas as "that little con artist." The eventual bottom line: Dantley at first refused to report to Dallas, missed three games, then limped along with the Mavericks to a 13-23 post-trade mark and 38-44 season record. Aguirre was a quiet and inconsistent contributor, but the Pistons were 31-6 post-trade in the regular season.

Farewell to the Teacher. Farewell to that body, hard and strong, and that face, which always seemed halfway between amusement and anger. Adrian Dantley came in with a bad reputation, and, ironically, he leaves in exchange for one. Known as selfish, moody and a ball-hog when he arrived in Detroit, he proved critics wrong, leading the Pistons to their best season ever, playing a role, muscling against giants, spinning and whirling and desiring his way to the hoop. He even sent himself to the hospital once diving for a basketball.

Diving? Adrian Dantley? And now, suddenly, he has been traded to Dallas for a guy named Mark Aguirre, who has a reputation for being . . . selfish, moody and a ball-hog. Go figure.

There will be those who say this is a smart trade in the long run but foolish in the short. There will be those who say the Pistons just secured themselves an NBA championship.

And nobody — to borrow some baseball vernacular — knows nuthin.' What really went on behind the scenes during Dantley's 2½ years in Detroit was rarely printed. It was mumbled. It was whispered. Like an uneasy marriage, Dantley Does Detroit was encouraging in the good times and stormy in the bad, so no one would give it the kiss of death until the very end. For weeks, Dantley knew he was gone. He told several teammates, "They're just waiting until the last minute."

And he was right. Why would the Pistons make this trade? Why would they cut loose last year's playoff star, their mentor to developing players, a guy who had proven his talents against everyone in the league? Why? Here's why. Because Dantley's years were advancing and his skills were not. Because his attitude was quiet at best, aloof at worst. Because Aguirre, nearly four years younger, was available. And because the Pistons seem convinced that other people's problems — i.e., William Bedford, Darryl Dawkins, even Dantley himself — can be rehabilitated in the waters of Camp Isiah.

And yes, let us not forget Isiah Thomas in this picture. If this trade proves anything, it is that the Pistons are Isiah's team — a sentence Dantley himself used to utter with regularity. That does not mean Thomas orchestrated this trade (despite what Dantley thinks). It does mean that Isiah stays and everybody else learns to work around him. Dantley was never much of a dance partner; Aguirre, abhorred by many of his Dallas teammates, was quoted after first learning of the deal as saying, "Great. It'll be great to join Isiah."

Interesting choice of words. There are 10 other guys here, remember?

Aguirre is certainly capable of brilliant basketball — when he wants to play. James Donaldson, his Mavericks teammate, said, "I'll look forward to having a new guy here who is willing to play hard every night." Hard? You never had to worry about hard with Dantley. Hard was the only game he knew to play. At his height (6-foot-5) and his position (small forward), what choice did he have? Guts. Confidence. He had them.

Here is the way Dantley saw it: "It's Isiah's team. He calls the shots. That guy (Aguirre) is his friend and he wants to play with his friend. If Chuck has to make a call, who do you think he's gonna side with? I didn't have any problem with Isiah. But Chuck wasn't playing me for a while." Dantley's trust in Daly was already thin, because he saw Isiah and Daly as a tandem.

Here is the way management saw it: Dantley had probably peaked. His best years were behind him. His moves were being anticipated by opposing teams and referees alike.

And then there were the personality conflicts. Daly will say of Dantley, "We got along fine," but they didn't. Daly found A.D. selfish and greedy and infatuated with money. So when Aguirre's name came up, and his personality was questioned, no doubt management said: "Hey, how much worse can it be than what we've got now? The guy's younger. His talent is there. He already likes Isiah. Why not?"

The trade was made. Farewell to the Teacher. ◆

Isiah Thomas got an earful when Dallas came to town six weeks after the Dantley-Aguirre trade. Moments after their chat, which neither would discuss, Thomas threw up an 18-foot air ball. But Detroit won handily, 90-77. Thomas scored 30 points, Dantley 18 and Aguirre 12.

The Pistons of the '80s always had been Isiah Thomas' team. But the "other guard," Joe Dumars, was the hero of Detroit's dismantling of the Los Angeles Lakers in the 1989 NBA Finals. The Lakers rode into the series on an 11-0 run — three series sweeps. But it was the Pistons who swept.

In the NBA Finals, Dumars averaged 27.3 points, shot 57.6 percent from the field, contributed six assists a game, earned a trip to Disney World, a shiny trophy, a new Jeep and a new contract for $8 million over six years.

GOING TO DISNEY WORLD!

By Johnette Howard

He is confident, understand. Like the times when he lets a jump shot go and immediately starts backpedaling downcourt, his wrist still cocked in mid-air because he knows, just knows, his shot is going in.

But when it came to winning the Most Valuable Player Award of the NBA Finals, well, guard Joe Dumars — the quietest Piston — would never presume to talk aloud about that. "Do you really think I've got it?" Dumars whispered to a reporter the day before the Pistons' series-clinching 105-97 victory in Game 4 at the Forum.

"Are you kidding?" the reporter answered.

No. Dumars wasn't. Not until he was clutching the silver-and-black trophy, walking toward a parted sea of teammates and Pistons supporters chanting, "Joe, Joe, Joe" in the champagne-soaked locker room, saying quietly to himself: "Anonymity. I just lost it."

Not that he was complaining. "We worked hard for it; it was our purpose coming into this series from Day 1," Dumars said. "And now, here we are. . . . I've always played offense. But when I first got here, they didn't need me to score a lot of points. I had to just work my way in. . . . Now, it couldn't be better."

Dumars, suddenly, was being applauded more for his torrid scoring than his defensive dirty work. He scored 22 points in Game 1 and another 33 in Game 2 — 26 in the first half. He started innocently enough in Game 3, then leveled the Lakers with a 21-point third quarter and finished with 31. He added another 23 points in the finale.

Still, as hot as he had been, Dumars approached Game 4 with some anxiety. In the long wait, his mind was consumed by the game, the game, the game — and the prickly uncertainty of how it would turn out. "I was tossing and turning all night last night," Dumars said in the afternoon, a baseball cap pushed back on his head. "I woke up at three in the morning, and I haven't been to bed since. I'm exhausted. You can feel the anticipation building. It's hard not to. My stomach is just rolling around inside."

In the last week, Dumars knows, he has become something of a revelation to the nation and its press. After Game 3, he had laughed and remarked how commonplace it has been to look across the locker room and see crowds around other players' lockers. "Now," he said, "they're standing around mine."

Was that bad? "Well," Dumars said, "it's not like it's gonna make me crumble."

The greatest wonder, to Dumars, is that all of this is being received as a big surprise. Four years into his pro career, Dumars has long quit reminding people he averaged more than 25 points during his last two college seasons at McNeese State. He also seems to think it would look ungainly to say the only reason he didn't score more before was he didn't try. But Isiah Thomas did that for him after Game 2: "When Joe first got here, Joe was pretty smart. He looked around and knew he'd have to play defense if he wanted to play. So that's what he did. It's just not all he can do."

And if the defensive-stopper image stuck, it may have been broadened forever with this series, too. But even so, the most egotistical thing Dumars will say is only: "It's like people are just finding out, 'Oh! Hey. He can play.'" Then he half-snorts, half-laughs. To Dumars, even that oversight is OK. Knowing what he is has always been enough. And he knew it even before Disney wanted to pay him $40,000 to say a few lines if the MVP Award came his way.

And when his last obligation to the Pistons is through, Dumars says he'll enjoy all this in his own way. He'll be on the first plane back home to southwest Louisiana. Back to Lake Charles, the small town where the heat rarely ebbs. Back to his midsummer night dinners of crawfish and catfish and conversation with his tried-and-true friends.

"All this may change my life but if it does, it will only last about a week down there," Dumars said. "People down there have to work for a living."

And Dumars? Forget Disney World. After a joyride of a series, the nation knows quiet Joe is as real as it gets. ◆

They had done it — a 105-97 victory over the Lakers for a four-game sweep of the NBA Finals, the Pistons' first championship since they entered the NBA as the Ft. Wayne Pistons in 1948. The ghosts of the Garden and the Forum had been exorcised at last. Champions! Bad Boys! It was time to party . . .

NOT BAD, BOYS

By Mitch Albom

Joe Dumars is gazing at his teammates on the dance floor and holding a champagne bottle, which should tell you how far this party has gone. Joey? Champagne? He lifts the bottle awkwardly to his lips.

"So you're drinking now?"

He lowers the bottle, stares at it, then laughs. "Look at me," he says, "I don't know what I'm doing. I'm no drinker. I don't even know how I got this thing!" He shakes his head in happiness. "Man, oh, man. . . . "

Bad Boys done good. Champions of the world. Out on the floor, Rick Mahorn is bumping and swaying like a Solid Gold dancer; John Salley, dressed in California shorts and a Detroit Bad Boys T-shirt, towers over the crowd with a funky roll, a woman on the left, a woman on the right, a woman in front. Dennis Rodman is off in the corner, talking to friends, still dressed in his uniform — even though the game ended five hours ago. "I don't want to take it off," he says, pointing to his number. "I don't want to take it off!"

Bad Boys done good. End of the rainbow. The Lakers had been swept, the champagne had been popped, the fantasy began to take on a real life, happy faces and teary eyes and music and yelling and laughter and . . . look out! There goes Jack McCloskey, the general manager, up on the table as the next record starts.

The table?

"You know you make me wanna
SHOUT!
Put my hands up and
SHOUT!
Throw my hands up and
SHOUT! . . . "

◆

Shout? There were five seconds left and the Boston Garden crowd was shouting, on its feet, roaring like the flames of hell, and Chuck Daly was frantically waving his arms, screaming madly, his voice lost in the noise. It was the 1987 Eastern Conference finals, and all he wanted was a time-out. Just a time-out. Come on, Isiah, LOOK AT ME, DAMN IT! But he was so far away and Isiah wasn't looking and Isiah lofted a pass inbounds, a soft pass, too soft, and the game and the series and the dreams were dashed before his very eyes when Larry Bird — who had the one thing the Pistons still lacked, championship mentality — zipped in front, stole the ball, whipped it to a streaking Dennis Johnson, who laid it up and in.

"I was watching the thing from mid-court," Dennis Rodman would later say, "and I saw Bird steal it, and I couldn't move. I was frozen. I was paralyzed. It was like a terrible dream, man. A terrible dream."

The dream turned nightmare. The series was lost. The Pistons went home. Growing up.

◆

Dennis Rodman punished the Lakers — averaging 10 rebounds a game during the finals — as he did the rest of the NBA during the season. In his third season, Rodman finished third in the voting for the Sixth Man and Defensive Player of the Year awards.

"SALLEY ON THE MICROPHONE, BABY!"

The crowd turns its head. Here is Spider John, the Pistons' answer to Dale Carnegie (How To Win Friends and Influence People? Simple. Geek 'em!), and he is up there with the disc jockeys, holding out a finger, inviting the whole city to his weekend parties — "Friday night at Landsdowne, Saturday at Maxie's, y'all!" — then delivering a rap he has been writing all season. "Everybody now," he urges, "BAAAD BOYS, BAAAD BOYS, BAAAD BOYS — pick it up!" ⬧

"BAAAD BOYS," joins the crowd.

"What's that, now?"

"BAAAD BOYS"

In the back of the room, wearing blue sunglasses and a white cap, is Bill Laimbeer, grinning, pointing, singing along, a little bit tipsy.

"Did you hear my post-game press conference?" he yells over the music.

"No."

"They said I made a jerk of myself."

He grins. Only Laimbeer could grin at a sentence like that.

"What did you say?"

"I told them this finally proved all you people wrong for all the stupid stuff you had written all year long about us."

"You said that to the national media?"

"Yep."

"Oh, well."

"You think I made a jerk out of myself? You know what?" he says, smiling and rising back up, as if to remind us that basketball players are taller than the rest of us. "The way I feel right now — screw 'em."

◆

Where is Isiah?

Over there, on the side of the room, one arm draped around his wife, the other draped around Matt Dobek, the Pistons' public relations director. Here is the picture of contentment, watching everything, the dancing, the food, a full-time smile on his face. For years Isiah attended parties like this for other teams, mostly for the Lakers, where his friend Magic Johnson would be soaked in glory, another ring for his finger, while Isiah stayed in the corner, trying to figure out the mystery of it all. How do they do it? How do we get it?

"It became my obsession," he says, licking his lips as if still tasting victory. "I could never understand the secret. Then one day it hits you, a light bulb just goes off."

He smiles. "I understand it now."

Once, years ago, Isiah said his fantasy would be to win a world championship, then duck out the back, jump in his car, and drive off to some faraway playground to watch little kids play basketball, remind himself how this all began. A few days before this year's championship series, a phone call came to the office from a kid at West Bloomfield High School. "You won't believe this," the kid gushed, "but we were playing basketball today and Isiah Thomas pulled up in his car and just sat there, watching us, and then he waved and drove away."

Maybe he knew.

◆

"I don't know, I don't know," he had said, his face pure pain, his ankle throbbing under the ice. Would he be able to play in Game 7? How could this have happened? Damn it all, why now? The Pistons had the world at their fingertips. They could stroke it, feel it, they were 57 seconds away from a championship in Game 6 against the Lakers at the Forum, a three-point lead, and they had lost the game on a questionable foul call.

Now the agony set in. Isiah Thomas had been brilliant, beyond brilliant, scoring 43 points, the final 11 on a horribly twisted ankle that was now, here, in the post-game locker room, swelling to the size of a grapefruit.

He hobbled on crutches for the next 48 hours, then taped the thing as tight as a rock, swallowed the pain, and went out there. Why me? Why now? Why must I be injured? He played gamely, he tried, he had the ball in his hands for a final desperation shot when the buzzer sounded and the court was mobbed by Lakers fans dancing on his grave.

Pistons lose Game 7. By three points. Why me?

Growing up.

◆

"Yo, Mr. Davidson, you drunk yet?" says Salley, grabbing the Pistons owner in a bear hug. "Good. Let's negotiate my new contract. I got a pen. You got a room." ➡

The feeling was fabulous at the Forum for John Salley and Isiah Thomas. Once better known for his fast-talking car commercials than his basketball skills, Salley came on strong in the playoffs. Thomas, despite breaking his hand in a late-season fight with Chicago center Bill Cartwright, averaged 18.2 playoff points.

Next page: Guard Joe Dumars, the 1989 Finals MVP, squared off with forward James Worthy, the 1988 Finals MVP. In '88, Worthy averaged 22.0 points, 7.4 rebounds and 4.4 assists. In '89, Dumars averaged 27.3 points, 1.8 rebounds and 6.0 assists.

Davidson cracks up, returns the hug, his face sweaty and red and absolutely delighted. All around, the non-players are as delirious as the players themselves. McCloskey is dancing. The trainers are singing. Assistant coaches Brendan Suhr and Brendan Malone are wandering in a happy circle, red-eyed, satisfied, stuffed.

And here comes Big Daddy. Chuck Daly. He has been through it all, and now, he is screaming, laughing, a woman comes up and begins dancing right by the Mexican food, and he briefly returns the dance, a delighted look on his face.

The coach. Is he ever truly appreciated? Daly has swallowed a thousand wasps in his time in Detroit, season after season, and they buzzed around his stomach driving him twitchy mad. But he never quit. He molded a group of guys that might not otherwise even like each other, much less commit to each other — Mahorn and Dumars? Laimbeer and Aguirre? Isiah and Edwards? — and he got them to play the most unglamorous part of the game, defense, together, in unison, with the ferocity of a mother lion. He has worked without a contract. He has worked for half of what the Rileys and Browns are getting. If he wasn't the coach of the year, nobody was.

"No one will ever know what we've been through here," he croaks. "God, I remember years ago, getting up one morning and we were 4-19. We got on the bus and I looked at Mike (Abdenour, the trainer) and he looked at me and we had nothing to say. We were that bad. . . . "

Dumars looks again at the champagne bottle and laughs. The music is pounding, the floor shakes with dancing feet.

"Man, oh, man," Dumars repeats. "You know, I was so excited about this, I didn't sleep at all last night. I can't believe it. I played the game on no sleep."

"What did you do when you finally got a moment alone?"

"I went to my room, I opened the window, I looked out on everything and I went 'Aaahhhhh.' "

That's a wrap, Detroit. Take their picture and paste it in your photo album: Isiah, Joe, Laimbeer, Rick, Mark, Worm, Salley, Fennis, John, Michael, Microwave, Buddha, the Brendans, and Chuck, and a cast of thousands. Wasn't their ride everything you dreamed it should be, quiet heroes and nasty villains, crazy calls and crazy balls, wild shots and muscle blocks, tough games and tight games and edge-of-your seat games? It was Boston swept, and Milwaukee swept, and Michael Jordan's one-man army, and, finally, the proud measure of a Lakers team that would surrender its crown only to the very best. The Pistons had to prove they were the very best. They were.

Aaahhhhh.

"I'm never gonna forget this," sighs Dumars, and he puts down the bottle, and follows the music to the party bath of glory in which they can all lay back and blow away the bubbles. World champions? The Detroit Pistons? Let the rest of the country blink. Michael Jackson penned the words that may sum it up best: Who's bad?

We are. ◆

Magic Johnson pulled his left hamstring with 4:39 left in the third quarter of Game 2 and the score tied. He played only five more minutes in the series. The Lakers' other starting guard, Byron Scott, tore a hamstring in a Game 1 practice and never played.

Power forward Rick Mahorn led the chants at a Palace rally two days after the Pistons beat the Lakers. Mahorn didn't know it at the time, but he was no longer the baddest of the Bad Boys. He had been taken by the Minnesota Timberwolves in the NBA's latest expansion draft.

BY THE NUMBERS

Detroit Pistons (NBA)

YEAR	W-L	PCT	FINISH	SCORING	POINTS	REBOUNDS	ASSISTS
1980	16-66	.195	6th, 34 GB Atlanta	McAdoo (21.7)	Long (1,337)	McAdoo (8.1)**	Money (4.2)
1981	21-61	.256	6th, 39 GB Milwaukee	Long (17.7)	Hubbard (1,161)	Hubbard (7.3)	Lee (4.4)
1982	39-43	.476	3rd, 16 GB Milwaukee	Long (21.9)	Tripucka (1,772)	Benson (8.7)	Thomas (7.8)
1983	37-45	.451	3rd, 14 GB Milwaukee	Tripucka (26.5)	Thomas (1,854)	Laimbeer (12.1)	Thomas (7.8)
1984	49-33	.598	2nd, 1 GB Milwaukee	Thomas (21.3) Tripucka (21.3)	Thomas (1,748)	Laimbeer (12.2)	Thomas (11.1)
1985	46-36	.561	2nd, 13 GB Milwaukee	Thomas (21.2)	Thomas (1,720)	Laimbeer (12.4)	Thomas (13.9)*
1986	46-36	.561	3rd, 11 GB Atlanta	Thomas (20.9)	Tripucka (1,622)	Laimbeer (13.1)*	Thomas (10.8)
1987	52-30	.634	2nd, 5 GB Atlanta	Dantley (21.5)	Dantley (1,742)	Laimbeer (11.6)	Thomas (10.0)
1988	54-28	.659	1st, 4 GA Atlanta, Chicago	Dantley (20.0)	Thomas (1,577)	Laimbeer (10.1)	Thomas (8.4)
1989	63-19	.768	1st, 6 GA Cleveland	Thomas (18.2)***	Thomas (1,458)***	Laimbeer (9.6)	Thomas (8.3)

Led the NBA
** *Bob Lanier averaged 8.8 rebounds but finished season in Milwaukee.*
*** *Adrian Dantley averaged 19.2 points but finished season in Dallas; Mark Aguirre scored 1,511 points but split season with Dallas and Detroit.*

Coaches: Dick Vitale (1979), 4-8 (.333); Richie Adubato (1979-80), 12-58 (.171); Scotty Robertson (1981-83), 97-149 (.394); Chuck Daly (1984-89), 310-182 (.630). Total: 423-397 (.516).

Post-season: Lost to New York, 3-2, in 1984 first round; beat New Jersey, 3-0, in 1985 first round; lost to Boston, 4-2, in 1985 Eastern Conference semifinals; lost to Atlanta, 3-1, in 1986 first round; beat Washington, 3-0, in 1987 first round; beat Atlanta, 4-1, in 1987 Eastern semifinals; lost to Boston, 4-3, in 1987 Eastern finals; beat Washington, 3-2, in 1988 first round; beat Chicago, 4-1, in 1988 Eastern semifinals; beat Boston, 4-2, in 1988 Eastern finals; lost to Los Angeles Lakers, 4-3, in 1988 Finals; beat Boston, 3-0, in 1989 first round; beat Milwaukee, 4-0, in 1989 Eastern semifinals; beat Chicago, 4-2, in 1989 Eastern finals; beat Lakers, 4-0, in 1989 Finals.

Award winners: Joe Dumars (guard), All-Rookie team (1986), All-Defense team (1989), Finals MVP (1989); Dennis Rodman (forward), All-Defense (1989); Isiah Thomas (guard), All-Rookie (1982), All-Star Game MVP (1984, 1986), All-NBA team (1984, 1985, 1986); Kelly Tripucka (forward), All-Rookie (1982). (All awards selected by the Basketball Writers Association of America.)

All-Star Game representatives: 1982 (Isiah Thomas, Kelly Tripucka); 1983 (Bill Laimbeer, Thomas); 1984 (Laimbeer, Thomas, Tripucka); 1985 (Laimbeer, Thomas); 1986 (Thomas); 1987 (Laimbeer, Thomas); 1988 (Thomas); 1989 (Thomas).

Hall of Fame inductees: Dave DeBusschere, forward (1983); Bob Houbregs, center (1987).

Worth noting: The Detroit Spirits won the Continental Basketball Association championship in 1983. They beat the Montana Golden Nuggets, 106-102, in Game 7 of the finals at Great Falls, Mont. The Spirits played at Cobo Arena, were coached by Gary Mazza and led by guard Tico Brown.